A HIDDEN REVOLUTION

A HIDDEN REVOLUTION

ELLIS RIVKIN

ABINGDON

NASHVILLE

A HIDDEN REVOLUTION

Copyright © 1978 by Ellis Rivkin

Library of Congress Cataloging in Publication Data

RIVKIN, ELLIS, 1918-
   A hidden revolution.
   Includes index.
   1. Pharisees. I. Title.
   BM175.P4R58   296.8'1   78-17180

ISBN 0-687-16970-4

Scripture quotations from the Old and New Testaments unless otherwise noted are from the Revised Standard Version Common Bible, copyrighted © 1973 by the Division of Christian Education of the National Council of Churches of Christ in the U.S.A., and used by permission.

Quotations from the Apocrypha are from the Revised Standard Version Aprocrypha, copyrighted © 1957 by the Division of Christian Education of the National Council of the Churches of Christ in the U.S.A., and used by permission.

Quotations from Josephus are from the Loeb Classics edition, published by Heinemann and Putnam, Heinemann and Harvard, and by Harvard University Press. Volume 8 © The President and Fellows of Harvard College 1963. Volume 9 © The President and Fellows of Harvard College 1965.

Passages from the Tannaitic Literature are the author's translation.

Portions of this book are based on material by the author which has appeared in several periodicals. Grateful acknowledgment for quotations and derivations is made to the following publications: *The Jewish Quarterly Review,* for "Pharisaism and the Crisis of the Individual in the Greco-Roman World," vol. LXI (1970-71); *Hebrew Union College Annual,* for "Defining the Pharisees: The Tannaitic Sources," vols. XL-XLI (1969-70); *Journal for the Scientific Study of Religion,* for "The Internal City: Judaism and Urbanization," vol. V (Spring 1966); and *Jewish Heritage,* for "Who Crucified Jesus?" vol. I (Fall 1958), and "Paul and the Parting of the Ways," vol. I (Winter 1959).

Acknowledgment is also made to KTAV Publishing House, Inc., for material derived from the Prolegomenon to *Judaism and Christianity,* ed. W. O. Oesterley and Erwin Rosenthal (rev. ed., 1969); and to Spertus College Press, for material from "The Pharisaic Revolution," in *Perspectives in Jewish Learning,* vol. II (1966).

MANUFACTURED BY THE PARTHENON PRESS AT
NASHVILLE, TENNESSEE, UNITED STATES OF AMERICA

To my pious and beloved parents,
of blessed memory,
for having nurtured me,
as to the Law, a Pharisee.

Contents

Acknowledgments 9
Preface 15
Introduction: Who Were the Pharisees? 25

Part I The Sources 29
  Chapter I Josephus 31
  Chapter II The New Testament 76
  Chapter III The Tannaitic Literature 125

Part II Historical Reconstruction 181
  Chapter IV From Definition to Historical
    Reconstruction 183
  Chapter V Ben Sira and Aaronide Hegemony 191

Part III Pharisaism: An Internal Revolution 209
  Chapter VI The Hidden Revolution 211
  Chapter VII On the *Cathedra* of Moses 253
  Chapter VIII "God So Loved the
    Individual . . . " 296

Notes 312
Bibliographical Note 330

Acknowledgments

In trying to recall all those who, at some time or other, gave a helping hand, whispered words of encouragement, tossed out an insight or an illuminating criticism, read this or that page, this or that chapter, or this or that draft, one does not, I must confess with sadness, remember them all. But since I do recall a great many, I see no virtue in withholding their names simply because there are some whose imprint is stamped on this work but whose names are for the nonce "forgotten." I can only hope that they will take to heart the Pharisaic admonition that we judge everyone on the scale of merit and that we withhold judgment until we find ourselves in the identical situation. I am certain that deep in the recesses of my unconscious all who have helped me are remembered, and a day may come when their names will surface and I shall be able to thank them personally.

Among those who helped me in so many subtle ways has been my dear friend, esteemed colleague, cherished confidant, and sturdy model, Professor Jacob R. Marcus. Dr. Marcus gently, patiently, and doggedly urged me to bring the Hidden Revolution out of hiding, and offered many practical suggestions as to how the manuscript could deal with technical data without loss of clarity. Dr. Nelson Glueck, of blessed memory, former President of the Hebrew Union College, nurturer of the spirit of free, critical, and audacious scholarship at the college, spurred me to test, not repress, unthinkable thoughts. There was never a time, when we chanced to meet, that his face did not light up when I shared with him my scholarly findings and my scholarly hopes, that he did not voice a "bravo" and a "go to it."

And then there have been my students—who through the years both in and out of my classes inspired me, challenged me, and always opened up for me roads not traveled, highways and byways not noted, and mental vistas not glimpsed. Of this I am sure, the image of the Pharisees would have been less clear, and their impact less evident had I taught less and researched more.

To my brother-in-law Dr. Herbert Zafren, Director of Libraries at the Hebrew Union College-Jewish Institute of Religion, who has been with the Pharisees since my undergraduate days, I am indebted for patiently applying the scalpel and for insisting that the husk be winnowed from the kernel.

Rabbi Jack Bemporad was my teacher even when he was my student, for he drew my attention to the broad philosophic implications of my mode of conceptualization and my methodological leanings. After the manuscript had been accepted and was going through the final editing process, he persuaded me to restructure the chapters on Josephus and on the New Testament—even though my editor had not requested any structural change. My willingness to undertake so arduous and time-consuming a task, when it could have been so easily shirked is, I suspect, the ultimate tribute to a rare mind and a devoted friend. I am truly grateful.

Rabbi Mayer Selekman has been a nurturing and supportive friend from the moment we met. In our discussions about the Pharisees, we were both drawn to the primordial quality of their achievement—their audacious breakthrough into novelty, their daring absorption into Judaism of Greco-Roman modes of thinking and Greco-Roman institutions, their judicious balancing or preservation *and* innovation, and their stirring proclamation that God holds out to the law-abiding individual eternal life for the soul and resurrection for the body. This sharing of awe of the Pharisees and what they had wrought was a constant source of inspiration and constant goad to share the good news about the Pharisees with others. Mayer offered gentle, relentless, and irresistable criticisms, and suffered with patient friendship the obstacles I designed, the rationalizations I contrived, and the stubborn resistance I stirred up, so the manuscript would remain unfinished. His patience has now been rewarded, and his enduring friendship reconfirmed.

Although my friendship with Connie Yaffe is far more recent, measured in months, not years, it matured precociously under the pressure of completing the manuscript by the end of August, 1977. As my research assistant, she threw all her energies and talents into helping me with the restructuring and the rewriting of chapters 2 and 3. This joint venture was, in retrospect, well worth the effort, since all who have read the two versions are agreed that the chapters are far more coherent, more clarifying, and more compelling. In addition, I must add, Connie painstakingly went through the entire manuscript on the prowl for undetected errors, unwished-for slips, and for non sequiturs lurking in the cracks and crannies of reasoned argument.

I also want to express my deep appreciation to Professors Michael Cook, Michael Meyer, Lewis M. Barth, Rabbi Barton G. Lee, Myron Greenberg, and Jane Fry, who were helpful in so many ways; David J. Gilner, whose "cuttings" only helped and whose prunings only enhanced; and Dr. David Altshuler, who skillfully scaled down the size of the manuscript so that the overarching thesis would be all the more impactful, and who was always ready cheerfully to check out the sources.

To Dr. Norman J. Cohen and Rabbi Gerald Brieger I am indebted for their sensing, quite correctly, that my case

11

for the Pharisaic Revolution would be strengthened if Simon the Hasmonean's elevation to the High Priesthood by a Great Synagogue, as recorded in I Macc. 14:27-45, was set down first in the chain of reasoning rather than at the end, where I had originally set it.

I am also grateful to my esteemed colleague Professor Ben Zion Wacholder who read parts of the original manuscript and wisely suggested that I dispense with an elaborate critical review of the scholarly literature and get on as quickly as possible with my own thesis.

My good friends Dr. Peter Topping (Charles Phelps Taft Professor of History and Later Greek Studies at the University of Cincinnati) and Dr. Martin Yaffe (Assistant Professor of Philosophy at North Texas State University) were most gracious in taking time away from urgent scholarly responsibilities to try their hand at unraveling an extremely difficult passage in Josephus' *Antiquities* —XVIII:4-11, 23-25.

To Helen Lederer and Yetta Gershune I am especially indebted. For many years before her retirement, Helen Lederer was my secretary and typed and retyped all the early drafts of the manuscript. Subsequently Yetta Gershune took over and typed the final drafts. Each in her own way was a joy to work with, because both Helen and Yetta were as committed to *A Hidden Revolution* as I was, if not, at times, more so.

I would like also to express my deep appreciation to all those many individuals at the Hebrew Union College who make the College a scholar's delight. Dr. Glueck's enduring commitment to scientific scholarship and his esteem for scholars are shared and sustained by his successor, Dr. Alfred Gottschalk. As a consequence, the entire staff of the college has always been dedicated to providing those support services which make creative scholarship possible. Especially noteworthy is the way in which the rich holdings of the library, under the direction of Dr. Herbert C. Zafren, are served up, with gracious dispatch, by a devoted and highly competent staff.

Acknowledgments

To Dr. Lloyd R. Bailey (Associate Professor of Old Testament at Duke Divinity School) I am most grateful for having invited me to write the article "Pharisees" for the supplementary volume of the *Interpreter's Dictionary of the Bible,* which led to Bailey's alerting Abingdon Press to the existence of a rough draft of my manuscript of *A Hidden Revolution* and urging Abingdon to snap it up before other publishers became aware of the "find." For this matchmaking I owe Professor Bailey abiding appreciation.

A Hidden Revolution bears the clear imprint on every page of students, friends, and teachers. The imprint of my extended family, however, is hidden from all who have not had the good fortune of knowing them intimately and living with them continuously. Yet it is their nurturing support, their intellectual prodding, their long-suffering patience, and their enduring love which threads through this book and weaves its warp and woof. Each one is deserving of mention, however elusive their specific contribution; for some have literally lived with this book for more than a generation, while others were born into it, and grew up enveloped by it. If, then, I single out my two daughters Roslyn and Sharon for special mention it is because they were actively involved with the shaping of the manuscript as they reacted with pointed criticism and gentle and patient love.

Zelda, my wife, is *sui generis.* She was an inspiration even *before* I took up with the Pharisees. I first met her at the Baltimore Hebrew College over shared Rashi texts and talmudic folios *à deux* at a time when I was still, as to the Law, a Pharisee and as to righteousness under the Law blameless. Zelda has remained an inspiration ever since. As for the Pharisees, she typed my original paper on the "Role of the Pharisees in the Development of the *Halakhah*" and was hooked. The Pharisees were always her favorites and the concept of *A Hidden Revolution* especially close to her heart. Her patience through the years was sorely tried when the completion of the

13

manuscript was delayed now for this, now for that "unreason." But she never gave up hope and never flagged in her loving support. She was always ready, eager, and able to read the various versions, offer constructive suggestions, and to reassure me that the manuscript in the fullness of time, if not sooner, would be completed. Simple justice thus dictated that *A Hidden Revolution* be dedicated to her, but she would not have it. It was her determined wish that the book be dedicated to my parents of blessed memory, because without them I could never have known the heart, the soul, and the mind of the Pharisees. And, after much reflection, I had to agree with her; so it is to their memory that I dedicate this book.

Preface

How does one write a preface for a book thirty-nine years aborning? For *A Hidden Revolution* was conceived more than a generation ago when, as a "know-it-all" sophomore at Johns Hopkins University, I undertook to write a term paper with the modest title *"The* History of the *Halakhah* from Ezra to Yavneh." It did not take me long, however, to recognize that I had perhaps embarked on a somewhat overambitious project, given the fact that there were other courses which I had to take and pass at the same time. With the permission of my Professor, Dr. Samuel Rosenblatt, I "narrowed" down the scope of the paper to the role of the Pharisees in the development of the *Halakhah.*

This decision, thirty-nine years ago, seeded *A Hidden Revolution.* I had already sensed that the Pharisees had carried through one of the most stunning revolutions in the history of humankind—a revolution they never acknowledged and of which they left no record other than their transmutation of Judaism. I was struck by this revolutionary quality when, in the course of my researches, I was drawn to Professor Solomon Zeitlin's seminal articles as holding the keys for unlocking an objective definition of the Pharisees and an adequate conceptualization of how, when, and why the Pharisees had emerged.

I felt that even though Zeitlin's views had had little or no impact on scholarly opinion, he was on the right track methodologically *and* conceptually. As a budding historian, I was impressed by Zeitlin's intuitive "feel" for the historically possible; as an admirer of those grand historians who had charted new paths in historiography, I detected in Zeitlin's writings a freshness of thought and a clarity of analysis that elevated him to the plane of those historians I wished to emulate. As a Jewish young man, bewildered by the triumph of Hitler, by the seeming collapse of Western civilization, and by the raucous claims of Marxist redeemers, I had become intensely interested in the dynamics of radical and revolutionary transformations throughout history. I was thus attuned to daring conceptualizations, pioneering methodologies, and the shock waves of revolution emanating from unseen sources.

Although in the years that followed, I drifted away from the Pharisees as I concentrated, during my graduate years, on the Renaissance and Baroque periods in Italy, the Pharisees were never out of sight or out of mind. The tug was always there, even when I was most absorbed with Leon da Modena and the Venetian Jews who were bursting with a creativity which two constraining ghettos, the *ghetto nuova* and the *ghetto vecchio,* could not hem in. The tug was there because the historical phenomena I was investigating could not be made intelligible without recourse to the Pharisees and their daring concept of the twofold Law, the Written and the Oral. It was not the Judaism of the Pentateuch that was enlivening Leon da Modena and his fellow Venetian Jews but the Judaism of the Mishnah and of the Talmud. Yet this revolutionary role of the Pharisees had never been explicitly spelled out.

The tug was also there because the problem of defining the Pharisees and the problem of determining the when, where, and why of Pharisaic origins were seemingly insurmountable unless a methodological breakthrough was forthcoming. This for me was alluring, since I had chosen to work in the Renaissance and Baroque periods only because this was Professor Frederic C. Lane's area of specialized research and teaching, and I was determined to study under Professor Lane so as to gain mastery of his analytical methodology. As paradoxical as it may seem, I concentrated in Italian history, so that I might gain access to those methodological tools that would in time—I hoped—enable me to solve the problem of the Pharisees.

My ongoing interest in the Pharisees was sustained when I accepted a postdoctoral research fellowship at the Dropsie College for Hebrew and Cognate Learning and for the first time met personally with Professor Zeitlin. Although I took no courses with him, I had occasion to chat with him almost daily when he would drop into the library, where I was doing my research on Leon da Modena's relationship to the *Kol Sakhal*. As was Zeitlin's wont, he would roam from the intertestamental period to the modern period, to the medieval, the geonic, the biblical, all the while tossing off profound learning as though it were common knowledge, and methodological gems as though they were the stock and trade of all scholars. For me these listening sessions—Zeitlin was not much given to hearing others out—were grand occasions for learning. Since I was so "high" on Zeitlin's insight and methodology, he seemed to regard me as a young scholar who, if taken under his wing, might mature into a scholar worthy of his commendation.

As was to be expected, the problems of the intertestamental period were always in the forefront of Zeitlin's mind, and he would share his thinking with me. However, as time went on, it more and more dawned upon me that I could not go along with Zeitlin's early dating of Pharisaic origins or with his unwillingness to call a revolution a revolution. I also was becoming aware that though Zeitlin intuitively applied a method capable of solving the fundamental problems of definition and origins, he had never made this method explicit. As a

17

consequence, he himself failed to follow his premises through to their logical conclusions. It thus occurred to me I might some day try my hand at developing an explicit methodology that would yield both an objective definition of the Pharisees and a compelling hypothesis of their origins as a revolutionary class.

Fortunately, when I joined the faculty of the Hebrew Union College, I was assigned the teaching of a two-year survey course in Jewish history. Year-in and year-out, I was teaching the intertestamental period to graduate-level students and, in doing so, had the ongoing opportunity of wrestling with the problem of the Pharisees. This wrestling became a serious preoccupation as I began to offer graduate seminars in the history of the intertestamental period, and as I noted that Professor Zeitlin had committed himself irrevocably to what seemed to me to be an unfinished definition of the Pharisees and a far too early date for their origins. It was at that point that I decided to write *A Hidden Revolution.*

Although I had decided to write *A Hidden Revolution* as early as 1959, the going was slow. Partly the slowness was attributable to what seemed to be higher priorities and partly to a fear that since I was not a specialist in the intertestamental period, I was oversanguine to believe that I could make a significant methodological and conceptual breakthrough on the Pharisees. I thus found it easier and wiser to test out my hypotheses in a series of articles published in the sixties and early seventies. The feedback being sufficiently reassuring, I tossed my fears aside and wrote a final draft of the book. I had come full circle: from an undergraduate writing a term paper on "The Role of the Pharisees in the Development of the *Halakhah*" to a professor of Jewish history writing a book on the Hidden Revolution of the Pharisees.

A Hidden Revolution is built on the inspiration, the insights, and the nurturing care of my four grand teachers, Drs. Louis L. Kaplan, Harry M. Orlinsky, Frederic C. Lane, and Solomon Zeitlin. These teachers built on the foundation of a love of learning for its own sake, instilled in me from infancy and childhood by my awesome and brilliant aunt, Anna E. Rivkin, and by my remarkable uncle Leon Rivkin. Dr. Kaplan was the teacher who first opened my eyes to a Jewish learning and creativity lying beyond the four ells of the *halakhah* and who goaded me to seek the unseen dimensions of Jewish historical experience in the complex interplay of the Jews with the societies, cultures, and civilizations within which their history had unfolded. Kaplan's stern counsel that I become a historian first, and only then a historian of the Jewish people, lest Jewish history be distorted, was profound wisdom then, no less profound wisdom now.

Dr. Orlinsky's impact was of a very different order. Although now an eminent Bible scholar, Orlinsky, freshly graduated from Dropsie College, was teaching Jewish history at the Baltimore Hebrew College when I first sat at his feet. I was then still deeply immersed in an orthodoxy of belief and practice which, to all appearances, was impermeable to critical historiography. Indeed, it was so impermeable that not even Dr. Kaplan could touch more than the edges with his philosophical and theological critique. Yet Orlinsky's critical analyses, dialectical thinking, and daring conceptualizations somehow found their counterpart in my own mind. As a consequence, although Orlinsky made no overt effort to dissolve my attachment to orthodox beliefs, I found myself more and more confronted with an unenviable choice: If the Jewish past had indeed been subject to the same laws of historical development as that of the non-Jewish, then the claims of orthodoxy were without sufficient grounds. If, on the other hand, the claims of orthodoxy were indeed true, then Orlinsky's reconstruction of Jewish history must needs be false. And since my mind recognized that Orlinsky's mode of thinking was right, and my heart was no less certain that the way of life I had been nurtured on and which I so deeply cherished was no less true, I was tossed into an inner conflict so deep and so painful that it was years before I could experience myself as a single person. Be that as it may, since I was unable to deny the tug of my mind, I was more and more drawn to Orlinsky's radical restructuring of Jewish history and became more and more excited by the clarifying effect of his mode of conceptualization and by the logic of his methodology.

It is little wonder, then, that all that I have written bears the imprint of Orlinsky's impact. Throughout the years, we have been very close and intimate friends and have continuously shared our thinking with each other. Orlinsky's imprimatur, I am sure, is evident in *A Hidden Revolution* wherever there is sound critical method, deep respect for the sources, and alluring conceptualization. I am truly grateful that when the die was cast, Orlinsky was at the right place, at the right time, for the right person.

My indebtedness to Dr. Frederic C. Lane I have long ceased to measure. The compound interest alone is by now staggering. When I first entered Johns Hopkins in 1938, I had no intention of becoming a historian. Semitics at that time was my goal. And then I heard Lane's first lecture, opening his two-year survey course in Western civilization, and then his second, his third, and his fourth. By the fifth lecture I had become so enthralled by the grandness of his design, the sharpness of his analysis, the telling power of his sources, and the clarity of his exposition that I said to myself, If this is what a historian can do— make the past and, by implication, the present intelligible—then it is a historian that I most want to be. So right there and then, I decided to become a historian so as to be able to learn from Lane all that I could absorb and understand. It is to be hoped that the final version of *A Hidden Revolution* is a tribute to Lane's total impact on my thinking. If, unwittingly, I have failed in this work to measure up to Lane's rigorous standards of scholarly excellence, I trust these failings will be recognized by all as mine, not Lane's.

I have earlier called attention to Dr. Solomon Zeitlin's contribution to *A Hidden Revolution.* I wish only to underline the point I made in my article entitled "Solomon Zeitlin's Contribution to the Historiography of the Second Commonwealth" (*Judaism,* 14 [Summer, 1965]), namely, that I regard Dr. Zeitlin as one of the truly seminal scholars of the modern age, not becaue he was necessarily right but because he championed a radical rethinking and restructuring of Jewish history in general and the history of the intertestamental period in particular. His errors were never free of truth and often as not illuminated more clearly how the problem might be solved. Similarly, his iconoclasm put all scholars on notice that their presuppositions were always being scrutinized and their handling of the sources always being weighed and measured.

There is an important stream of influence other than the intellectual that prepared me for my perspective on the Pharisees. It is my early life, which was embedded in the context of the twofold Law. My father and mother, to whom this book is dedicated, lived the life of the twofold Law, believed that the loving God and Father had revealed to Israel on Sinai this way of life, and they looked forward with sturdy faith to life eternal for the soul in the world to come, and for the body on that glorious day when the dead would be quickened and restored to life. For them, as for me, the prayer uttered thrice daily ("He sustains life with His grace, revives the dead with His boundless mercy, supports the falling, heals the sick, loosens the bound, and keeps his faith with those who sleep in the dust. Who is like unto Thee master of mighty acts, and who bears resemblance unto Thee, O King, Who deadens and enlivens and causes salvation to flower? And Thou art indeed utterly trustworthy to resurrect the dead. Praised be Thou, O Lord, Who causes the dead to come to life") was no anemic pietude, no metaphysical illusion, no irritating embarrassment. My parents, my grandmother, my uncles, Leon and Will, and my aunt believed with perfect faith that God had the power and the wish to resurrect every individual who had faith in his power and in his promise. These were the beliefs to which I was committed long before I could utter a word or comprehend an idea. I was as totally embraced by the Law and as immersed in faith as Paul had been.

I lived the life of the twofold Law; I believed in its divine source; I had faith in a Father-God who would lift *my* soul into the world to come and raise *my* body from the dead. When my grandmother died, I, as a child of nine, was as certain that her soul was in heaven as I was certain that she had died. And what a source of comfort that belief!

But along with the promise and the hope was the terror. Eternal life and resurrection was stored up for the righteous; eternal suffering awaited the sinner. How could I or anyone be certain that, dangling on the edge of choice between good and evil, I had not been lured into a sinfulness beyond redemption. On the unerring scales of God's justice, would my righteousness offset my sinfulness and tip the scales to eternal life, or would the heavy weight of this or that sin, alone or in combination, bring the scales down on the side of eternal punishment? I oscillated between the ecstacy of the Law fulfilled and the agony lest, frail, finite, and impulse-ridden, I would fall short of what the Law demanded of me. How, standing before God's judgment on Yom Kippur, I prayed that his mercy triumph over his justice and grant me one more year at least to make amends and to pile up good deeds without measure so that his trust in me would have been justified. In my home, sin was no trifle; the Law no ethnic nicety or charming custom; belief in God no whimsy. My eternal, not mortal life, was day and night and night and day always on the line.

It was because I lived the life of the twofold Law,

believed in the God of the twofold Law, hoped for eternal life, and dreaded eternal punishment that I could discover *A Hidden Revolution*. Whereas other scholars, Jewish and Christian, list the belief in resurrection as a Pharisaic tenet, they do not convey what the belief in resurrection means to an individual who believes literally that God will raise the dead. These scholars do not communicate what such good news must have meant to Jews nurtured on the Pentateuchal proclamation that rewards and punishments are to be meted out in this world only. Indeed, scholars have tended to play down Pharisaism as a religion of personal salvation lest it be confused, either to its advantage or disadvantage, with Christianity. Pharisaic Judaism, so goes the refrain, was first and foremost a "this-worldly" religion, while Christianity is an "other-worldly" religion. Instead of seeing Christianity as a variation on the Pharisaic theme of eternal life and resurrection, scholars see Judaism as preeminently the religion of a people, and Christianity, a religion of salvation for the individual.

The notion of *A Hidden Revolution* was thus seeded by my early life in Judaism.

But even when my intellectual development made it impossible for me to accept the claims of the twofold Law to be God's immutable revelation, I never forgot the awesome experience of living under this Law, the glow of goodness which the fulfillment of a divine commandment brought in its train or the serene joy of glimpsing a life without end. When, therefore, I gained access to the tools of modern critical scholarship, I used these tools to reveal that the primordial power of Pharisaism lay in its proclamation that God so loved the individual that he revealed to Israel a twofold Law which, if internalized and obeyed, would lead to eternal life for the soul and resurrection for the body. It was this triadic teaching that so stirred the Jews that they abandoned the literal, written Pentateuch for a Law that had never been written down. It was this triadic teaching that stirred Paul to

23

substitute Christ for the twofold Law. It was this triadic teaching that almost two thousand years later gave my family the strength to follow the twofold Law, whatever the sacrifice and however demanding the discipline. It was this triadic teaching on which I was nurtured and upon which I still look back with such reverent awe. And it is this nurture and this awe that, along with the tools of modern scholarship, give me some grounds for hoping that my *subjective* experience makes an *objective* definition and portrait of the Pharisees possible.

It is thus with the deepest feelings of gratitude for having been brought up as to the Law a Pharisee and for having experienced the joy and the trembling before the Father-God who cares that I dedicate this book in loving memory of the pious souls of my beloved mother and revered father.

NOTE: To facilitate reading, diacritical marks for transliterated Hebrew have been omitted.

Introduction:

Who Were the Pharisees?

Then said Jesus to the crowds and to his disciples, "The Scribes and Pharisees sit on [the *cathedra* of Moses]; so practice and observe whatever they tell you, but not what they do; for they preach but do not practice."

"Woe to you, Scribes and Pharisees, hypocrites! For you are like whitewashed tombs, which outwardly appear beautiful, but within they are full of dead men's bones and all uncleanness. So you outwardly appear righteous to men, but within you are full of hypocrisy and iniquity."

—Matthew 23:1-3, 27-28

[The Pharisees] have very great influences with the masses, and whatever they do about divine worship, or prayers, or sacrifices, they perform in accordance with the interpretation [of the Pharisees]. . . . [The views of the Sadducees] are received by only a few, but these are of the highest rank. But they are hardly able to do anything so to speak, for when they become magistrates, as they are unwillingly and by force sometimes obliged to do, they conform to the teachings of the Pharisees, because the populace would not otherwise put up with them.

—Josephus, *Antiquities* XVIII 15, 17

It is related of a Sadducean High Priest that he prepared the incense outside [the Holy of Holies], and only then did he bring it inside the Holy of Holies. When he came out he was very happy [for he had performed the ritual in accordance with Sadducean procedure]. His father met him [and disapproving of his act] said to him: "Although we are Sadducees, we fear the Pharisees. . . .

—Yoma 19*b*

Who were the Pharisees? This question has puzzled generations of scholars; for the answer carries with it the key to the understanding of a crucial epoch in the history of Judaism, of Christianity, and of Western civilization. In the Gospel accounts of Jesus, the Pharisees argue with him, irritate him, and participate in his downfall. Indeed, the Pharisees so stirred up the hatred of Jesus' disciples that the refrain "Scribes, Pharisees, hypocrites" (Matt. 23:13, 15, 23, 25, 27, 29) ultimately became a byword, and the description of them (Matt. 23:27, 33) as "whitewashed tombs" and as "serpents," "vipers," destined for Gehenna ultimately became their hallmark. The Pharisees are accused of hounding the followers of Jesus, scourging them in the synagogues, and persecuting them from town to town (Matt. 23:24). Yet this very Gospel of Matthew which condemns them most bitterly affirms that they sit on the *cathedra* of Moses and should therefore be obeyed (Matt. 23:2).

The Pharisees are thus firmly embedded in the sacred texts of Christianity. They appear in all four Gospels as dangerous opponents of Jesus. They appear in Acts in connection with both Peter and Paul. In his Epistle to the Philippians (3:5; cf. Gal. 1:13-14), Paul affirms that he had been a Pharisee and a persecutor of the Church before his tranformation. The New Testament thus ties the birth of Christianity umbilically to the Pharisees and their teachings.

The Pharisees are even more significant for the role they play in the development of Judaism and in the history of the Jewish people. They loom large in the writings of Josephus. The Tannaitic Literature—the Mishnah, the Tosefta, the so-called Tannaitic Midrash, and the *beraitoth*—confirms their vital relationship to Jewish law and lore. According to Josephus, the Pharisees had played an active role in the early years of John Hyrcanus' High Priesthood; had assumed the leadership of a major rebellion against Alexander Jannaeus (103-76 B.C.); and had been restored to power by

Salome Alexandra (76-67). The Pharisees also counted among themselves such outstanding legal authorities as Simon ben Shetach, Shemaiah and Abtalion, Hillel and Shammai, and Rabban Gamaliel. The authoritative corpus of Jewish Oral Law, the Mishnah, testifies to their enduring impact on the development of normative Judaism. Indeed, all the varied forms of Judaism flourishing today are historically interconnected with the Pharisees; for only the Judaism of the Pharisees survived antiquity. It was this form of Judaism that confronted the medieval Christian Church. Hence, all the vicissitudes that have marked Jewish-Christian relations are rooted in an antagonism which had had its beginnings in the hostility marring the relationship between Jesus and the Pharisees.

It is no wonder, then, that scholars have perennially searched for an answer to the question, Who were the Pharisees? Yet the sources that might have provided an answer are few in number, contradictory, highly subjective, and scanty in details. No source defines the name, pinpoints the origin, tells the story, describes the institutions, or pens the lives of the leading Pharisees.

Although Josephus, the Tannaitic Literature, and the New Testament bear witness to the importance of the Pharisees, they do not articulate for us a clear and unambiguous definition. Our sources are rich in emotion-laden adjectives but poor in rendering the meaning of the noun. Little wonder then that scholars have come up with conflicting definitions.

Among these competing formulations, the one that has proved to be the most appealing to Jewish and Christian scholars defines the Pharisees as a confraternity of Jews who separated themselves from the *am ha-aretz,* the masses, because of the greater strictness exercised by the Pharisees in observing the laws of ritual purity. Hence, it is argued, their Hebrew name, *Perushim,* "Separatists," and the Greek name, *Pharisaoi* (a transliteration from the Hebrew with Greek plural ending, *oi*), are expressive of who and what they were. In support of this definition, scholars cite a seemingly definitive text from Mishnah Hagigah 2:7, which puts the *Perushim* as those who are most scrupulous in observing the laws of ritual purity in juxtaposition to the *am ha-aretz.* These scholars likewise adduce other tannaitic texts that would seem to confirm this definition, even though in these texts the Pharisees are called *haberim,* "associates." These *haberim,* like *Perushim,* appear in the Mishnah, so these scholars claim, as a confraternity separating themselves from the *am ha-aretz,* the masses who were suspected of nontithing.[1]

This *consensual* definition of the Pharisees *as a sect,* or a confraternity, fails to visualize them as a class of audacious revolutionaries who stirred the masses to embrace the bold concept of the two-fold Law, the Written and the Oral, and to hearken to the "gospel" of eternal life and resurrection. The conventional definition scarcely conjures up the image of a scholar class that transmuted the priestly Judaism of the onefold Law, the Pentateuch, and seeded the soil in which Christianity took root.

Yet the Pharisees were such a class. They were revolutionaries, even though their revolution has remained hidden behind the opaque obscurity of our sources. Once the Pharisees have been defined by a methodology, both rigorous and objective, however, their role as revolutionaries may very well become self-evident. And once so defined, the sources will reveal, rather than conceal, the momentous revolution which they wrought.

Part I

The Sources

Chapter I

Josephus

Josephus, the New Testament, and the Tannaitic Literature are the only sources that can be legitimately drawn upon for the construction of an objective definition of the Pharisees. They are the only sources that can lay claim to contemporaneity or near contemporaneity. They are the only sources using the term *Pharisees* that derive from a time when the Pharisees flourished. *No other sources qualify.* The apocryphal and pseudepigraphic writings, though contemporaneous in part, *never* mention the Pharisees by name. The Babylonian and Palestinian Talmuds, though mentioning the Pharisees by name, reflect the teaching activities of the so-called *Amoraim* who were active only after the Mishnah had already been compiled around A.D. 210; hence, these sources cannot be drawn upon to aid us in building an objective definition of the Pharisees. Nor can we look either to the Church Fathers or to the author of the scholion to Megillat Ta'anit since, living as they did long after the Pharisees had ceased to be known as such, these writers had no first-hand knowledge of them.

Three sources—Josephus, the New Testament, and the Tannaitic Literature—and these three sources only, will be drawn upon to construct our definition of the Pharisees. Each of these sources will be cited, for the most part, in full and thoroughly analyzed, source by source, in successive chapters. With each of these sources, beginning with Josephus, we shall build our definition as though the other sources had not survived antiquity. Only after we have constructed three definitions, independently drawn from Josephus, the New Testament, and the Tannaitic Literature, will we then compare each of the definitions with the others. Should it turn out that these definitions are congruent with one another, then shall we not have cogent grounds for postulating that such a definition is truly viable and as objective as the nature of our sources allow? And once in possession of such a definition, shall we not have at our disposal a benchmark allowing us to probe gently and judiciously for a satisfying resolution to the problems of Pharisaic origins, for which no sources exist, and of the history of the Pharisees, however sketchy, which until now has eluded us?

We shall begin our analysis with the writings of Josephus, since, in contrast to the New Testament and the Tannaitic Literature, Josephus refracts the Pharisees from many angles of vision: (1) He was himself a follower of the Pharisees; hence, he knew them from within. (2) He was an observer of the day-to-day role of the Pharisees and their leaders before, during, and after the Jewish revolt against Rome. (3) He was a self-conscious historian who, in constructing the Jewish past, drew upon sources that told of the activities of the Pharisees long before his own time. Neither the writers of the New Testament nor the sages whose teachings are to be found in the Tannaitic Literature looked upon the Pharisees from so many angles. The New Testament writers saw the Pharisees as the stumbling blocks, barring Jesus from reaching out to the people. The *Tannaim* of the Tannaitic Literature for their part portray for us the Pharisees only insofar as they are umbilically tied to the Oral Law and the Oral Lore. Since, then, Josephus' refraction is multi- rather than uni-lensed, we shall begin our analysis with the writings of Josephus: *The Jewish War, The Antiquities,*

and *The Life,* the three books in which the Pharisees are
mentioned by name.

Josephus did not write a history of the Pharisees;
nonetheless, in the course of narrating the history of the
Jews in *War* and *Antiquities,* he felt compelled to deal with
them. This compulsion, however, seems to have been
infrequent; for the only sustained account of their activity
is confined to the series of events that followed on the rift
between John Hyrcanus and the Pharisees. The Pharisees are pictured by Josephus as playing a significant role
in a rebellion against Alexander Janneus and in a
subsequent reconciliation with Salome Alexandra. After
the death of Salome Alexandra, Josephus mentions the
Pharisees only sporadically.

Josephus thus limits his interest in the Pharisees to
their involvement in those kinds of events Josephus
considered to be the stuff of history. When John
Hyrcanus broke with the Pharisees, and they in turn rose
up in revolt, first against him, and then against
Alexander Jannaeus, they were making history. Consequently, Josephus considered it his duty as a historian to
weave them into his narrative. So, too, when Salome
Alexandra allocates considerable power to the Pharisees,
Josephus considers them appropriate subjects for the
historian's pen. But when they are not directly involved
with the surface of change, they are of little relevance for
a historian with Josephus' concept of history. A single act
of Herod's was, for Josephus, of greater historical import
than a hundred years of Pharisaic activity.

Yet as sparing as Josephus is of historical data
pertaining to the Pharisees, he does share with us some
precious information drawn from sources at his disposal.
These data allow us to reconstruct an image of the
Pharisees elicited from the role they had played prior to
Josephus' day. Since this phase of analysis will be carried
through chronologically, parallel passages in *War* and in
Antiquities will be treated side by side.

The earliest chronological reference to the Pharisees is found in the *Antiquities,* where they are brought in, along with the Sadducees and the Essenes, for no ascertainable reason. Josephus had just quoted a letter sent by Jonathan the Hasmonean to the Lacedaemonians, a letter that makes no reference to any of these religious groupings. Nor had the Pharisees, Sadducees, or Essenes been involved in the subject matter either of the preceding narrative or of the narrative following this intrusive passage. Josephus inserts this passage abruptly without any apparent reason. Indeed the only connective is chronological:

Now at this time there were three schools of thought [or ways of life, *haereseis*][1] among the Jews, which held different opinions concerning human affairs; the first being that of the Pharisees, the second that of the Sadducees, and the third that of the Essenes. As for the Pharisees, they say that certain events are the work of Fate, but not all; as to other events, it depends upon ourselves whether they shall take place or not. The Essenes, however, declares that Fate is mistress of all things, and that nothing befalls men unless it be in accordance with her decree. But the Sadducees do away with Fate, holding that there is no such thing and that human actions are not achieved in accordance with her decree, but that all things lie within our power, so that we ourselves are responsible for our well-being, while we suffer misfortune through our own thoughtlessness. Of these matters, however, I have given a more detailed account in the second book of the *Jewish History.* (*Ant.* XIII:171-3)

This passage is very important because it links the Pharisees to the Hasmonean epoch. Josephus had hitherto never made mention of the Pharisees, Sadducees, or Essenes. By introducing the three *haereseis* here as fully functioning in the times of Jonathan, Josephus is alerting us to the fact that he must have had some source other than I or II Maccabees recording the existence of the Pharisees. Since he had found this chronological connection in some other source, Josephus felt constrained to insert this datum into his history. But since it had no direct relation to the events he was narrating, he could not blend this information into his account. He therefore thrust it in abruptly as a dangling paragraph suspended between Jonathan's letter to the Spartans and Jonathan's resumption of warfare with Demetrius' generals.

Following on this interjection, Josephus takes no further notice of the Pharisees until he tells us of the split between them and John Hyrcanus in *Ant.* XIII:288-98:

As for Hyrcanus, the envy of the Jews was aroused against him by his own successes and those of his sons; particularly hostile to him were the Pharisees, who are one of the Jewish schools *[haereseis]*, as we have related above. And so great is their influence with the masses that even when they speak against a king or high priest, they immediately gain credence. Hyrcanus too was a disciple of theirs, and was greatly loved by them. And once he invited them to a feast and entertained them hospitably, and when he saw that they were having a very good time, he began by saying that they knew he wished to be righteous and in everything he did tried to please God and them—for the Pharisees thus believes; at the same time he begged them, if they observed him doing anything wrong or straying from the right path, to lead him back to it and correct him. But they testified to his being altogether virtuous, and he was delighted with their praise. However, one of the guests, named Eleazar, who had an evil nature and took pleasure in dissension, said, "Since you have asked to be told the truth, if you wish to be rightoues *[dikaios]*, give up the high-priesthood and be content with governing the people." And when Hyrcanus asked him for what reason he should give up the high-priesthood, he replied, "Because we have heard from our elders that your mother was a captive in the reign of Antiochus Epiphanes." But the story was false, and Hyrcanus was furious with the man, while all the Pharisees were very indignant.

Then a certain Jonathan, one of Hyrcanus' close friends, belonging to the school *[haereseos]* of Sadducees, who hold opinions opposed to those of the Pharisees, said that it had been with the general approval of all the Pharisees that Eleazar had made his slanderous statements; and this, he added, would be clear to Hyrcanus if he inquired of them what punishment Eleazar deserved for what he had said. And so Hyrcanus asked the Pharisees what penalty they thought he deserved—for, he said, he would be convinced that the slanderous statement had not been made with their approval if they fixed the penalty commensurate with the crime—, and they replied that Eleazar deserved stripes and chains; for they did not think it right to sentence a man to death for calumny, and anyway the Pharisees are naturally lenient in the matter of punishments. At this Hyrcanus became very angry and began to believe that the fellow had slandered him with their approval. And Jonathan in particular inflamed his anger, and so worked upon him that he brought him to join the Sadducaean party and desert the Pharisees, and to abrogate the laws *[nomima;* author's trans.*]* which they had established for the people, and punish those who observed them. Out of this, of course *[oun]*, grew the hatred of the masses for him and his sons, but of this we shall speak hereafter. For the present I wish merely to explain that the Pharisees had passed on to the people certain laws handed down by former generations and not recorded in the Laws of Moses *[hoti nomima tina paredosan to demo hoc Pharisaioi ek pateron diadoxes]*, for which reasons they are rejected by the Sadducaean group, who hold that only those laws should be considered valid which were written down (in Scripture), and that those which had been handed down by former generations should not be observed *[legon ekeina dein hegeisthai nomima ta gegraximena, ta d'ek paradoseos ton pateron me terein]*. And concerning these matters the two parties came to have controversies and serious differences, the Sadducees having the confidence of the wealthy alone but no following among the populace, while the Pharisees have the support of the masses *[plethos]*. But of these two schools and of the Essenes a detailed account has been given in the second book of my *Judaica.*

Josephus' account of the split between John Hyrcanus, the Hasmonean, and the Pharisees is worthy of the closest scrutiny. This event had occurred sometime before the death of John Hyrcanus in 104 B.C., hence about two hundred years before Josephus wrote the *Antiquities.* Josephus was thus absolutely dependent on sources he had at hand. He therefore included this incident not because of his interest in the Pharisees per se but because he felt compelled as a historian to narrate all facts he deemed relevant for understanding historical events. The break between John Hyrcanus and the Pharisees was an important political event; for it involved a High Priest and ruler, John Hyrcanus, and its ultimate outcome was a violent civil war which lasted a generation. Events such as these—sedition, rebellion, revolution, and mass upheaval—were for Josephus the very stuff of history, requiring skillful narration.

Josephus was thus constrained by his concept of historical relevance to give a causal explanation of the split and the uprisings that followed. He therefore offers his readers an episode, found in some source, that seemed to account for the violent hostility that ensued. It is immaterial whether we are satisfied with this causal link, since the fact that a rebellion broke out when the rupture occurred proves conclusively that the Pharisees must have had a large, powerful, and dedicated following among the people. And when to this fact is added the sustained armed rebellion that plagued the entire reign of Alexander Janneus, it is evident that the Pharisees must have been capable of arousing loyalties to themselves and to their unwritten laws of such intensity that the people were willing to rise up against a Hasmonean High Priest and ethnarch.

Josephus' account thus contains three levels of communication: (1) the rebellion itself, which followed on John's split with the Pharisees; (2) the description of the incident purportedly causing the rupture; and (3) the clarifying exposition of Josephus as to reasons why the Pharisees and Sadducees were hostile to each other.

Let us now analyze each level of communication to elicit data for constructing a definition of the Pharisees.

On the episodic level, the Pharisees appear to have enjoyed an intimate relationship with John Hyrcanus since he prided himself on being one of their disciples. Sometime during his High Priesthood, a clash occurred between him and the Pharisees which was of so serious a nature that he abandoned them for the Sadducees and abrogated the unwritten laws they had established for the masses. Indeed, he went so far as to punish those who observed them. The uprising that followed on

John's abrogation of the unwritten laws testifies to the strong hold the Pharisees had upon the masses.

That this uprising was no slight affair is made starkly evident in Josephus' account in the *War*. Though the cause of the outbreaks is not explicitly connected with John's rupture with the Pharisees, it is clear that the events are to be read in the light of the robust treatment in *Antiquities*. This is how Josephus describes the rebellion in *War:* "The prosperous fortunes of John and his sons, however, provoked a sedition among his envious countrymen, large numbers of whom held meetings to oppose them and continued to agitate, until the smouldering flames burst out in open war and the rebels were defeated . . ." (*War* I:67).

The events themselves thus demonstrate that the people were agitated and disturbed by the fall of the Pharisees from the elevated status they had enjoyed. Violent uprisings and open warfare occur when intense loyalties are affected. Accordingly, the Pharisees must have gained wide mass support *prior* to the rupture; indeed, they must have enjoyed their initial close relationship with John Hyrcanus because they were held in such high esteem by the people.

If, then, we ask ourselves what the distinguishing characteristics of the Pharisees were as revealed by the structure of events, we are struck by the fact that they had been responsible for promulgating *nomima* for the people. They were thus legislators, lawmakers. These laws were distinctively theirs, distinguishable from laws that John Hyrcanus established in their stead. Since John Hyrcanus continued on as High Priest and as an adherent of the Sadducees, the laws that superseded the Pharisaic laws must have been Sadducean. The Pharisees are thus identifiable as a scholar class who had had the authority to establish laws for the people, an authority challenged only when John Hyrcanus abrogated these laws and punished those who obeyed them. The Pharisees must therefore have been extremely powerful and influential if their laws could have had such sanction; for their laws were operational, not academic. These laws were not merely for experts but for the masses as well. In breaking with the Pharisees, John Hyrcanus was thus challenging the *functioning* legal system and replacing it with another. So drastic an alteration in the life of the people was bound to have traumatic consequences.

Utilizing Josephus' data with an eye only to the events themselves, one must therefore conclude that the Pharisees were powerful legislators and men of affairs. They were not passive academicians but determined leaders who had successfully gained for their unwritten laws the tenacious support of the masses—leaders who had not hesitated to resist John's decree declaring that these laws were no longer binding and threatening those who remained loyal to them with punishment.

From the outset, Josephus, or his source, makes it clear that the Pharisees are a *haeresis* who enjoy the strong support of the masses. They have but to take a stand against king or High Priest, and the masses side with them. And when John Hyrcanus abrogates the laws of the Pharisees, this stirs them to hatred of John and of his sons. It is when this latter fact is recorded that Josephus, or his source, uses the Greek *oun* ("wherefore," "to be sure") so as to underscore the well-known source of the hatred of the masses for John and his sons.

The Pharisees have a mass following. They are also teachers of justice, advocates of pleasing God, instructors as to the just or proper way of life, underwriters of virtue, philosophers of religion. John Hyrcanus is pictured as being their disciple, a *mathetes,* who looks to them for religious and moral guidance.

We learn more. The Pharisees are well-disposed to John Hyrcanus; indeed, they "loved him greatly." They are indignant when Eleazar slanders John and they are ready to mete out stripes and chains as punishments. They refrain from inflicting more severe punishment because of their principles, a natural leniency in matters of punishment and an especial regard for the taking of a human life. Slander, however reprehensible it might be, did not justify capital punishment, irrespective of the rank of the slandered one.

The Pharisees were those who determined the laws applicable to crime and its punishment. Not only are they asked by John to indicate the punishment they would favor in this instance, but their well-known leniency in criminal matters is clearly alluded to in explanation of their calling for only stripes and chains. They are advocates of a particular legal orientation in criminal law.

There may be more information in this passage. The story as given by Josephus puts the blame for the slander on a single individual, Eleazar, who is described as having an evil nature. The Pharisees as such are not held responsible for the charge. Indeed, they are pictured as disassociating themselves from Eleazar's statement and as being indignant. John's Sadduceean friend, however, accuses the Pharisees of believing the slander, and it is this accusation that prompts John to test the Pharisees. Their failure to recommend the death penalty—a penalty the Sadducees presumably would have countenanced*—is taken by John as evidence of their participation in the slander.

This account reveals John Hyrcanus as taking initiative in breaking with the Pharisees. The Pharisees had done all that was in their power to demonstrate their rejection of Eleazar's charge. John, however, was looking for a pretext, and he found it.

Of greatest importance, however, in this account of the split between John Hyrcanus and the Pharisees is

---

*When Exod. 22:28 ("You shall not revile God, nor curse a ruler of your people") is juxtaposed to Lev. 24:15-16 ("Whoever curses his God shall bear his sin. He who blasphemes the Lord shall be put to death"), one can discern the scriptural justification for the death penalty, since John Hyrcanus, a prince and High Priest, had been reviled. Hence the Sadducees, upholding literality, could expose the Pharisees as lax in undergirding John's rule.

Josephus' explanation of the essential differences that divided the Pharisees from the Sadducees. It takes the form of a descriptive aside, for the narrative is temporarily halted so as to clarify for the reader the significance of John Hyrcanus' break with the Pharisees and his adherence to the Sadducees. Josephus had to explain why John's abrogation of the laws of the Pharisees should have stirred up such intense hatred of the masses. Consequently he bypasses all but the essential difference that separated the Pharisees from the Sadducees. This root disagreement revolved around the authority of the Unwritten Law.

Since Josephus was confronted with the need to relate the Pharisees and the Sadducees to events of great significance, he was called upon by these events themselves to offer a definition of the Pharisees and the Sadducees that would offer the reader a causal explanation. He needed to put his finger on the crucial differentiation between the two *haereseis,* the sort of differentiation that alone could stir up such intense loyalty and such bitter hostility. He had to offer an explanation that accounted for the violent response of the masses to a decision on the part of a High Priest and ruler to abandon one *haeresis* for another. The definition Josephus gives us here is, therefore, of a decisive character. And the core of this definition is that the Pharisees and the Sadducees were the protagonists of two conflicting systems of law.

Josephus is as explicit as he can be: the Pharisees and the Sadducees were hostile to each other because they violently disagreed as to the authority of the so-called Unwritten Law. The Unwritten Law was championed by the Pharisees. The laws were not to be found in the laws of Moses. They were laws that had been transmitted in unwritten form, laws that hailed back to the "Fathers." The Pharisees had transmitted these laws to the masses who accepted them as authoritative.

The Sadducees rejected the Unwritten Law. Only the

laws written in the Pentateuch were binding. The *paradosis ton pateron,* the transmitted laws of the fathers, the unwritten laws, were *not* to be obeyed. "And concerning these matters," concludes Josephus, "they [the Pharisees and Sadducees] came to have controversies *[zeteseis]* and serious differences *[diaphoras megalas]*."

Basic, deep-rooted differences over the Law—these, according to Josephus, divided the Pharisees from the Sadducees. The unwritten laws, transmitted by the Pharisees from the "Fathers," had so captured the loyalty of the masses that they were willing to lay down their lives to seek the restoration of these laws. The Sadducees, by contrast, had little sympathy among the masses.

Two systems of law in collision thus account for the unleashing of a bitter civil war. The written and the unwritten laws could *not* be *simultaneously* obeyed when they commanded very different acts. No wonder, then, that when John Hyrcanus abrogated the Unwritten Law of the Pharisees and adopted the Written Law as espoused by the Sadducees, the masses reacted violently. They regarded the Unwritten Law as binding and resented its abrogation. As devoted followers of the Pharisees, who were now out of favor, they were appalled at the prospect of violating what they considered to be divinely sanctioned Law. They were being threatened with punishment if they persisted in observing the Unwritten Law. Josephus underscores this bitterness of the masses when he says, "Out of this, of course *[oun]*, grew the hatred of the masses *[tou plethous]* for him [John Hyrcanus] *and* his sons [Aristobulus I and Alexander Jannaeus]" (italics added).

This view of the Pharisees as active, aggressive, and determined champions of that Unwritten Law is further confirmed by the structure of events that followed John Hyrcanus' death. John had successfully put down the spontaneous outburst of violence that had followed in the wake of his abrogation of the Pharisaic unwritten

Law and of his going over to the Sadducees and their literal reading of the Pentateuch. His successor, Judah Aristobulus, who served as High Priest and declared himself king, may have been spared armed insurrection, but with Alexander Jannaeus' accession to the throne and to the High Priesthood, the smouldering hatred of the masses burst into flames of sustained rebellion as the Pharisees sought to recapture their authority.

Josephus deals with these events in both the *War* and *Antiquities.* We shall analyze the account in *Antiquities* first because it alone narrates the activity of the Pharisees and their supporters while Alexander Janneus was still alive. Although *War* presupposes such activity, it does not deal explicitly with it.

The role of the Pharisees in the rebellion of the people against Alexander is brought out in Josephus' account of Alexander's deathbed advice to his wife Salome, who was to become queen after his death:

And when the queen saw that he [Alexander] was on the point of death and no longer held to any hope of recovery, she wept and beat her breast, lamenting the bereavement that was about to befall her and her children, and said to him, "To whom are you thus leaving me and your children, who are in need of help from others, *especially* when you know how hostile the nation feels toward you!" Thereupon he advised her to follow his suggestions for keeping the throne secure for herself and her children and to conceal his death from the soldiers until she had captured the fortress. And then, he said, on her return from Jerusalem as from a splendid victory, she should yield a certain amount of power to the Pharisees, for if they praised her in return for this sign of regard, they would dispose the nation favourably toward her. These men, he assured her, had so much influence with their fellow-Jews that they could injure those whom they hated and help those to whom they were friendly; *for they had the complete confidence of the masses when they spoke harshly of any person, even when they did so out of envy; and he himself, he added, had come into conflict with the nation because these men had been badly treated by him.* "And so," he said, "when you come to Jerusalem, send for their partisans, and showing them my dead body, permit them, with every sign of sincerity, to treat me as they please, whether they wish to dishonour my corpse by leaving it unburied because of the many injuries they have suffered at my hands, or in their anger wish to offer my dead body any other form of indignity. Promise them also that you will not take any *action,* while you are on the throne, without their consent. If you speak to them in this manner, I shall receive from them a more splendid burial than I should from you; for once they have the power to do so, they will not choose to treat my corpse badly, and at the same time you will reign securely." With this exhortation to his wife he died, after reigning twenty-seven years, at the age of forty-nine. (*Ant.* XIII:399-404; italics added)

Josephus, on the basis of the source or sources available to him, has Alexander testify to the power of the Pharisees, a power that derived from their popularity with the masses. The stubborn rebellion of the nation had its roots in Alexander's ill treatment of them. A shift in policy according them a decisive decision-making role was certain to bring an end to the hostility. Indeed, in return for such power, the Pharisees would be willing to recognize the legitimacy of the monarchy and to give Alexander a splendid funeral. Even more. They would rehabilitate the honor of Alexander and convince the masses that he had indeed been a great ruler.

And, according to Josephus, the Pharisees did just that:

Thereupon Alexandra, after capturing the fortress, conferred with the Pharisees as her husband had suggested, and by placing in their hands all that concerned his corpse and the royal power, stilled their anger against Alexander, and made them her well-wishers and friends. And they in turn went to the people and made public speeches in which they recounted the deeds of Alexander, and said that in him they had lost a just king, and by their eulogies they so greatly moved the people to mourn and lament that they gave him a more splendid burial than had been given any of the kings before him. . . . As for the queen herself, she was loved by the masses because she was thought to disapprove of the crimes committed by her husband. (*Ant.* XIII:405-7)

The masses are pictured as utterly trusting the decision of their Pharisaic leaders. They are even willing to mourn for the very monarch they had hated. And they are only too happy to bestow on Salome Alexandra their affection for restoring the Pharisees to power. The Pharisees thus appear to have had the full confidence and support of the people.

Josephus then gives a clear account of how the Pharisees used their power:

Alexandra then appointed Hyrcanus as high priest because of his greater age but more especially because of his lack of energy; and she permitted the Pharisees to do as they liked in all matters, and also commanded the people to obey them; *and whatever laws [nomima;* author's trans.*], introduced by the Pharisees in accordance with the tradition of their fathers [kata ten patroan paradosin], had been abolished by her father-in-law Hyrcanus, these she again restored.* And so, while she had the title of sovereign, the Pharisees had the power. For example, they recalled exiles, and freed prisoners, and, in a word, in no way differed from absolute rulers. Nevertheless, the queen took thought for the welfare of the kingdom and recruited a large force of mercenaries and also made her own force twice as large, with the result that she struck terror into the local rulers around her and received hostages from them. And throughout the entire country there was quiet except for the Pharisees; for they worked upon the feelings of the queen and tried to persuade her to kill those who had urged Alexander to put the eight hundred to death.* Later they themselves cut down one of them, named Diogenes, and his death was followed by that of one after the other, until the leading citizens came to the palace [and bitterly protested these actions]. (*Ant.* XIII:408-11; italics added)

The source Josephus used was not favorably disposed to the Pharisees. Yet he did not tamper with it even though he himself was a Pharisee. This source reports a series of acts that involve the Pharisees. These acts are all of a determined and aggressive character. They are goal-oriented, and they display a sophisticated awareness of the realities of power. The Pharisees knew what they wanted, and moved decisively to break up the

*Cf. *Ant.* XIII:380-81; *War* I:97-98.

anti-Pharisaic clique which had enjoyed the confidence of Alexander.

The Pharisees appear to have had two aims: (1) to restore the Unwritten Law, and (2) to crush the opposition. With Salome Alexandra's support, the Unwritten Law, "the traditions of the Fathers," was reintroduced. The legal system thereby underwent another complete transformation as the Sadducean Written Law was replaced by the Pharisaic twofold Law, the Written and the Oral. The Pharisees thus once again sat in Moses' seat.

Coupled with their restoration of the Unwritten Law, the Pharisees took other steps to consolidate their power. They brought back the exiled and released the imprisoned. They instituted what appeared to their opponents to be a reign of terror. They wanted put to death those who had instigated Alexander's brutal crucifixion of the eight hundred. And apparently they carried out their designs. They are held responsible for having slaughtered Diogenes and with having brought about the death of any number of others. They struck such terror into the heart of the aristocracy that a delegation led by Aristobulus beseeched Queen Salome Alexandra to take steps to prevent the total annihilation of those who had demonstrated their valor on the field of battle and had stood loyally by Alexander in times of danger.

The source used by Josephus is hostile to the Pharisees. Nevertheless, if the acts it reports are true, the Pharisees must have been alert to the problems of power and to the decisive character of violence. They may have given the dead Alexander a grand funeral, but they were fully aware of the danger to their supremacy from living opponents. They therefore did not hesitate to put to death as many of their enemies as possible. The Pharisees appear as the champions of a system of law which was meant to function. And to make certain that it would, the Pharisees resorted to means designed to achieve their end.

This picture of the Pharisees as men of action is confirmed by the parallel account given by Josephus in his *War:*

Alexander bequeathed the kingdom to his wife Alexandra, being convinced that the Jews would bow to her authority as they would to no other, because by her utter lack of his brutality and by her opposition to his crimes she had won the affections of the populace. Nor was he mistaken in these expectations; for this frail woman firmly held the reins of government, thanks to her reputation for piety. She was indeed, the very strictest observer of the national traditions and would deprive of office any offenders against the sacred laws. Of the two sons whom she had by Alexander, she appointed the elder, Hyrcanus, high priest, out of consideration alike for his age and his disposition, which was too lethargic to be troubled about public affairs; the younger, Aristobulus, as a hot-head, she confined to a private life.

Beside Alexandra, and growing as she grew, arose the Pharisees, a body of Jews *[suntagma ti Ioudaion]* with the reputation of excelling the rest of their nation in the observances of religion, and as exact exponent of the laws *[kai tous nomous akribesteron aphegeisthai]*. To them, being herself intensely religious, she listened with too great deference; while they, gradually taking advantage of an ingenuous woman, became at length the real administrators of the state, at liberty to banish and to recall, to loose and to bind, whom they would. In short, the enjoyments of royal authority were theirs; its expenses and burthen fell to Alexandra. She proved, however, to be a wonderful administrator in larger affairs, and, by continual recruiting doubled her army, besides collecting a considerable body of foreign troops, so that she not only strengthened her own nation, but became a formidable foe to foreign potentates. But if she ruled the nation, the Pharisees ruled her.

Thus they put to death Diogenes, a distinguished man who had been a friend of Alexander, accusing him of having advised the king to crucify his eight hundred victims. They further urged Alexandra to make away with the others who had instigated Alexander to punish those men; and as she from superstitious motives always gave way, they proceeded to kill whomsoever they would. The most eminent of the citizens thus imperilled sought refuge with Aristobulus, who persuaded his mother to spare their lives in consideration of their rank, but, if she was not satisfied of their innocence, to expel them from the city. Their security being thus guaranteed, they dispersed about the country. (*War* I:107-14)

Although this account does not contain the deathbed speech of Alexander with its explicit advice to restore the Pharisees to power, it conveys much the same idea. The Hasmoneans had lost the support of the masses because of their break with the Pharisees. If the monarchy wished to avoid continuous civil war, it would have to make its peace with the Pharisees. Alexandra is thus pictured as holding firmly the reins of government because of her reputation for *eusebes,* "piety," and for her strict adherence to the laws. And there can be little doubt that the offenders against the sacred laws whom she removed from office were Sadducees.

The Pharisees whom she favors are determined to wield the power allotted them. Josephus' source attributes to them complete control over the state and fingers them as the real power behind Salome. They do as they please, putting to death not only Diogenes but many others. Alexandra is pictured as meekly submitting because of her religious nature.

There are hints, however, that Salome was no ingenuous woman. Her skills as an administrator of the foreign affairs of the realm are praised by the very source that exposes her as a helpless pawn of the Pharisees. Her shrewd assessment of the mood of the masses probably accounts for her support of the Pharisees far more satisfactorily than her religious naïveté.

The Pharisees, however Salome's relationship to them is explained, apparently did have considerable authority to liquidate their most hated opponents. They were, for Josephus' source, a *suntagma,* a body or band of Jews who were known for their *eusebes,* their piety, and for their exact, or precise or accurate *(akribesteron),* exposition of the laws. But clearly they were a group that did not see any contradiction between *eusebes* and administrating the affairs of state, nor between being exact expositors of the laws and putting Diogenes to death. They are a *suntagma* that is determined to have its exposition of the laws recognized as authoritative, and its *eusebes* the model for their fellow Jews.

The *eusebes* of the Pharisees and their exact exposition of the laws are thus far removed from irenic contemplation. No objection is raised by them to Salome's concern with larger affairs, her doubling the size of the army, and the hiring of large numbers of foreign mercenaries. The Pharisees are not averse to her building a strong nation, formidable to foreign potentates. The Pharisees appeared to Josephus' source as pious, legal experts seeking to rule a people and taking the steps necessary to achieve their aim.

The Pharisees in the time of John Hyrcanus, Alexander Jannaeus, and Salome Alexandra were a law-making, scholar class capable of stirring up and abetting rebellion against king and High Priest, sanctioning the use of violence to attain power and authority, maneuvering shrewdly to effect a compromise with Salome Alexandra, and liquidating their enemies. They must, at the same time, have been men who could arouse intense loyalty and evoke sustained support for their leadership. If, after a generation, all efforts at suppressing the rebellion by violence had failed and the Hasmonean dynasty was compelled to make their peace with the Pharisees, it is evident that the Pharisees tapped deep wellsprings of loyalty and devotion among the masses.

The role of the Pharisees looms large in that segment of history beginning with John Hyrcanus and ending with Salome Alexandra. They are very much in the forefront of events. The surface of history is continuously churned by their activities. They are making what Josephus and his fellow historians conceived to be history, for they are affecting the functioning of political, dynastic, and military affairs. But the moment that this aspect of their activity dwindles in importance, they cease to be relevant for Josephus, and he never again accords them more than passing mention. And when he does, it is with reference to some event of political significance.

He thus briefly refers to the Pharisees Samaias and Pollion because of their special relationship to Herod. As a politically significant individual, Herod is very much the concern of Josephus; and since the Pharisees Samaias and Pollion impinged meaningfully on Herod's career, Josephus feels constrained to mention these incidents.

According to Josephus (*Ant.* XIV:168-83), when Herod was brought to trial on the charge that he had unlawfully killed Ezekias, an insurrectionary leader, and many of his men, "someone named Samaias, an upright man," urged the members of the council (sanhedrin) to convict Herod. Yet,

> when Herod assumed royal power, he killed Hyrcanus and all the other members of the Synhedrion with the exception of Samaias. Him he held in the greatest honour, both because of his uprightness and because when the city was later besieged by Herod and Sossius, he advised the people to admit Herod, and said that on account of their sins they would not be able to escape him. (*Ant.* XIV:175-76)

In *Ant.* XV:3-4, Josephus further informs us that when Herod gained mastery of all Judea, he especially honored Pollion the Pharisee and his disciple Samaias,* because they had advised their fellow Jews to admit Herod into Jerusalem. His regard went so far that when Pollion and Samaias and their disciples refused to take the oath of loyalty to Herod, they went unpunished (XV:370).

In the course of the narrative, Josephus informs us at one point that Samaias was an upright man and, for that reason, superior to fear. We also learn that Pollion and Samaias were related to each other as teacher to disciple, and that Pollion and Samaias had a following of disciples.

---

*In *Ant.* XIV:168-83, it is Samaias who calls for Herod's conviction. Substantively, it makes no difference whether it was Samaias or Pollion since in either case we are dealing with a teacher-disciple relationship.

50

Since Pollion and Samaias are referred to as Pharisees, it is apparent that the Pharisees were scholars.

More significantly, however, Pollion and Samaias emerge as powerful men of affairs. When Samaias, or Pollion, arose before the sanhedrin and warned his co-councillors that if they acquitted Herod, Herod would some day wreak vengeance upon them, he speaks as a sophisticated man of affairs, fully alive to problems of power.

The subsequent relationship to Herod underwrites Samaias' political sophistication. Herod was never deterred by kindness when his power was at stake. He killed even when he was not threatened. If, then, he spared Samaias and Pollion even though Samaias, or Pollion, had called for his execution, it could only have been because these scholars had secured and enhanced his power. They had sided with him at a crucial time. They had thrown their support to him rather than to the Hasmonean Antigonus. Their influence must have been great enough to have made a difference. The text in Josephus leaves little doubt that they must have performed an extraordinary service for Herod; for the treatment accorded them is in stark contrast to that meted out to others:

When Herod had got the rule of all Judaea into his hands, he showed special favour to those of the city populace which had been on his side while he was still a commoner, but those who chose the side of his opponents he harried and punished without ceasing for a single day. *Especially honoured* by him were Pollion the Pharisee, and his disciple Samaias, for during the siege of Jerusalem these men had advised the citizens to admit Herod, and for this they now received their reward. This same Pollion had once, when Herod was on trial for his life, reproachfully foretold to Hyrcanus and the judges that if Herod's life were spared, he would [one day] persecute them all. And in time this turned out to be so, for God fulfilled his words. (*Ant.* XV:2-4; italics added)

Herod's relatedness to Pollion and Samaias was thus not passive and neutral. He accorded them a status higher than that accorded to his other well-wishers and supporters: "Most honored by him was the Pharisee Pollion and his disciple Samaias."

That this respect was no passing fancy is proved by Herod's freeing of Pollion and Samaias and their disciples from an oath of loyalty. Seventeen years had passed since Herod had taken over Jerusalem and still Pollion and Samaias were treated with special consideration:

He also tried to persuade Pollion the Pharisee and Samaias and most of their disciples to take the oath, but they would not agree to this, and yet they were not punished as were the others who refused, for they were shown consideration on Pollion's account. (*Ant.* XV:370)

Herod, not Pollion and Samaias, is the one to give in! Pollion and Samaias simply refused to take the oath, and Herod, who was so ruthless whenever his person and power were concerned, backs down and exempts them and their disciples from the oath. And the reason? His respect and esteem for Pollion stays his hand from punishing *them,* though he, "by one means or another made away" with all other recalcitrants—except for the Essenes whom Herod held in honor, but for other reasons.

This exemption testifies to the great power and influence exercised by Pollion and Samaias. As Pharisees, their opinion must have carried great weight with the masses, and consequently Herod felt that he needed their support. To have punished them for refusing to take the oath would presumably have meant an invitation to civil war no less fierce than that which had marked the tragic reign of Alexander Jannaeus. Too astute a ruler to provoke the entire people to rebellion, Herod was willing to forego a formal oath of loyalty so long as he was convinced that Pollion and Samaias and their disciples were loyal in fact. They had already demonstrated their commitment to Herod when they had urged the masses to side with Herod against Antigonus. For though the city had to be taken by storm, its defenses must have been considerably weakened by the defection of Pollion, Samaias, and their followers. Only if one were to assume a naïve, tender-hearted, religiously devout Herod, a Herod who forgave and forgot, a Herod indifferent to power, i.e., a nonexistent Herod, could one account for Herod's veneration and regard for Pollion and Samaias by considerations other than that of the very real power they exercised.

The power of the Pharisees was thus real indeed. Even so despotic a ruler as Herod had to bend before it, even though the Pharisees no longer enjoyed quite the same relationship to the throne that had been theirs during Salome Alexandra's reign.

Once again our source demands that in defining the Pharisees, we include qualities allowing for active leadership and a high degree of political sophistication.

Josephus does not again pick up on the Pharisees until he is compelled to deal with the rise of a novel *haeresis,* i.e., a school of thought championed by Judas of Galilee. Josephus calls this *haeresis* simply the Fourth Philosophy:

Under his [Coponius'; A.D. 6-9] administration, a Galilaean named Judas incited his countrymen to revolt, upbraiding them as cowards for consenting to pay tribute to the Romans and tolerating mortal masters, after having God for their lord. This man was a sophist who founded a *haeresis** of his own, having nothing in common with the others. (*War* II:118)

Since Josehus had written his *War* to describe how the Jews had been driven to rebel against Rome, he was compelled to draw the attention of his readers to that "philosophy" of Judaism which had been the first to call upon the people to take up arms against Rome. Having thus made reference to a Fourth Philosophy, Josephus had little choice but to apprise his readers of the other

---

*Thackeray translates haeresis as "sect."

three "philosophies" which had been in existence long before Judas of Galilee had raised the standard of revolt. As a consequence, we have set before us additional raw material for a definition of the Pharisees:

> Of the two first-named schools, the Pharisees, who are considered the most accurate interpreters of the laws, and hold the position of the leading *haeresis,* attribute everything to Fate and to God; they hold that to act rightly or otherwise rests, indeed, for the most part with men, but that in each action Fate co-operates. Every soul, they maintain, is imperishable, but the soul of the good alone passes into another body, while the souls of the wicked suffer eternal punishment. (*War* II:162-63)

Josephus then turns to the Sadducees to point out the contrast:

> The Sadducees, the second of the orders, do away with Fate altogether, and remove God beyond, not merely the commission, but the very sight of evil. They maintain that man has the free choice of good or evil, and that it rests with each man's will whether he follows the one or the other. As for the persistence of the soul after death, penalties in the underworld, and rewards, they will have none of them. (*War* II:164-65)

Having contrasted their beliefs, Josephus goes on to point out another difference.

> The Pharisees are affectionate to each other and cultivate harmonious relations with the community. The Sadducees, on the contrary, are, even among themselves, rather boorish in their behaviour, and in their intercourse with their peers are as rude as to aliens.
> Such is what I have to say on the Jewish philosophical schools. (*War* II:166)

The Pharisees, according to Josephus, are a *haeresis,* and, as such, hold to doctrines that differentiate them from the other *haereseis.* [1] What is their hallmark? What is their most prominent feature? Is it their accurate interpretation of the laws? Or their views on free will and Providence, or belief in the immortality of the soul? Or is

it perhaps their friendliness to each other and their efforts
to cultivate harmonious relations with the community?

One cannot say for certain, since Josephus does not
underwrite any one of these as being the primary
characteristic. Each feature, therefore, must be analyzed
separately and made ready for future use in the
construction of Josephus' definition of the Pharisees.

The Pharisees must have been scholars. Josephus
leaves no doubt about this. He says of them that they are
deemed to be the most accurate, precise, or exact
interpreters or expounders of the laws, even though he
fails to give any example of their precision, accuracy, or
exactitude. Josephus does not tell us whether they are
interpreters of the Pentateuchal text, i.e., exegetes, or
expounders of the laws, i.e., those teaching the laws
without recourse to the Pentateuchal text, or both. The
Greek word *exegeisthai* can support either meaning. But
Josephus does evoke a picture of a class of scholars whose
meticulous interest in the laws has gained for them a
reputation as the most expert.

These scholars, according to Josephus, were also
philalailoi, "friendly to each other," and practiced
concord toward the community. They stand out in sharp
contrast to the Sadducees, who are coarse to each other
and rude to their compatriots.

The Pharisees, in Josephus' eyes, were friendly
expounders or interpreters of the laws who held definite
beliefs about God and man. "The Pharisees," Josephus
informs us, "attribute everything to Fate and to God;
they hold that to act rightly or otherwise rests, indeed for
the most part with men, but that in each action Fate
cooperates" (*War* I:162). For the Pharisees, God was
active in the universe and in the life of man. Man can
choose between good and evil, but the consequence of
his choice in this world is not certain. Here Fate plays a
part. Yet God is not indifferent to man's actions, for he
has, for the good man, another body awaiting the
imperishable soul, even as he has eternal punishment

readied for the wicked: "Every soul is imperishable, but the soul of the good alone passes into another body, while the souls of the wicked suffer eternal punishments" (*War* I:163).

The Pharisees thus taught that God cared for the individual, rewarding the good and punishing the wicked. In this world, the acts of the righteous do not necessarily reap a good harvest, for whatever occurs involves both Fate and God. These acts, however, do not escape God's sight anymore than do those of the wicked who may in this life be favored by Fate. God's justice will be evident to the immortal soul after death, even though it may have been indiscernible in one's lifetime.

The Sadducees, according to Josephus, offered no such solace to the individual. The Sadducees eliminate the role of Fate. God for them could in no wise be party to the evil of the world. Man can choose either good or evil. It is a decision that he makes freely, and he reaps its consequences during his lifetime.

Although the exact meaning of these doctrines espoused by the Pharisees and Sadducees on God, Fate, and free will is somewhat ambiguous, Josephus does convey the idea that the Pharisees believed in a God who cared for each and every individual, while the Sadducees believed in a God who shared no equivalent concern.

Josephus' second descriptive aside is to be found in *Antiquities.* He interjects it into the historical narrative, much as he did in the *War.* Since Josephus is compelled to treat the emergence of the revolutionary movement under Judas, and since he once again calls this movement a *haeresis,* he temporarily pauses in his history to explain to the reader some of the characteristics of the other *haereseis,* the Pharisees, Sadducees, and Essenes. Here is his description of the Pharisees:[2]

The Pharisees live modestly, forswearing luxury. They adhere devotedly to the good doctrines which have been transmitted orally to them, holding to and prizing their own teachings.

56

They show great respect to their elders, refraining from rashly contradicting what these elders have taught.

Although the Pharisees believe that, by and large, all things are brought about by Fate, they nonetheless allow some role for the human will. For they find it seemly that God should have allowed for some fusion of the council-chamber of Fate, on the one hand, and the virtue and vice of human conduct on the other.

The Pharisees believe that souls are immortal, and that men are punished or rewarded in the underworld in accordance with the virtue or the vice they practised during their lifetime: eternal punishment being the lot of evil souls; the opportunity for resurrection the destiny of good souls.

These views [of the Pharisees] have been so persuasive with the populace that whatsoever pertains to prayers and sacrifices are performed in accordance with the exposition of the Pharisees, Indeed, the city dwellers bear such testimony to the great virtue of the Pharisees that they emulate the nobility of the Pharisaic way of life and adhere to their teachings.

As for the Sadducees, they believe that the soul perishes with the body. Furthermore, they are on guard lest there be any alteration whatsoever in the laws. Indeed they reckon it a virtue to debate with the teachers of wisdom [namely, the Pharisees] whom they hound. Though few in number, the Sadducees hold positions of esteem. Yet they are powerless. For even when they exercise authority, they submit, however unwillingly, to the teachings of the Pharisees, since otherwise the populace would not put up with them. (*Ant.* XVIII:12-17; author's rendering)

Josephus paints here a pleasing picture of the Pharisees in these passages. They appear as scholars and teachers who are concerned with divine worship, prayer, and sacrifices. They have strong beliefs about the immortality of the soul and the eternal rewards for the virtuous and eternal punishments for the wicked. They show respect for the opinions of those more advanced in years, and they do not contradict their teachings. They have such enthusiastic support from the masses that their exposition of the laws regulates all public religious ceremonies. They are beloved and praised by the cities because of the beauty of their lives and the excellence of their teachings. Their power is so great that even the

Sadducees, when they hold public office, must adhere to Pharisaic views. And this power stems from the fact that the people at large adhere to their teachings.

In another passage of *Antiquities,* when speaking of the emergence of the Fourth Philosophy, Josephus reveals to us the attitude of the Pharisees toward the Roman state:

Quirinius also visited Judaea, which had been annexed to Syria, in order to make an assessment of the property of the Jews and to liquidate the estate of Archelaus. Although the Jews were at first shocked to hear of the registration of property, they gradually condescended, yielding to the arguments of the high priest Joazar, the son of Boethus, to go no further in opposition. So those who were convinced by him declared, without shilly-shallying, the value of their property. But a certain Judas, a Gaulanite from a city named Gamala, who had enlisted the aid of Saddok, a Pharisee, threw himself into the cause of rebellion. They said that the assessment carried with it a status amounting to downright slavery, no less, and appealed to the nation to make a bid for independence. They urged that in case of success the Jews would have laid the foundation of prosperity, while if they failed to obtain any such boon, they would win honour and renown for their lofty aim; and that Heaven would be their zealous helper to no lesser end than the furthering of their enterprise until it succeeded—all the more if with high devotion in their hearts they stood firm and did not shrink from the bloodshed that might be necessary. Since the populace, when they heard their appeals, responded gladly, the plot to strike boldly made serious progress; and so these men sowed the seed of every kind of misery, which so afflicted the nation that words are inadequate. When wars are set afoot that are bound to rage beyond control, and when friends are done away with who might have alleviated the suffering, when raids are made by great hordes of brigands and men of the highest standing are assassinated, it is supposed to be the common welfare that is upheld, but the truth is that in such cases the motive is private gain. They sowed the seed from which sprang strife between factions and the slaughter of fellow citizens. Some were slain in civil strife, for these men madly had recourse to butchery of each other and of themselves from a longing not to be outdone by their opponents; others were slain by the enemy in war. Then came famine, reserved to exhibit the last degree of shamelessness, followed by the storming and razing of cities until at last the very temple of God was ravaged by the enemy's fire through this revolt. Here is a lesson that an innovation and reform in ancestral traditions weighs heavily in the scale in leading to the destruction of the congregation of the people. *In this case certainly, Judas and Saddok started among us an intrusive fourth school of philosophy;* and when they had won an abundance of devotees, they filled the body politic immediately with tumult, also planting the seeds of those troubles which subsequently overtook it, all because of the novelty of this hitherto unknown philosophy that I shall now describe. My reason for giving this brief account of it is chiefly that the zeal which Judas and Saddok inspired in the younger element meant the ruin of our cause. (*Ant.* XVIII:2b-10; italics added)

Josephus then proceeds to describe the *haereseis* that had been long in existence and then returns to the fourth *haeresis:*

As for the fourth of the philosophies, Judas the Galilaean set himself up as leader of it. *This school agrees in all other respects with the opinions of the Pharisees, except that they have a passion for liberty that is almost unconquerable, since they are convinced that God alone is their leader and master.* They think little of submitting to death in unusual forms and permitting vengeance to fall on kinsmen and friends if only they may avoid calling any man master. Inasmuch as most people have seen the steadfastness of their resolution amid such circumstances, I may forgo any further account. For I have no fear that anything reported of them will be considered incredible. The danger is, rather, that report may minimize the indifference with which they accept the grinding misery of pain. The folly that ensued began to afflict the nation after Gessius Florus, who was governor, had by his overbearing and lawless actions provoked a desperate rebellion against the Romans. Such is the number of the schools of philosophy among the Jews. (*Ant.* XVIII:23-25; italics added)

The Fourth Philosophy refused to see the issue as one that involved God at all. As a consequence, some of their followers were so aroused by this policy that they formed another *haeresis,* one that agreed with Pharisaic notions except for Pharisaic acquiescence to Roman rule. The Fourth Philosophy, according to Josephus, had an inviolable attachment to political freedom, which presumably the Pharisees did not. The Fourth Philosophy, unlike the Pharisees, considered that submission to Rome was a denial of God's sovereignty. The difference on this issue, however, was so crucial that the followers of Judas and Saddok could no longer be viewed as Pharisees, despite their agreement on all other notions. As the adherents of a new *haeresis,* they were deemed to be a separate and distinct school of thought.

The Pharisees, exponents of the principle that the Roman state exercised legitimate authority so long as religious law was not violated, made every effort to restrain the people from revolting against Rome.

Thereupon the principal citizens assembled with the chief priests and the most notable Pharisees to deliberate on the position of affairs, now that they were faced with what seemed irreparable disaster. Deciding to try the effect of an appeal to the revolutionaries, they called the people together before the bronze gate. . . . They began by expressing the keenest indignation at the audacity of this revolt and at their country being thus threatened with so serious a war. They then proceeded to expose the absurdity of the alleged pretext. Their forefathers, they said, had adorned the sanctuary mainly at the expense of aliens and had always accepted the gifts of foreign nations; not only had they never taken the sacrilegious step of forbidding anyone to offer sacrifice, but they had set up around the Temple the dedicatory offerings which were still to be seen and had remained there for so long a time. But now here were these men, who were provoking the arms of the Romans and courting a war with them, introducing a strange innovation into their religion, and, besides endangering the city, laying it open to the charge of impiety, if Jews henceforth were to be the only people to allow no alien the right of sacrifice or worship. (*War* II:411-14)

Josephus reaffirms that the Pharisees were opposed to rebellion against state authority. He claims that the most notable Pharisees made every effort to dissuade the people from embarking on a course of action which was bound to alienate Rome. The Pharisees argued that to refuse an oblation offered by a foreigner would be a violation of long-established precedent. Josephus likewise makes clear that the appeal of the Pharisees was ineffective in cooling the revolutionary fervor of the masses.

Unfortunately, Josephus is not as helpful as we should have liked. He refers to the Pharisee notables *(dunatoi),* but he neither spells out who these notables were nor clarifies the question as to whether the notables spoke for all the Pharisees or only for themselves. Nevertheless, it is evident that these notables must have intervened because they had influence with the masses. It had been hoped that their authority might still the clamor of the people for a defiant act against Rome.

Josephus thus is consistent in picturing the Pharisees as devotees of the laws even as they support Roman authority so long as these laws are not violated. In this instance, the Pharisaic notables insisted that the laws regulating the cultus had always allowed foreigners to have their offerings sacrificed in the Temple.

Josephus records the actions of the Pharisaic notables on the eve of the revolt against Rome, at a time when they still felt there was a chance of checking what, for him, were the reckless and irresponsible demands of the masses. Once, however, the die was cast and open rebellion had broken out, some of the Pharisee notables not only joined the revolution but assumed a role of leadership. Josephus reports that Simon the son of Gamaliel, a notable Pharisee, had a decisive voice in the top leadership of the revolt prior to the loss of Galilee, and was indefatigable in his efforts to steer a moderate course when the Zealots pressed for the overthrow of the provisional revolutionary assembly.

In recording the activities of Simon son of Gamaliel, Josephus sheds valuable light on the kind of men the Pharisees were. Simon emerges as a politician and statesman, an astute man of affairs, an aggressive and agile leader as well as a respected expert on the laws. He is alert to the subtleties of power and parries the shrewd tactics of Josephus and of Ananias:

61

Meanwhile, the hatred borne me [i.e., Josephus] by John, son of Levi, who was aggrieved at my success, was growing more intense, and he determined at all costs to have me removed. Accordingly, after fortifying his native town of Gischala, he dispatched his brother Simon and Jonathan, son of Sisenna, with about a hundred armed men, to Jerusalem, to Simon, son of Gamaliel, to entreat him to induce the national assembly of Jerusalem to deprive me of the command of Galilee and to vote for his appointment to the post. This Simon was a native of Jerusalem, of a very illustrious family, and of the *haeresis* of the Pharisees, who have the reputation of being unrivalled experts in their country's laws *[hoi peri ta patria nomima dokousin ton allon akribeia diapherein]*. A man highly gifted with intelligence and judgment, he could by sheer genius retrieve an unfortunate situation in affairs of state. He was John's old and intimate friend, and, at the time, was at variance with me. On receiving this application he exerted himself to persuade the high-priests Ananus and Jesus, son of Gamalas, and some others of their party to clip my sprouting wings and not suffer me to mount to the pinnacle of fame. He observed that my removal from Galilee would be to their advantage, and urged them to act without delay, for fear that I should get wind of their plans and march with a large army upon Jerusalem. Such was Simon's advice. In reply, Ananus, the high-priest, represented the difficulties of the action suggested in view of the testimonials from many of the chief priests and leaders of the people to my capacity as a general; adding that to accuse a man against whom no just charge could be brought was a dishonourable proceeding.

On hearing this speech of Ananus, Simon implored the embassy to keep to themselves and not divulge what had passed at the conference; asserting that he would see to it that I was speedily superseded in Galilee. Then calling up John's brother he instructed him to send presents to Ananus and his friends, as a likely method of inducing them to change their minds. Indeed Simon eventually achieved his purpose; for, as the result of bribery, Ananus and his party agreed to expel me from Galilee, while every one else in the city remained ignorant of the plot. The scheme agreed upon was to send a deputation comprising persons of different classes of society but of equal standing in education *[te paideia d'homious]*. Two of them, Jonathan and Ananias, were from the lower ranks and adherents of the Pharisees; the third, Jozar, also a Pharisee, came of a priestly family; the youngest, Simon, was descended from high priests. Their instructions were to approach the Galilaeans and ascertain the reason for their devotion to me. If they attributed it to my being a native of Jerusalem, they were to reply that so were all four of them; if to my expert knowledge of their laws, they should retort that neither were they ignorant of the customs of their fathers; if, again, they asserted that their affection was due to my priestly office, they should answer that two of them were likewise priests. (*Life* 190-98)

Josephus thus pictures Simon as anything but an academic recluse. We see no saintly figure here! Nor does the following description of Simon, seeking to stem the Zealot bid for power, evoke images of passive piety.

This latest outrage [the elevation of a simple villager to the post of High Priest by the Zealots] was more than the people could stand, and as if for the overthrow of a despotism one and all were not roused. For their leaders of outstanding reputation, such as Gorion, son of Joseph, and Symeon [probably Simon], son of Gamaliel, by public addresses to the whole assembly and by private visits to individuals, urged them to delay no longer to punish these wreckers of liberty and purge the sanctuary of its bloodstained polluters. Their efforts were supported by the most eminent of the high priests, Jesus, son of Gamalas and Ananus, son of Ananus, who at their meetings vehemently upbraided the people for their apathy and incited them against the Zealots; for so these miscreants called themselves, as though they were zealous in the cause of virtue and not for vice in its basest and most extravagant form. (*War* IV:158-61)

Simon the son of Gamaliel is no quietist in Josephus' book. He had very definite ideas as to how the revolution should be conducted, and he was aggressive in countering the tendencies toward excessive radicalism. Although he was unsuccessful—the Zealots did gain ascendency—he did not passively submit to the turn of events but fought determinedly against them.

In constructing a definition of the Pharisees from Josephus' data, we must give careful consideration to Josephus' portrait of this leading Pharisee, namely, Simon son of Gamaliel. Simon does not cease being a Pharisee when he acts as a political leader; his vigorous actions are not out of keeping with his expertness in the laws. Josephus clearly does not see any contradiction between the Simon who "could by sheer genius retrieve an unfortunate situation in affairs of state" and the Simon who adhered to such Pharisaic principles as resurrection and accurate exposition and interpretation of the laws.

The Pharisees as activists emerge also in Josephus' mention of the composition of the delegation appointed to oust Josephus from control of Galilee. Josephus tells us specifically that three of the four delegates were Pharisees. They are sent to carry out a *political* assignment, the nature of which necessitated that experts on the laws be present. Two of the Pharisees, at least, were to act as such experts so as to undercut any claims by Josephus of superior competence. Such a mission in the midst of a revolution and directed against the general of Galilee could have been entrusted only to men whose qualities were not limited to academic knowledge. Yet Josephus sees nothing strange in Pharisees being assigned so dangerous a task but rather takes it for granted. In his mind, Pharisees were not pietistic religionists far removed from the clash of arms and the jostlings for command but aggresive participants.

And indeed Josephus never pictures them other than as men of affairs. We have already seen that he speaks of them as "*striving* earnestly to put into *practice* their teachings"; as regulating "all that pertains to divine worship, prayers and sacrifices"; as teaching even magistrates with Sadducean leanings the laws to be followed. The fact that Pharisees were at first opposed to the rebellion against Rome and only subsequently gave it their support does not imply that they were either quietists or indifferent to the outcome of events. Indeed, they were most active in their efforts to stop the revolt. They did not stand idly by but used all their influence to deter the masses. And when this tactic failed, they did not surrender leadership but accommodated themselves to the new situation and attempted to guide the revolution in the direction of moderation. And when, with the loss of Galilee, the Zealots emerged with their demand for more radical measures, Simon the son of Gamaliel vigorously opposed them.

Josephus not only adds a new dimension to the Pharisaic image in his delineation of Simon ben Gamaliel's role, but he reaffirms certain distinguishing characteristics that he has already set forth in his descriptive asides. Thus he once again refers to the Pharisees as a *haeresis,* a school of thought, and not a sect. And when he wishes to give a highly condensed mark of identification as to who these Pharisees were, he says that they are those "who have the reputation of being unrivalled experts in their country's laws."

These experts were drawn from all classes of society. Some, like Simon son of Gamaliel, came from illustrious families, while others, like Jonathan and Ananias, came from the lower classes, the *demotikoi.* They could even be, as were Joazar and Josephus, of priestly stock. What united them was an identical education *(paideia d'homoious),* presumably one which conentrated on achieving expertness in the laws *(nomima).* The Pharisaic link to the masses, stressed by Josephus elsewhere, is thus concretely reaffirmed here.

The Pharisees as Josephus knew them from personal experience were thus a scholar class, experts in the expounding and in the interpretation of the laws, whose teachings determined the manner in which the institutions of Judaism functioned. The Pharisees advocated doctrines that called for a life of moderation lived in accordance with their doctrines. They assured their adherents that one had the freedom to choose between good and evil and that one's soul would be either rewarded or punished after death on the basis of this choice. The Pharisees encouraged gregariousness and social harmony and sought to live lives of goodness and virtue. Their laws and their teachings won them the support of the masses and, consequently, they were the dominant *haeresis* in Josephus' day. Although they urged the masses to be loyal to the Roman state, they did actively support the rebellion once it had broken out.

There is one final passage in Josephus which sheds light on the Pharisees in a most intimate way, since it is a recollection of Josephus' adolescent years when, as a precocious youth, he was struggling to determine for himself which of the *haereseis* would yield for him religious satisfaction. Here is how he describes his search in the autobiography, the *Life,* which he penned in the sunset of his life:

At about the age of sixteen I determined to gain personal experience of the several schools of thought [i.e., ways of life] into which our nation is divided. These, as I have frequently mentioned, are three in number—the first that of the Pharisees, the second that of the Sadducees, and the third that of the Essenes. I thought that, after a thorough investigation, I should be in a position to select the best. So I submitted myself to hard training and much pain and passed through the three. Not content, however, with the experience thus gained, on hearing of one named Bannus, who dwelt in the wilderness, wearing only such clothing as trees provided, feeding on such things as grew of themselves, and using frequent ablutions of cold water, by day and night, for purity's sake, I became his devoted disciple. With him I lived for three years and, having accomplished my purpose, returned to the city. Being now in my nineteenth year I began to follow the legal system of the Pharisees, a school of thought [i.e., a way of life] having points of resemblance to what the Greeks call the Stoic school. (*Life* 9-12; author's rendering)

What do we learn of the Pharisees from this passage? It seems that (1) they are a *haeresis,* one of the three schools of thought in the sense of ways of religious life that flourished among the Jews; (2) that their teachings resemble those of the Stoics in some points, but presumably not in others; (3) that in following the Pharisees one does not join something, but one governs oneself by a system of laws. This information is scanty indeed. Josephus does not tell us precisely what a *haeresis* is; he does not tell us on what points the Pharisees have teachings similar to the Stoics; he does not even tell us what specifically one did when one decided to govern his life by the system of laws of the Pharisees. But one point must not be overlooked. Josephus does not use any word which means "to join an association," or "to become a member of a confraternity." He merely says that in his nineteenth year, he began *politeuesthai te Pharisaoi-katakolouthon,* to follow the system of law, or way of life, or constitution, as taught by the Pharisees. This constitution, as we have already learned from Josephus himself (cf. *Ant.* XIII:297-98), was the twofold Law, that is, the Written Law and the Oral Law.

Now that we have set down and analyzed in detail all those passages in which Josephus deals with the Pharisees, we are ready to formulate a definition.[3] In doing so, however, we shall first draw up a definition derived from the structure of action and then that which follows from the purely descriptive asides. The reason for this procedure is to underline the fact that whereas the pattern of action must necessarily yield a definition that is true, for if the pattern of action is true, i.e., if the Pharisees did indeed act as Josephus or his sources affirm that they did, they must have been the sort of people that could do what they did, quite apart from any rationale or explanation they or others might give for their actions. Thus, if the Pharisees did indeed put Diogenes to death, then they must have been willing to use force to achieve their ends, even if these ends may have been to eliminate the use of force, and even if such an act may have been motivated by a highly elevated concept of justice.

By contrast, the purely descriptive statements may contain more elusive and ambiguous elements. Thus, the views of the Pharisees with respect to free will and life after death do not necessarily follow from an analysis of the structure of action. We cannot say that the Pharisees must have been thus and so because they held these beliefs in the same say that we affirm that the Pharisees must have been thus and so because they rebelled against John Hyrcanus when he abrogated their laws. The descriptive statements are not necessarily incompatible with those yielding an action pattern; indeed, the motives for the acts may very likely have been the belief system. They are, however, less compelling, since contradictory beliefs, in contrast to contradictory actions, can coexist. One cannot both put Diogenes to death and spare his life, but one can affirm in words that death is life.

When we focus on the structure of action, whether occurring before Josephus' day or during his lifetime, we discover that the Pharisees were active, aggressive, and determined protagonists of a system of laws uniquely their own, as the following situations make manifest.

First, their system of law must have been functioning on the eve of their quarrel with John Hyrcanus, for he abrogated "the laws *[nomima]* which the Pharisees had legislated for the masses." This abrogation was the signal for riots and insurrections.

Second, their distinctive laws were restored by Salome Alexandra when the Pharisees returned to power. They are specifically referred to as being the very laws John Hyrcanus had abrogated.

Third, these laws are *operative* during Josephus' lifetime, for he affirms that "everything that pertains to divine worship, prayers, and sacrifices is carried out in accordance with their interpretation" and that the Sadducees, when serving in positions of authority, reluctantly follow Pharisaic teachings.

The Pharisees thus emerge as those concerned with the *functioning* of laws. Their concern for the laws is so intense that they are ready to resort to violent rebellion when these laws are endangered. The vivid memory of a generation of civil war under Alexander Jannaeus restrained all subsequent rulers, whether they were Hasmoneans, Herodians, or procurators, from tampering with the laws of the Pharisees. When their laws were touched, the Pharisees were never passive.

The laws the Pharisees championed were the unwritten laws, the laws handed down from the "Fathers," transmitted orally and not committed to writing. These laws differed *radically* from the laws recorded in the Pentateuch, and for this reason they were rejected by the Sadducees. That these unwritten laws of the Pharisees were radically different is evident from the agitated reaction to their abrogation and their replacement by the Written Law alone. The Pharisees did not deny the authority of the Pentateuch, but they most emphatically insisted that the unwritten laws were binding, and they were willing to fight to the death for their belief.

The Pharisees as active, militant protagonists of the Unwritten Law had the support of the masses. This fact is reitereated by Josephus whenever the Pharisees are related to the structure of action. The Pharisaic laws are referred to as those instituted for the masses; their abrogation as the obvious cause of the hatred of the masses for John Hyrcanus and his sons; their reinstitution a signal for support to Salome Alexandra. The masses look to the Pharisees as their leaders and willingly follow their advice. They are willing to forgive Alexander Jannaeus his crimes when the Pharisees urge them to. They accept Alexandra as a queen because she adhered to the Pharisees. They will not put up with Sadducean magistrates unless they follow Pharisaic precedent, and they can be counted upon to resist any tampering with the Pharisaic regulations for worship, prayer, and sacrifices.

Indeed, until the actual outbreak of the rebellion against Rome, the Pharisees appear to have had the full confidence of the masses. Only when some Pharisaic leaders opposed the revolt did the people at large refuse to heed. When, however, such Pharisaic leaders as Simon son of Gamaliel joined the revolt, the masses once again looked to the Pharisees as their leaders. Of the delegation of four sent to depose Josephus, three were

Pharisees, and they were being sent to remove a general who was himself a follower of the Pharisees!

The definition of the Pharisees thus far substantiated by the structure of action is the following: *The Pharisees were the active protagonists of the Unwritten Law who enjoyed, except for a brief interval, the wholehearted confidence and support of the masses.*

They were also a scholar class. This, too, is substantiated by the pattern of action. As champions of the unwritten laws, Pharisees must have been those who knew the laws and taught them. Josephus makes this point time and time again. John Hyrcanus is referred to as their disciple. Pollion is called the pupil of Samaias, and Samaias the pupil of Pollion. Likewise, Josephus refers to them as "the most accurate interpreters of the laws," "unrivalled experts in their country's laws," "the most precise exponents of the laws." And, of course, they are consistently called a *haeresis,* a school of thought, which philosophizes and expounds *logoi,* teachings. A scholar class they most assuredly were, but a scholar class which led and directed the people, and which stood on militant guard to protect the authority of the Unwritten Law. The picture of Simon son of Gamaliel devising the overthrow of Josephus and taking the lead against the Zealots is very much one with that of the Pharisaic leaders who had cut down Diogenes more than a century before and who had compelled the Hasmonean family to restore their unwritten laws.

The pattern of action likewise reveals the position of the Pharisees with regard to the state. The acts of the Pharisees indicate that they were at first positively oriented toward John Hyrcanus. This would mean that they approved of his being ruler and High Priest, at least at the outset. Hostility toward John and Alexander is directly linked to the abrogation of the Unwritten Law and their link with the Sadducees. Similarly, friendship toward Salome Alexandra goes hand in hand with the restoration of the Unwritten Law and the ousting of the

Sadducees. The Pharisees show themselves to be favorably disposed to the monarchy (though no monarchy had as yet existed when they broke with John); to a Hasmonean High Priest (Hyrcanus II); and to the foreign policy of Alexandra. Pollion and Samaias seek to clip Herod's wings but subsequently urge the people to open the gates to Herod and Rome and abandon Antigonus, the Hasmonean. Once Herod is in power, Pollion and Samaias are presumably given a free hand with respect to the Unwritten Law, and are even excused from the oath of loyalty. After Herod's death, the Pharisees take so firm a stand in support of the rights of the Romans to take a census and exact tribute that a fourth *haeresis* arises which differed from the Pharisees on this issue alone. And even on the eve of the revolt against Rome, some of the Pharisaic leaders urge the people to submit to Roman authority. Once, however, the rebellion is in full swing, some Pharisees, at least, play an active role in it.

The Pharisees clearly had no principled objection to state power as such. They did not hesitate to wield it or influence it whenever they could. They were not committed to any specific form of government. They did not oppose a strong state with a powerful army, even if a good part of it was made up of mercenaries. They did not have any principled objections to a vigorous foreign policy. Nor did they have any enduring loyaltes to a specific family. They both supported and opposed the Hasmoneans. They were loyal to Herod, but equally loyal to the procurators. They at times favored rebellion against constituted authority, and at times they denounced it.

The Pharisees thus had no hard and fast position on the state. They had apparently a single concern, and this alone determined their policy of action. This concern was the status of the unwritten laws. The state that left them untouched deserved support; the state that tampered with them courted rebellion. The Pharisees were a scholar class committed to the unwritten laws, and this

71

commitment motivated their conduct. And precisely because they were so committed, they had to face the loss of some of their following, those who, for one reason or another, placed loyalty to a dynasty, e.g., those who remained steadfastly loyal to Antigonus even when Samaias and Pollion went over to Herod, above their loyalty to the Unwritten Law, or who valued political independence more than the Unwritten Law. The pattern of action reveals that the Pharisees identified themselves as the protagonists of the Unwritten Law, the traditions of the "Fathers," and they guided their policies accordingly.

The Unwritten Law thus emerges from the pattern of action as the core of Pharisaism. Yet Josephus never tells us, nor does he explicity draw on sources that would tell us, what specifically these laws happened to be. Nor does he enlighten us as to how they had been transmitted, or as to who the "Fathers" had been. He gives no clue as to whether the Pharisees had some institution that preserved and administered these laws; nor does he inform us as to whether the Pharisees also legislated Unwritten laws. The only example of how an Unwritten law might differ from a written law is Josephus' reference to the fact that the Pharisees considered flogging to be a sufficient punishment for calumny, since the Pharisees, according to Josephus, were naturally lenient in matters of punishment. The implication is clear that the Sadducees would have meted out the death penalty to the slanderer of a High Priest.

Although it is regrettable that Josephus felt no need to communicate to his readers the Unwritten laws of the Pharisees, the significance of their existence is not to be overlooked. A system of laws that functions within a society binds its members together in a very definitive way and determines the pattern of social and institutional interaction. The cultic service in the Temple will be the kind of service that the operational laws demand; the fate of a criminal, the outcome of the application of the laws; the decision of magistrates, the execution of the laws. The structure of society thus must have undergone a radical transformation when John Hyrcanus abrogated the unwritten laws, and an equally radical transformation must have followed when these laws were restored. Josephus may not have given us a detailed account of these transformations, but, by the bare reference, in a sentence or two, to the abrogation and the restoration of the Unwritten Law, he compels us to visualize in a very concrete way what this must have meant for society.

So much, then, for the definition of the Pharisees as derived from the structure of action. Josephus, however, communicates information of another kind. He tells us of what the Pharisees believed and what values they espoused. These beliefs and values, however, do not necessarily flow from the pattern of action. The interconnection of events does not reveal that the Pharisees believed in reward and punishment after death, but it does reveal that the Pharisees were an aggressive scholar class dedicated to the propagation of their system of law. This, of course, does not mean that Josephus is not communicating accurate information about the beliefs of the Pharisees; it does mean that this information is not nearly as decisive for determining the basic or essential definition of the Pharisees as that which emerges out of their activity. This distinction must be underlined because in his descriptive asides Josephus does not mention specifically that the crucial difference between the Pharisees and Sadducees was their position on the status of the Unwritten Law. Josephus does refer, however, to the Pharisees in these asides as "the most accurate interpreters of the laws," but he does not indicate that this meant that the Pharisees were the champions of the Unwritten Law. Josephus points out this crucial difference *only* when he is attempting to clarify for his readers the reasons why John Hyrcanus' decision to abrogate the laws of the Pharisees and to go over to the Sadducees should have unleashed a civil war.

When, therefore, Josephus refers to the Pharisees and their expertness in the laws, it must be assumed that the unwritten laws are meant. And when he affirms that cultus, prayer, and worship were carried out in accordance with the interpretations of the Pharisees, the unwritten laws are likewise implied. And when the Sadducees reluctantly serve as magistrates and adhere to the Pharisaic notions, the unwritten laws must be these notions.

The other doctrines of the Pharisees reported by Josephus must not be permitted to usurp the primacy of the role of the Unwritten Law merely because Josephus devotes more sentences to these doctrines. The *quantity* of description must not overwhelm the decisive *quality* of a core doctrine. Merely because Josephus writes more about the Pharisaic views on free will than he does about their unwritten laws does not mean that these views outweigh the other in the construction of a definition.

Let us now collate these data which Josephus provides and build them into the definition: The Pharisees were a *haeresis,* a school of thought, that had the support of the majority of the population. The *haeresis* was noted (1) for its expert interpretation and expounding of the law; (2) for its advocacy of moderation and reason; (3) for its dedication to justice *(dikaios)* and virtue *(arete)*; (4) for its encouragement of mutuality and friendliness *(philaleloi)*; and (5) for its belief in reward and punishment after death. It also taught that although man was free to pursue either good or evil, the outcome was uncertain because Fate played a role. The virtuous man therefore might· fare ill while the wicked man might enjoy well-being. The *haeresis* of the Pharisees thus appears as a body of men learned in the laws and teachers of religious doctrines which are conducive to the practice of justice and virtue in this world and which promise the individual immortality for his soul in the world to come and resurrection for his body. In seeking to find an equivalent *haeresis* in the Greco-Roman world, Josephus intimates that the Pharisees most resembled the Stoics. Presumably, a Stoic sage would not be too unlike a Pharisee.

Josephus has yielded us the raw material for constructing a definition of the Pharisees. The definition is not necessarily accurate, but it is a definition built on the communications of one who was himself a Pharisee, who had the opportunity of observing other Pharisees, who found records pertaining to Pharisees before his time, and who felt compelled by his duty as a historian to communicate some of his knowledge about the Pharisees to others. The definition derived from Josephus must therefore be given very serious consideration in the construction of an objective definition of the Pharisees. How much consideration depends on the definitions derived from the two other sources that have a right to be heard, namely, the New Testament and the Tannaitic Literature.

Chapter II

The New Testament

The New Testament is a very different kind of source from Josephus. It is a collection of several books written by different writers at different times and with different purposes. With the exception of the authentic Pauline Epistles, the authors are unknown. Not a single one of these books was written by a historian whose preeminent concern was factual accuracy. These writers, unlike Josephus, looked upon themselves as the bearers of a message about Jesus, his ministry on earth, his crucifixion, his resurrection, and his second coming. They were motivated by the need to spread the "good news," to defend themselves from their persecutors, and to paint a portrait of Jesus worthy of veneration and evocative of belief.

Nor do the authors of the New Testament have any intrinsic interest in the Pharisees. Unlike Josephus, they did not feel compelled to give some explanation of who the Pharisees were. They only recorded the role of the Pharisees in the life and death of Jesus and in the history of the early church. For these writers, the Pharisees were those Jews who had vexed Jesus during his lifetime and who had participated in bringing about his crucifixion. For them the Pharisees were objects of hostility. What, then, did these writers perceive?

PAUL

We shall begin with the testimony of Paul, since his Epistles are the only sources in the New Testament whose authorship is certain and whose dating is ascertainable within reasonable limits. But of even more crucial importance is the fact that Paul, by his own confession, had been a Pharisee. As such Paul is our most precious source for the Pharisees in the entire New Testament. He bears direct witness to the Pharisees in an Epistle that he himself composed and whose authenticity has not been questioned by scholars. The reference to the Pharisees is brief, but it communicates vital information. In the Epistles to the Philippians (3:2-7), Paul writes:

Look out for the dogs, look out for the evil-workers, look out for those who mutilate the flesh. For we are the true circumcision, who worship God in spirit, and glory in Christ Jesus, and put no confidence in the flesh. Though I myself have reason for confidence in the flesh also. If any other man thinks that he has reason for confidence in the flesh, I have more: cicumcised on the eighth day, of the people of Israel, of the tribe of Benjamin, a Hebrew born of Hebrews; as to the law a Pharisee, as to zeal a persecutor of the church, as to righteousness under the law blameless. But whatever gain I had, I counted as loss for the sake of Christ.

Paul, in striving to establish his right to reject the need for circumcision, spreads before the Philippians his Jewish credentials. He is determined to still the opposition by an impressive listing of his Jewish ties: circumcised on the eighth day, a full-fledged member of the people of Israel, of the tribe of Benjamin, indeed a Hebrew born of Hebrews (no convert he). And then to make crystal-clear his relationship to the Law, Paul affirms that he was a Pharisee, who could pride himself on his steadfast loyalty—"as to righteousness under the law blameless."

We thus have Paul's own clear-cut statement to the effect that he had been a Pharisee and that to be a Pharisee meant to hold a specific conception of the Law, one differentiated from other concepts. Paul implies that the highest goal set by this Law was "righteousness," "law-abiding" *(dikaiosune)*, a goal Paul triumphantly proclaims to have achieved: his righteousness under this Law had been without blemish.

Paul does not mention the Pharisees specifically in any other Epistle, though he has much to say about the Law. Nor does he communicate the distinguishing features of the Pharisaic conception of the Law. Nevertheless, in one passage, even though he does not use the term *Pharisees* explicitly, Paul does convey by implication what this distinction was. In his Epistle to the Galatians (1:13-14), Paul writes:

For you have heard of my former life in Judaism, how I persecuted the church of God violently and tried to destroy it; and I advanced in Judaism beyond many of my own age among my people, so extremely zealous was I for the traditions *[paradoseon]* of my fathers.

This passage parallels that in Philippians not only because it is autobiographical but also because it, too, stresses Paul's intense attachment to Judaism going hand-in-hand with his violent hatred of the church. The Judaism Paul speaks of in Galatians must have been identical with the Judaism of Philippians, namely, that of the Pharisees. However, whereas Paul refers to it as the Law of the Pharisees in Philippians, he identifies it with the "traditions of the fathers" *(ton patrikon paradoseon)* in Galatians. And since the term *paradosis* is used by both Josephus *(Ant.* XIII:297, 408) and Mark (7:3, 5, 8, 9, 13) to designate the nonwritten Law, it is evident that Paul is reiterating that as to the Law he had been a Pharisee.

From Paul's brief mention of his Pharisaic background, we derive the following definitions of the Pharisees: The Pharisees are those who hold to a specific and differentiable concept of the Law, one that affirms the authority of the *paradosis,* the "tradition" of the Fathers, and one which has righteousness, *dikaisune,* under this

Law as its dominant goal. And since Paul is unique among New Testament writers in that we know him by name, and we can date his ministry with relative precision, and have before us his own testimony, the definition of the Pharisees elicited from Philippians and Galatians has an overriding claim to priority.

THE SYNOPTIC GOSPELS AND ACTS

The Synoptic Gospels and Acts likewise bear witness to the Pharisees as an historical reality; but this witness is mediated through an oral tradition and through those who cast these writings in their final form. The Synoptic Gospels and Acts do indeed purport to record verbatim events and controversies, but, however accurate they may be, they are not in their present form necessarily the literal words either of Jesus or of the eyewitnesses to his ministry. The Pharisees as known to the authors of the Synoptic Gospels and Acts in their day may have been retrojected to the time of Jesus and his immediate disciples. We can never be certain, therefore, whether the Pharisees as depicted in the Synoptic Gospels and in Acts were indeed the Pharisees whom Jesus and his disciples had known.

Each of the Synoptic Gospels and Acts contains incidents and conversations involving the Pharisees. Each of the Gospels is hostile, but they differ both as to the quantity of the data they communicate and the hostility they express. Mark contains the least data and is the least hostile; Matthew contains the most data and is, at the same time, the most hostile. Luke, as can be gathered, is midway. Though these quantitative and qualitative differences do exist, the Synoptic Gospels and Acts picture the Pharisees in much the same way. Thus no datum in Matthew is incompatible with the overall data in Mark or Luke. Since there is no such agreement between the Synoptic Gospels and Acts and the Gospel of John, the Fourth Gospel will be analyzed separately.

The Synoptic Gospels and Acts present the reader with

a loosely connected series of episodes from the life of Jesus leading ultimately to his arrest, trial, crucifixion, and resurrection. Though the Gospels differ in content, they do not differ in form. None gives us a chronological biography, only an episodic one. The Pharisees therefore appear in those episodes of Jesus' career where he does some act or utters some statement that is challenging or provocative or worthy of approbation. It is thus impossible to link these episodes to any specific point in Jesus' career, with the exception, of course, of the arrest, trial, and crucifixion.

At the outset it must be stressed that for the purposes of extracting data to define the Pharisees, the problem of dating the sources is *relatively* unimportant. An intensification of hatred for the Pharisees might very well have grown out of experiences that followed the death of Jesus, and hence not be attributable to Jesus himself. But this makes little difference, for we are concerned in this study with identifying the Pharisees, and not with determining the intensity of Jesus' hostility toward them or with the dating. *So long as the Synoptics do not confront us with contradictory data, or with mutually exclusive images, we can bypass both the problem of the degree of hostility toward the Pharisees and of the dating of the sources.* Thus the Gospel of John will be treated separately, not because he is generally thought to be later than the Synoptics but because his picture of the Pharisees is at variance with that drawn in the Synoptics.

At the very beginning, however, we are confronted with a crucial methodological problem. The Pharisees are specifically mentioned throughout the Synoptics, but so are the Scribes. Frequently the Scribes and Pharisees are linked together as in the oft repeated *"Pharisaoi kai grammateis,"* though not invariably so. Sometimes the Pharisees are mentioned without the Scribes, and sometimes the Scribes are mentioned without the Pharisees. For the purpose of constructing a definition of the Pharisees, we must take into account every passage in which the name *Pharisee* occurs, but what status are we to assign to the Scribes? Are the Scribes identical with the Pharisees? Are the Scribes a distinct class among the Pharisees, but Pharisees nonetheless? Or are some, but not all, Scribes-Pharisees?

Since scholars are in sharp disagreement, we cannot permit the definition of the Pharisees to be jeopardized by resort to any text that does not specifically use the term *Pharisees.* At the outset, therefore, we shall build the definition of the Pharisees from the Synoptic Gospels and Acts by confining our analysis to the passages that use the word *Pharisees.* After a definition has been established through this procedure, we shall then be in a position to grapple with the problem of the meaning of the term *Scribes.*

Since, as pointed out above, neither the degree of hostility toward the Pharisees nor the dating of the sources is vital to our enterprise, we shall begin our analysis with Matthew 23, since it etches a full portrait of the Pharisees rather than a bare sketch:

The scribes and the Pharisees sit on Moses' seat; so practice and observe whatever they tell you, but not what they do; for they preach but do not practice. They bind heavy burdens, hard to bear, and lay them on men's shoulders; but they themselves will not move them with their finger.

They do all their deeds to be seen by men; for they make their phylacteries broad and their fringes long, and they love the place of honor at feasts and the best seats in the synagogues, and salutations in the market places, and being called rabbi by men. But you are not to be called rabbi, for you have one teacher, and you are all brethren. And call no man your father on earth, for you have one Father, who is in heaven. Neither be called masters, for you have one master, the Christ. He who is greatest among you shall be your servant; whoever exalts himself will be humbled, and whoever humbles himself will be exalted.

But woe to you, scribes and Pharisees, hypocrites! because you shut the kingdom of heaven against men; for you neither enter yourselves, nor allow those who would enter to go in. Woe to you, scribes and Pharisees, hypocrites! for you traverse sea and land to make a single proselyte, and when he becomes a proselyte, you make him twice as much a child of hell as yourselves.

Woe to you, blind guides, who say "If anyone swears by the temple, it is nothing; but if anyone swears by the gold of the temple, he is bound by his oath." You blind fools! For which is greater, the gold or the temple that has made the gold sacred? And you say, "If anyone swears by the altar, it is nothing; but if anyone swears by the gift that is on the altar, he is bound by his oath." You blind men! For which is greater, the gift or the altar that makes the gift sacred? So he who swears by the altar, swears by it and everything on it; and he who swears by the temple, swears by it and by him who dwells in it; and he who swears by heaven, swears by the throne of God and by him who sits on it.

Woe to you, scribes and Pharisees, hypocrites! for you tithe mint and dill and cummin, and have neglected the weightier matters of the law, justice and mercy and faith; *these you ought to have done, without neglecting the others.* You blind guides, straining out a gnat and swallowing a camel!

Woe to you, scribe and Pharisees, hypocrites! for you cleanse the outside of the cup and of the plate, but inside you are full of extortion and rapacity. You blind Pharisee! first cleanse the inside of the cup and of the plate, that the outside may also be clean.

Woe to you, scribes and Pharisees, hypocrites! for you are like whitewashed tombs, which outwardly appear beautiful, but within they are full of dead men's bones and all uncleanness. So you also outwardly appear *righteous* to men, but within you are full of hypocrisy and iniquity.

Woe to you, scribes and Pharisees, hypocrites! for you build the tombs of the prophets and adorn the monuments of the righteous, saying, "If we had lived in the days of our fathers, we would not have taken part with them in shedding the blood of the prophets." Thus you witness against yourselves, that you are the sons of those who murdered the prophets. Fill up, then, the measure of your fathers. You serpents, you brood of vipers, how are you to escape being sentenced to hell? Therefore, I send you prophets and wise men and scribes *[grammateis],* some of whom you will kill and crucify, and some you will scourge in your synagogues and persecute from town to town, that upon you may come all the righteous blood shed on earth, from the blood of innocent Abel to the blood of Zechariah the son of Barachiah, whom you murdered between the sanctuary and the altar. Truly, I say to you, all this will come upon this generation.

O Jerusalem, Jerusalem, killing the prophets and stoning those who are sent to you! How often would I have gathered your children together as a hen gathers her brood under her wings, and you would not! Behold, your house is forsaken and desolate. For I tell you, you will not see me again, until I say, "Blessed be he who comes in the name of the Lord." (Matt. 23:2-39; italics added)

The hatred for the Pharisees is all-consuming. Matthew excoriates them as hypocrites, whitewashed tombs, serpents, vipers—all images evocative of distrust, rejection, disgust, even horror. And from the point of view of Matthew, the actions that he attributes to the Pharisees fully justified his venom, for he believes the Pharisees were so hostile to Jesus that they were capable of killing, crucifying, scourging, and persecuting those prophets, wise men, and scribes who presumably taught and preached in Jesus' name. It is therefore all the more remarkable that Matthew should bind the Christians to the Pharisees by affirming that the Scribes and Pharisees sit in Moses' seat. Indeed, the Pharisees arouse his hatred because they are in charge of the Law and have the support of the people. And Matthew not only refuses to challenge their ultimate authority but insists that no provocation— not scourging, not persecution, not even death—is sufficient justification for loosening the ties binding the followers of Jesus to the Pharisees.

The Pharisees for Matthew are authoritative leaders. They are the scholar class. Their power and their importance are crystallized in the simple affirmation that they sit in Moses' seat, and it is for this reason that even the Christians who hate them must practice and observe whatever they tell them to do. Indeed, even if the Pharisees are seen as hypocrites, this can serve as no excuse for failing to heed the commands of the Pharisees. For the Pharisees are clothed with the authority of Moses and therefore must be heeded. Hell may be their ultimate reward, but the followers of Jesus must obey them in the interim.

That the Pharisees were a class of leaders for all the people arouses the hostility of Matthew. The fact that they wore their phylacteries broad and their fringes long; that they assumed the seat of honor at feasts and the best seats in the synagogues; that they were saluted in the market place and called rabbi, testifies to their leadership role, a role Matthew surrounds with hypocritical intent "they do all their deeds to be seen by men." Indeed, the Pharisees are so powerful as leaders that they have successfully parried the message of Jesus, for Matthew holds them responsible for shutting the door to the kingdom of heaven for those who might otherwise have sought entry. The Pharisees may be blind leaders, but they are leaders and guides nonetheless.

And their leadership involves the right to determine the Law, even though there may be no direct Mosaic sanction for it: Pharisees tithe mint, dill, and cummin, despite the fact that these are not specifically prescribed by the Pentateuch. And such tithing is not condemned by Matthew, even though he berates the Pharisees for neglecting the weightier matters of the Law.

Only in the matter of swearing does Matthew take exception to the Pharisaic formulation in such a way that might imply a defiant act. He has Jesus ridicule the Pharisees for attributing greater weight to the gold in the Temple than to the Temple itself and to gifts on the altar than to the altar itself. In any event, since this section is introduced by "Woe to you, blind guides," it under-scores the fact that the Pharisaic formulas were the norm.

Matthew's intense bitterness toward the Pharisees does not stem from their being some sect absorbed in their own piety and avoiding contamination by the ritually careless *am ha-aretz,* but rather from the fact that they are *the* authoritative experts on the Law. The Pharisees are those whom the people look up to with such respect that the followers of Jesus find themselves killed, crucfied, scourged, and persecuted while the mass of people seemingly acquiesce. In contrast to the followers of Jesus, the majority of the Jews apparently were convinced that the Pharisees were inwardly what they appeared outwardly. And Matthew cannot be equalled for his representation of what the Pharisees appeared to be, precisely because he insists that the outer appearance falsifies the inner reality. The Pharisees are clean-looking, for they cleanse the outside of the cup and plate, but for Matthew, their inner selves are full of extortion and rapacity. He would have his readers perceive them as whitewashed tombs which outwardly appear beautiful, and this accounts for the fact that most Jews are taken in by what they see. Matthew "knows" that they are in reality whitewashed tombs full of dead men's bones and uncleanness, but clearly this perception of their inner reality is not shared by the average Jew. If it had been, there would be no need for Matthew's tirade, which desperately seeks to convince others that the beauty of the Pharisees is a deceptive facade. "They outwardly appear righteous to men"—to observe them and their conduct is to be taken in, for they give ample concrete evidence that they are indeed righteous. Matthew's insistence that they are full of hypocrisy and iniquity is by no means obvious to the unwarned observer. Indeed, the concrete evidence that Matthew brings for the inner rottenness of the Pharisees could have been convincing only to those who already shared Matthew's evaluation, for it derives primarily from the Phariasaic persecution of the Christians.

Matthew's outburst against the Pharisees thus offers us the following definition: The Pharisees were a scholar class invested with the authority to determine the divine Law and appearing to be both pious and righteous. Their behavior is thus comprehensible. Having determined that the Christians were undermining the Law, the Pharisees, by virtue of their authority as *the* scholar class, sought to crush the movement by whatever means might be necessary.

Matthew, it is to be noted, denounces the Pharisees for

many things, but he does not include among these the charge that they were especially meticulous about the laws of ritual purity or that they separated themselves from the masses or that they wished to have nothing to do with the Gentiles. To the contrary. The purity Matthew attributes to them is the seeming purity of their outward stance, the apparent goodness and righteousness of their lives, the unblemished appearance of their public conduct. Their relationship to the masses is that of respected leaders to loyal followers. The Pharisees set the standard and they enjoy the honors and the privileges that attend on their model behavior. Far from avoiding the people, the Pharisees, according to Matthew, make every effort to be seen by them. They may very well seek out the places of honor in the synagogues, but in doing so they are participating with the people at large in religious communion. And as for the Gentiles, Matthew eloquently testifies that the Pharisees go to great pains to seek them as proselytes. The Pharisees, if we are to follow Matthew, are distinguished not for their concern with Levitical purity, not for their desire to separate from the masses or the Gentiles, but for the power they wield as the authoritative spokesmen for the Law, a power so great that they can successfully expel the Christians from the synagogues and unleash against them a persecution so violent that to followers of Jesus, such as Matthew, they did appear to be a brood of vipers and serpents.

Of one Pharisaic tenet, Matthew leaves no doubt: prophecy had come to an end; hence, anyone claiming to be a prophet was a deceiver to be exposed and exterminated. The Pharisees venerated the prophets of old, for they were true prophets. But those claiming to be prophets in their own day, as well as those wise men and scribes who confirmed their claims, are to be killed, crucified, scourged, and persecuted. "O Jerusalem, Jerusalem, killing the prophets and stoning those who are sent to you" expresses Matthew's bitter recognition that the Pharisees and not the followers of Jesus determined the credentials of a prophet, and the majority of the people upheld the Pharisaic tenet that prophecy had long since come to an end and was not about to revive.

The twenty-third chapter of Matthew was chosen first for analysis because nowhere in all the Gospels does the hatred of the Pharisees reach such a violent crescendo, and yet nowhere else in the Gospels is the authority and the power of the Pharisees more starkly manifest. The hate itself guarantees that the core of Pharisaism will be exposed. And exposed it is. The Pharisees sit on Moses' seat and they therefore have the authority to do what they please and to have the support of the people. If Matthew underwrites this authority even after the Pharisees have killed, crucified, scourged, and persecuted the Christian leaders—practice and observe whatever they tell you because they sit in Moses' seat is Matthew's admonishment—how much more so must this authority have been respected by the non-Christian Jews!

No less striking is Matthew's crisp warning directly linked to the Law and to Jesus' affirmation of its immutability in the following passage:

Think not that I have come to abolish the law and the prophets; I have come not to abolish them but to fulfill them. For truly I say to you, till heaven and earth pass away, not an iota, not a dot, will pass from the law till all is accomplished. Whoever then relaxes one of the least of these commandments and teaches men so shall be called least in the kingdom of heaven; but he who does them and teaches them shall be called great in the kingdom of heaven. For I tell you, unless your righteousness exceeds that of the scribes and Pharisees, you will never enter the kingdom of heaven. (Matt. 5:17-20)

The Pharisees are the measure of the Law! Their righteousness is undeviating loyalty to jot and tittle, to even the least of the commandments. *The followers of Jesus are charged to accept the Pharisees as the models for the legally normative.* The Christian is to ground his righteousness in Pharisaic righteousness. He must begin with the

Pharisaic system of Law as the immutable foundation upholding his own mode of life. If he questions the Pharisaic concept of the immutability of the Law or the binding quality of its most minute commandments, he shall be called least in the kingdom of heaven. And should he fail to exceed the Pharisaic standard of righteousness, he will not enter the kingdom at all. The Pharisees are here no sect but the legal norm-makers and the practicing exemplars of the norm.

Matthew's picture of the Pharisees is confirmed throughout the Synoptic Gospels, now with more, now with less clarity. This will become evident as we cull the texts dealing with the Pharisees in the order of their pictorial clarity. Such an ordering is justified since, as pointed out above, critical concerns over the authorship and dating of the Synoptics and Acts need not concern us so long as the depiction of the Pharisees is compatible with that drawn from Paul's testimony, namely, that the Pharisees were the spokesmen for the *paradosis* of the Fathers.

With this in mind, we turn first to Mark 7 where the *paradosis* of the elders is seen to be the hallmark of the Pharisees:

Now when the Pharisees gathered together to him with some of the scribes *[kai tines ton grammateon],** who had come from Jerusalem, they saw that some of his disciples ate with hands defiled, that is, unwashed. (For the Pharisees, and all the Jews, do not eat unless they wash their hands, observing the *tradition of the elders [kratountes ten paradosin ton presbuteron];* and when they come from the market place, they do not eat unless they purify themselves; and there are many other traditions which they observe, the washing of cups and pots and vessels of bronze.)
And the Pharisees and the scribes *[hoi pharisaioi kai hoi grammateis]* asked him, "Why do your disciples not walk

---

*For the relationship of the Pharisees to the Scribes, see below, subsection "Scribes, Pharisees, Hypocrites."

according to the *tradition of the elders [kata ten paradosin ton presbyteron]*, but eat with hands defiled?" And he said to them, "Well did Isaiah prophesy of you hypocrites, as it is written, 'This people honors me with their lips, but their heart is far from me; in vain do they worship me, teaching as doctrines the precepts of men. You leave the commandment of God, and hold fast to the tradition of men *[krateite ten paradosin ton anthropon]*."

And he said to them, "You have a fine way of rejecting the commandment of God, in order to keep your tradition *[ten paradosin humon]!* For Moses said, 'Honor your father and your mother'; and, 'He who speaks evil of father or mother, let him surely die'; but you say, 'If a man tells his father or his mother, What you would have gained from me is Corban' (that is, given to God)—and then you no longer permit him to do anything for his father or mother, thus making void the word of God through *your tradition* which you hand on *[te paradosei humon he paredokate]*. And many such things you do."

And he called the people to him again, and said to them, "Hear me, all of you, and understand: there is nothing outside a man which by going into him can defile him; but the things which come out of a man are what defile him. . . . For from within, out of the heart of man, come evil thoughts, fornication, theft, murder, adultery, coveting, wickedness, deceit, licentiousness, envy, slander, pride, foolishness. All these things come from within and defile a man." (Mark 7:1-23; italics added)

The Scribes and the Pharisees are those who adhere to the traditions of the elders, the *paradoseos ton presbyteron.* This *paradosis* is especially associated with them, for Jesus twice refers to it as "your tradition," a tradition valued so highly that it takes precedence over the literal words of Moses. The Scribes and the Pharisees are charged with substituting for divine precepts those which have been contrived by men. They nullify and make void *(Kratountes)* the very word of God *(ton logon tou theou).*

By subordinating God's commands to their *paradosis,* the Pharisees expose themselves to the charge of hypocrisy, since they praise God and worship him yet usurp his authority! God's Law does not command that one must eat with undefiled hands, but since the *paradosis* does so command, the Pharisees are all wrought up over the failure of Jesus' disciples to wash their hands. They most decidedly demand that one hold fast to the *paradosis,* even though unsupported by biblical writ.

The *paradosis,* according to the Gospel of Mark, contains not only laws that are not to be found in Scripture but laws that even violate crucial commands of the Pentateuch. The Pharisees with their *paradosis* make it possible for a man to withhold honor from his father or mother. It attaches more significance to the sanctity of a vow than to the exhortation of Moses. The Pentateuch, God's revelation to Moses, is made a handmaiden to the *paradosis* of the Pharisees.

Paradoxically, the *paradosis* of the elders which required hand washing before eating reveals the Pharisees as those who mitigated the strict ritual purity laws of the Pentateuch which required both a ritual bath and the setting of the sun for cleansing, not those who prided themselves on their meticulous observance of the laws of ritual purity. As we shall see in the chapter dealing with the Tannaitic Literature, the "uncleanness of hands" was designed to reduce the laws of ritual purity for nonpriests virtually to the mere washing of hands.

The Scribes and the Pharisees thus appear as the champions of the *paradosis,* "the Tradition," laws not to be found written down in the Pentateuch. These laws they have received from previous generations and will in turn transmit to the generations that follow. And these unwritten laws are supreme; they cannot be overridden by an appeal to the written laws of the Pentateuch.

The Gospel of Mark thus leaves no doubt that the Pharisees are terribly concerned with upholding the authority of the *paradosis.* But so are the Scribes—a clear indication that the Scribes and the Pharisees are one and the same.*

---

*Compare the Markan passages to the parallel passages in Matt. 15:1-20.

For full discussion about the Scribes and Pharisees being one and the same, see below, subsection "Scribes, Pharisees, Hypocrites."

Indeed, throughout Mark, Luke, Matthew, and Acts, the Pharisees appear as the authoritative spokesmen of God's Law. Again and again, they seek to expose Jesus as one who, by challenging the teachings of the Pharisees, would set himself up as an authority in his own right. This is evident when the Pharisees seek to determine Jesus' stand on the legality of divorce.

And the Pharisees came up and in order to test him asked, "Is it lawful *[exestin]* for a man to divorce his wife?" He answered them, "What did Moses command you?" They said, "Moses allowed a man to write a certificate of divorce, and to put her away" But Jesus said to them, "For your hardness of heart he wrote you this commandment. But from the beginning of creation, 'God made them male and female.' 'For this reason a man shall leave his father and mother and be joined to his wife, and the two shall become one? So they are no longer two but one flesh. What therefore God has joined toether, let not man put asunder."
And in the house the disciples asked him again about this matter. And he said to them, "Whoever divorces his wife and marries another, commits adultery against her; and if she divorces her husband and marries another, she commits adultery." (Mark 10:2-12)

Jesus, in this instance, is not attacking the *paradosis*, "the Tradition," but the very command of Moses. The Pharisees stand guard in this instance over the integrity of the Written Law, the Pentateuch. For this reason, they test Jesus; they are seeking to determine whether he is undermining the Law. And his answer could leave little doubt that he set himself up as an independent authority, pitting a nonlegal passage in Genesis against a legal passage in Deuteronomy.

The Pharisees were also disturbed by what seemed to them to be Jesus' disregard of the laws regulating sabbath observance:

One sabbath [Jesus] was going through the grainfields; and as they made their way his disciples began to pluck ears of grain.

And the Pharisees said to him, "Look, why are they doing what is not lawful on the sabbath?" And he said to them, "Have you never read what David did, when he was in need and was hungry, he and those who were with him: how he entered the house of God, when Abiathar was high priest, and at the bread of the Presence, which is not lawful for any but the priests to eat, and also gave it to those who were with him?" And he said to them, "The sabbath was made for man, not man for the sabbath; so the Son of man is lord even of the sabbath." (Mark 2:23-28)

The Pharisees here appear as those having a special relationship to the Law. It is simply taken for granted that this is an area of their legitimate concern. They want to know what kind of teacher Jesus is if he permits his disciples to defy the Law, which is assumed to be both authoritative and well-known. And Jesus in his reply does not challenge the legitimacy of the Law but invokes his authority as the Son of man to dispense with the Law. He apparently alludes to a dictum that the Pharisees themselves accepted, namely, that the sabbath is made for man and not man for the sabbath, to justify the special prerogatives of the Son of man to dispense with the sabbath laws whenever he saw fit, even as the Pharisees allowed, in certain instances involving life or death for the suspension of sabbath laws.

The Pharisees in this episode, as in the previous one, are scholars and legal authorities. They are not ordinary rank-and-file members of some society or denomination but authoritative spokesmen of the Law, religious leaders terribly concerned lest the law be violated, especially if such violation is sanctioned by a teacher with a following of disciples.

This aspect of their concern is underlined even more forcefully in the episode where Jesus himself violates the sabbath law:

Again he entered the synagogue, and a man was there who had a withered hand. And they [the Pharisees] watched him, to see whether he would heal him on the sabbath, so that they might

accuse him. And he said to the man who had the withered
hand, "Come here." And he said to them, "Is it lawful *[exestin]*
on the sabbath to do good or to do harm, to save life or to kill?"
But they were silent. And he looked around at them with anger,
grieved at their hardness heart, and said to the man, "Stretch
out your hand." He stretched it out, and his hand was restored.
The Pharisees went out, and immediately held counsel with the
Herodians against him, how to destroy him. (Mark 3:1-6)

In the very act of turning to the Pharisees with this
question, Jesus was testifying to their authoritative
knowledge of the laws. The Pharisees are thus those who
know the laws and their application.

The status of the laws is the source of the hostility of
Jesus for the Pharisees and of theirs for him. Did Jesus
have the right to take the laws into his own hands and to
dispense with them solely on the basis of personal
authority, an authority that inhered within him? This
question likewise looms large when the Pharisees
confront Jesus with the fact that Jesus' disciples do not
observe the appropriate fasts:

Now John's disciples and the Pharisees were fasting; and the
people came and said to him, "Why do John's disciples and the
disciples of the Pharisees fast, but your disciples do not fast?"
And Jesus said to them, "Can the wedding guests fast while the
bridegroom is with them? As long as they have the bridegroom
with them, they cannot fast. The days will come, when the
bridegroom is taken away from them, and they will fast in that
day." (Mark 2:18-20)

The Pharisees stand guard over the laws; they also
respect the sovereignty of the state. The coin-of-Caesar
episode, as reported in the Gospel of Mark, clearly
conveys this loyalty:

And they sent to him some of the Pharisees and some of the
Herodians, to entrap him in his talk. And they came and said to
him, "Teacher, we know that you are true, and care for no man;
for you do not regard the position of men, but truly teach the
way of God. Is it lawful *[exestin]* to pay taxes to Caesar, or not?

Should we pay them or should we not?" But knowing their hypocrisy, he said to them, "Whose likeness and inscription is this?" They said to him, "Caesar's." Jesus said to them, "Render to Caesar the things that are Caesar's, and to God the things that are God's." And they were amazed at him. (Mark 12:13-17)

The Pharisees are linked to the Herodians and both are tied to Caesar and his tribute. It would appear that the Pharisees considered it lawful to pay the tribute to Caesar. A *didaskalos,* such as Jesus, would have no basis in the laws to advocate on his own personal authority the withholding of the tribute. The test was clearly designed to determine whether Jesus would challenge the authority of the state on religious grounds.

In the course of recording this episode, the author of the Gospel of Mark presents the Pharisees as extremely clever, indeed as hypocrites. They thus attempt to beguile Jesus by appealing to his sense of self–esteem and assuring him that he is a teacher of the way of God. They show themselves to be artful debaters, though no match for Jesus—at least so the Gospel of Mark would have us believe.

The Pharisees also appear as authoritative figures when they demand that Jesus prove his special relationship to God by insisting that he provide a sign from heaven:

The Pharisees came and began to argue with him, seeing from him a sign from heaven, to test him. And he sighed deeply in his spirit, and said. "Why does this generation seek for a sign? Truly, I say to you, no sign shall be given to this generation." And he left them, and getting into the boat again he departed to the other side.

Now they had forgotten to bring bread; and they had only one loaf with them in the boat. And he cautioned them, saying, "Take heed, beware of the leaven of the Pharisees and the leaven of Herod." (8:11-15)

Once again the Pharisees appear as those who concern themselves with the credentials of a *didaskalos,* "a teacher." Jesus had been going about driving out demons, healing the sick, and performing miracles. Many people presumably were impressed. The Pharisees challenge Jesus to prove that he has divine authority for his claims. They demand that he perform a miracle for them. This he refuses to do on the grounds that for this generation no decisive sign from heaven will be forthcoming. And he warns his disciples that they must beware of the leaven of the Pharisees and the leaven of Herod. They must be on the alert lest the teachings of the Pharisees lure them away from him. The seemingly appropriate request that Jesus prove his divine selection should not ensnare them.

The Pharisees are thus men of authority and importance. The attitude that they take toward a teacher will have important consequences. They are listened to. And their linkage with Herod, now reaffirmed, implies some connection with the state authorities.

Even more fundamental than the attitude of the Pharisees with respect to state sovereignty was their belief in the resurrection of the dead, since this belief brought them into conflict with the Sadducees who rejected such a notion out of hand. Ironically, this Pharisaic belief is championed so effectively by Jesus in a confrontation with the Sadducees that he wins the approbation of the Pharisees themselves. The full text is deserving of citation since it gives us some sense of the kind of debate attested to in the Tannaitic Literature as having taken place between the Pharisees and Sadducees:

The same day Sadducees came to him, who say that there is no resurrection; and they asked him a question, saying, "Teacher, Moses said, "If a man dies, having no children, his brother must marry the widow, and raise up children for his brother.' Now there were seven brothers among us; the first married, and died, and having no children left his wife to his brother. So too the second and third, down to the seventh. After them all, the woman died. In the resurrection, therefore, to which of the seven will she be wife? For they all had her."

But Jesus answered them, "You are wrong, because you know neither the scriptures nor the power of God. For in the resurrection they neither marry nor are given in marriage, but are like angels in heaven. And as for the resurrection of the dead, have you not read what was said to you by God, 'I am the God of Abraham, and the God of Isaac, and the God of Jacob'? He is not God of the dead, but of the living." And when the crowd heard it, they were astonished at his teaching.

But when the Pharisees heard that he had silenced the Sadducees, they came together. And one of them, a lawyer, asked him a question, to test him. "Teacher, which is the great commandment in the law?" And he said to him, 'You shall love the Lord your God with all your heart, and with all your soul, and with all your mind. This is the great and first commandment. And a second is like it, You shall love your neighbor as yourself. On these two commandments depend all the law and the prophets." (Matt. 22:23-40)

This clash between the Pharisees and the Sadducees over the belief in resurrection is strongly echoed in Acts 22:30 and 23:6-10:

But on the morrow, desiring to know the real reason why the Jews accused him, he unbound him, and commanded the chief priests and all the council [Sanhedrin] to meet, and he brought Paul down and set him before them.

But when Paul perceived that one part were Sadducees and the other Pharisees, he cried out in the council, "Brethren, I am a Pharisee, a son of Pharisees; with respect to the hope and the resurrection of the dead I am on trial." And when he said this, a dissension arose between the Pharisees and the Sadducees; and the assembly was divided. For the Sadducees say that there is no resurrection *[anastasin],* nor angel, nor spirit; but the Pharisees acknowledge them all. Then a great clamor arose; and some of the scribes of the Pharisees' party stood up and contended, "We find nothing wrong in this man. What if a spirit or an angel spoke to him?" And when the dissension became violent, the tribune, afraid that Paul would be torn in pieces by them, commanded the soldiers to go down and take him by force from among them and bring him into the barracks.

It is to be noted that in the first instance Jesus so effectively bespeaks the Pharisaic belief that he wins the approbation of the Pharisees. Likewise in the second instance, Paul's exclamation that he was being persecuted because of his belief in the resurrection of the dead provokes a violent clash between the Pharisees and the Sadducees. We are left in no doubt that on this doctrine the Pharisees, Jesus, and Paul saw eye to eye.

The other beliefs of the Pharisees emerge from a further analysis of the Synoptic Gospels and Acts. Thus we learn that the Pharisees believed in demons (Matt. 9:32-34); affirmed that God alone could forgive sins (Luke 5:17-21); and disapproved of eating and drinking with tax collectors and sinners (Matt. 9:10-13; Luke 5:29-32; 15:1-2); consider loving God and their fellow man as the prime commandments (Matt. 22:35-40); insist that the Messiah must be a descendant of David (Matt. 21:4-45).

It is striking that nowhere in the Synoptic Gospels or in Acts do we ever find the Pharisees separating themselves from the masses of people or devoting themselves to the minute observances of the laws of ritual purity not followed by the people at large. Indeed, the only instance involving ritual purity (Mark 7:1-13) involves the requirement that the hands be washed before eating. It is ironic that not only is this law one that is to be observed by all Jews, but as has been pointed out above, it represents a mitigation of the strict ritual purity laws set down in the Pentateuch.

The picture of the Pharisees as drawn from the Synoptic Gospels and Acts thus shows them to be the authoritative teachers of the twofold Law, the Written Law and the Tradition of the elders, i.e., the Oral Law. The picture is thus no different from that which we had already glimpsed in Paul's Epistles. Indeed, the portrait of Gamaliel sketched by the author of Acts would seem to be an accurate representation: Gamaliel was a Pharisee, a teacher of the Law, "held in honor by all the people" (Acts 5:34), the very Gamaliel who in Acts 22:14 is proclaimed by Paul to have been the teacher who educated him "according to the strict manner of the law of our fathers."

Similarly, the author of Acts was conveying the hallmark of Pharisaism when he has Paul affirm (Acts 26:5) that it represented the most accurate *haeresis* of Judaism: "They have known for a long time . . . that according to the most accurate *haeresis* of our religion I have lived as a Pharisee" (author's translation).

JOHN

The Gospel of John offers us Pharisees who do not possess the distinguishing features ascribed to them by the Synoptics and Acts. The Pharisees in John seem to have no distinguishing features at all. They seem to be a name, not a reality.They appear as hardly more than a synonym for *Jews.* They are not even differentiated from the Sadducees! They never challenge Jesus on points of the Law but only on his claims to having been sent by God. The only tangible datum that John reveals about them is that they were leaders whose authority with the people was great.

This power and authority of John's otherwise feature-less Pharisees is evident in each passage in which they appear. Thus the Pharisees are held responsible for sending the Jews, priests, and Levites to ply John the Baptist with questions as to his identity (John 1:24). The Pharisees are clearly influential, but no reason is given for their influence. So, too, Nicodemus is referred to as "a man of the Pharisees and a ruler of the Jews." Unlike his fellow Pharisees, he believes Jesus is a teacher come from God seeking to understand his mission (John 3:1-2). Indeed, he intervenes with the Pharisees, beseeching them to give Jesus a hearing before rejecting Jesus' claims to be the Christ (John 7:50-52). But all we can derive from this account is that as a Pharisee, Nicodemus was an authoritative teacher, for Jesus asks him, "Are you a teacher of Israel, and yet you do not understand this?" (John 3:10). But as to what the content of the teaching might be, nothing is said.

Likewise, the Pharisees appear in John as those who know the Law and wield authority:

The officers then went back to the chief priests and Pharisees who said to them, "Why did you not bring him?" The officers answered, "No man ever spoke like this man!" The Pharisees answered them, "Are you led astray, you also? Have any of the authorities or the Pharisees believed in him? But this crowd, who do not know the law, are accursed." Nicodemus, who had gone to him before, and who was one of them, said to them, "Does our law judge a man without first giving him a hearing and learning what he does?" They replied, "Are you from Galilee too? Search and you will see that no prophet is to rise from Galilee." (John 7:45-52)

Again Jesus spoke to them, saying, "I am the light of the world; he who follows me will not walk in darkness but will have the light of life." The Pharisees then said to him, "You are bearing witness to yourself; your testimony is not true." Jesus answered, "Even if I do bear witness to myself, my testimony is true, for I know whence I have come and whither I am going, but you do not know whence I come or whither I am going. You judge according to the flesh, I judge no one. Yet even if I do judge, my judgment is true, for it is not I alone that judge, but I and he who sent me. In your law it is written that the testimony of two men is true; I bear witness to myself, and the Father who sent me bears witness to me." They said to him therefore, "Where is your Father?" Jesus answered, "You know neither me or my Father; if you knew me, you would know my Father also." These words he spoke in the treasury, as he taught in the temple; but no one arrested him, because his hour had not yet come. (John 8:12-20)

In this passage the Pharisees are linked to the authorities in general. They determine the beliefs that are legitimate. They are contrasted with the crowd who do not know the Law and who are accursed for defying the Law. And even when in his account of Jesus' healing on the sabbath day (chapter 9) John seems to refer to the Pharisees as though they and all the Jews were one and the same, the Pharisees nonetheless are pictured as legal authorities.

John clearly conveys the notion that the Pharisees were the leaders to whom the people would go to get things done. They were those who had the authority to evaluate Jesus' acts and to put a stop to them. They have such influence that they, along with the chief priests, have the authority to convoke the council and take steps to silence Jesus. Thus John testifies to the *power* of the Pharisees, though he does not communicate to us any doctrine that would *differentiate* them from the chief priests or from any other grouping in Judaism. Indeed, the only division among the Jews that John recognizes is that between those who believed in Jesus and those who rejected him.

It seems, then, that for John, the Pharisees are authority figures who can be drawn upon to serve John's polemical and didactic purposes. Thus, whereas throughout the Synoptics the Pharisees demand that Jesus prove his prophetic or messianic claims by performing "signs," which he refuses to do, John has Jesus perform signs of so definitive a character that even the Pharisees cannot deny their persuasive power. The Pharisees themselves are made to testify in favor of Jesus' claim:

Many of the Jews, therefore, who had come with Mary and had seen what he did [i.e., raised Lazarus from the dead], believed in him; but some of them went to the Pharisees and told them what Jesus had done. So the chief priests and Pharisees gathered the council [sanhedrin], and said, "What are we to do? For this man performs mnay signs. If we let him go on thus, every one will believe in him, and the Romans will come and destroy both our holy place and our nation." But one of them, Caiaphas, who was high priest that year, said to them, "You know nothing at all; you do not understand that it is expedient for you that one man should die for the people, and that the whole nation should not perish." He did not say this of his own accord, but being high priest that year he prophesied that Jesus should die for the nation, and not for the nation only, but to gather into one the children of God who are scattered abroad. So from that day on they took counsel how to put him to death. (John 11:45-53)

The Pharisees for John are, along with the chief priests, the leaders of the Jews. They want Jesus put out of the way because he was so successful with the people. This is vividly portrayed in John's account of Jesus' entry into Jerusalem.

The next day a great crowd who had come to the feast heard that Jesus was coming to Jerusalem. So they took branches of palm trees and went out to meet him, crying, "Hosanna! Blessed is he who comes in the name of the Lord, even the King of Israel!"
And Jesus found a young ass and sat upon it; as it is written,
"Fear not daughter of Zion;
behold, your king is coming,
sitting on an ass's colt!"
His disciples did not understand this at first; but when Jesus was glorified, then they remembered that this had been written of him and had been done to him. The crowd that had been with him when he called Lazarus out of the tomb and raised him from the dead bore witness. The reason why the crowd went to meet him was that they heard he had done this sign. The Pharisees then said to one another, "You see that you can do nothing; look, the world has gone after him." (John 12:12-19)

The Pharisees thus see their leadership threatened by Jesus' success in raising Lazarus from the dead. Not only, according to John, is the sign which Jesus has performed winning over the Jews but the world as well. Indeed, John would have us believe that many more would have openly acknowledged the evidence of the "signs" had not the fear of the Pharisees restrained them:

Nevertheless, many even of the authorities believed in him, but for fear of the Pharisees they did not confess it, lest they should be put out of the synagogue; for they loved the praise of men more than the praise of God. (John 12:42-43)

In this passage, John reveals *his* basic definition of the Pharisees. They are the rulers of the synagogue. They determine who is and who is not welcome. They have the power to exclude from the synagogue those whom they deem heretical. Their authority is so thoroughly entrenched that they strike fear into the hearts even of those who may have been impressed by Jesus' signs. Little wonder, then, that the Pharisees would seek to preserve their power by having Jesus put to death.

The Pharisees appear only one more time in John's Gospel, when they are held responsible, along with the chief priests, for the contingent of soldiers and officers that are put at Judas' disposal (John 18:3). They are thus conceived of as wielding great authority. Nevertheless, they are nowhere to be found in John's report of the trial and crucifixion. Instead we find the high priest Annas given a central role along with the high priests and the Jews in general. Even when the Law is mentioned, the Jews, and not the Pharisees, are made to speak (John 18:31-32; 19:7).

John's concept of the Pharisees is thus seen to be at variance with that offered us by the Synoptics. They are *not* differentiated from the Sadducees. They are *not* identified with the *paradosis,* "the Tradition." They are *not* challenging Jesus for his defiance of the laws. They are *not* scolded for being hypocrites. They are not once linked to the Scribes but only to the High Priest. If only the Gospel of John were available to us, we would not suspect the characteristics that loom so large in the Synoptics and Acts.

Nevertheless, there is nothing in John that precludes these characteristics! John underscores their power; indeed, he portrays them as possessing an authority that is challenged *only* by Jesus and the Jews who were drawn to him. John does not seem to know of any religious authority other than the Pharisees. Even the chief priests and the High Priests appear in a secondary role, as functionaries. The Pharisees are pictured as the religious leaders of *all* the Jews, as if there were no Sadducees. Nonetheless, John's definition of the Pharisees is not necessarily at odds with that of the Synoptics, since it does not incorporate characteristics that are incompatible with the Synoptic image.

If John's Gospel was written after the destruction of the Temple and in the Diaspora, the Pharisees may very well have been the only religious authorities recognized by the Jews. In the period after the destruction of the Temple and in the Diaspora, there may have been *only* the Jews who followed the Pharisees and the Jews who followed Jesus and to the extent that John's Gospel was a polemical work against the Jews, he was only concerned with countering the arguments of the Pharisees, for no other *Jewish* arguments existed in the postdestruction period.

One link, however, does exist binding the Pharisees of John to the Pharisees of the Synoptics. John unequivocally assigns to the Pharisees control over the synagogue: "Nevertheless many even of the authorities believed in him, but for fear of the Pharisees they did not confess it, *lest they should be put out of the synagogue"* (12:42-43; italics added). Now since the synagogue was *exclusively* a Pharisaic institution, then John's Pharisees must be identical with the Pharisees of the Synoptics, i.e.,‍ whatever Judaism was preached in the synagogue was the Judaism of John's Pharisees. In John's day the *paradosis,* and Judaism were seemingly one and the same, there being no longer any Sadducees to challenge this claim. There was no longer any need to differentiate the teachings of the Pharisees from the teachings of the Sadducees. The belief in resurrection was no longer challenged by a viable school of thought.* The struggle between the Jews and the Christians in John revolves around the question of whether Jesus was the son of the Father sent to die for the sins of man, and not around his challenge to the *paradosis.* John is attempting to explain how it was that the Jews rejected Jesus despite the many signs that he displayed of his divine nature. And the explanation he gives is that their religious leaders, the

---

*Such a supposition is strengthened by the fact that throughout his *Against Apion,* written more than two decades after the destruction of the Temple and at a time when the Sadducees had ceased to be a viable *haeresis* among the Jews, Josephus writes as though all Jews were followers of the Pharisaic system. Thus, for example, he takes for granted that all Jews believe in eternal life and resurrection.

Pharisees, were so frightened of his impact on the mass of Jews that they sought his death and threatened those who believed in him with exclusion from their synagogue. John pits Christ against the Pharisees; Christianity against Judaism. Two religions are locked in combat. There is no longer, as in the Synoptics, a doctrinal or legal struggle within Judaism itself.

This, then, is the definition of the Pharisees that can be extracted from John: The Pharisees were a class of men held to be the religious authorities in the time of Jesus, controlling the synagogue and possessing sufficient power to bring about, in conjunction with the High Priests, the arrest of Jesus. It is a class with such influence over the Jews that even the miraculous signs of Jesus' divinity were disbelieved.

SCRIBES, PHARISEES, HYPOCRITES

Thus far our pursuit of a definition of the Pharisees in Paul, the Synoptics, Acts, and John has confined itself exclusively to passages where the term *Pharisees* is used. Although the Pharisees are frequently conjoined with the Scribes in the Synoptics and Acts, we made no systematic effort to explore the relationship between the two. And this for a very good reason: the Pharisees at times are conjoined with the Scribes; at times the Pharisees stand alone; and at other times the Scribes are mentioned, but the Pharisees not. Similarly, when we turn to the Gospel of John, we find references to the Pharisees but not the Scribes, and when we turn to Paul we find the term *Pharisees* but not *Scribes*. The problem, therefore, is whether (1) the Scribes and the Pharisees are one and the same, i.e., the terms are synonymous; or (2) the Scribes are a grouping within the Pharisees; or (3) some Scribes are Pharisees but other Scribes are not. Most, if not all, scholars have argued that the Scribes were either a grouping within the Pharisees, or that there were Scribes who were not Pharisees at all. No scholar, however, to

my knowledge, has claimed that the terms Pharisees and
Scribes are absolutely equivalent.[1]

Is there some objective method by which this problem
can be solved? Perhaps the analysis that follows will
suggest the possibility, at least, that such a method can be
designed.

The basic principle is simple: If the Scribes hold the
identical views as the Pharisees when the two are
conjoined, and if the Scribes hold identical views as the
Pharisees when they are not conjoined, and if the Scribes
never express views that are contrary to the expressed
views of the Pharisees, then the terms may be deemed
synonymous. And the same principle holds true for
actions. Since, as will be evident, a thorough analysis of
all the texts in the Gospels and Acts demonstrates that all
three of the above conditions are met, the Pharisees and
the Scribes must have been one and the same.

Let us first analyze those passages where the Scribes
are *not* linked with the Pharisees and build up a
definition of Scribes from these passages only. Such
analysis reveals that the Scribes were teachers.

And they went into Capernaum; and immediately on the
sabbath he [Jesus] entered the synagogue and taught. And they
were astonished at his teaching, for he taught them as one who
had authority *[exousian]*, and not as the scribes. And
immediately there was in their synagogue a man with an
unclean spirit; and he cried out, "What have you to do with us,
Jesus of Nazareth? Have you come to destroy us? I know who
you are, the Holy One of God." But Jesus rebuked him, saying,
"Be silent and come out of him!" And the unclean spirit,
convulsing him and crying with a loud voice, came out of him.
And they were all amazed, so that they questioned among
themselves, saying, "What is this? A new teaching! With
authority he commands even the unclean spirits, and they obey
him." And at once his fame spread everywhere throughout all
the surrounding region of Galilee. (Mark 1:21-28)

The role of the Scribes as authoritative teachers is
reechoed in the following dialogue between Jesus and his
disciples:

And they asked him, "Why do the scribes say that first Elijah must come?" And he said to them, "Elijah does come first to restore all things; and how is it written of the Son of man that he should suffer many things and be treated with contempt? But I tell you that Elijah has come, and they did to him whatever they pleased, as it is written of him." (Mark 9:11-13)

Likewise we note that the Scribes are experts in religious doctrine, as is evident from the following passage in Mark:

And when Jesus saw their faith, he said to the paralytic, "My son, your sins are forgiven." Now some of the scribes were sitting there, questioning in their hearts, "Why does this man speak thus? It is blasphemy! Who can forgive sins but God alone?" And immediately Jesus, perceiving in his spirit that they thus questioned within themselves, said to them, "Why do you question thus in your hearts? Which is easier, to say to the paralytic, 'Your sins are forgiven,' or to say, 'Rise, take up your pallet and walk'? But that you may know that the Son of man has authority on earth to forgive sins"—he said to the paralytic—"I say to you, rise, take up your pallet and go home." (Mark 2:5-11)

The Scribes also appear as experts when they are called in to pass judgment on the meaning of Jesus' strange behavior:

Then he [Jesus] went home; and the crowd came together again, so that they could not even eat. And when his friends heard it, they went out to seize him, for people were saying, "He is beside himself." And the scribes who came down from Jerusalem said, "He is possessed by Beelzebul, and by the prince of demons he casts out demons." And he called them to him, and said to them in parables, "How can Satan cast out Satan? If a kingdom is divided against itself, that kingdom cannot stand. And if a house is divided against itself, that kingdom cannot stand. And if a house is divided against itself, that house will not be able to stand. And if Satan has risen up against himself and is divided, he cannot stand, but is coming to and end. But no one can enter a strong man's house and plunder his goods, unless he first binds the strong man; then indeed he may plunder his house.

"Truly, I say to you, all sins will be fogiven the sons of men, and whatever blasphemies they utter; but whoever blasphemes against the Holy Spirit never has forgiveness, but is guilty of an eternal sin"—for they had said, "He has an unclean spirit." (Mark 3:19*b*-30)

So prestigious, in fact, were the teachings of the Scribes that Jesus must parry the Pharisaic teaching that Elijah must come prior to the coming of the Son of man by affirming it: the Scribes are right; Elijah must come before the Son of man; and Elijah had, according to Mark, indeed come. Hence there could be no challenge to Jesus' claims to being the Son of man.

An equivalent testimony to the authority of the Scribes is to be found in Jesus' challenge to their exegesis:

And as Jesus taught in the temple, he said, "How can the scribes say that the Christ is the son of David? David himself, inspired by the Holy Spirit, declared,
> 'The Lord said to my Lord,
> Sit at my right hand,
> till I put thy enemies under thy feet.'
David himself called him Lord; so how is he his son?" And the great throng heard him gladly. (Mark 12:35-37)

Nowhere, however, is the prestige of the Scribes more apparent than in the following passage denouncing them:

And in his teaching *[didache]* he said, "Beware of the scribes, who like to go about in long robes, and to have salutations in the market places and the best seats in the synagogues and the places of honor at feasts, who devour widows' houses and for a pretense make long prayers. They will receive the greater condemnation." (Mark 12:38-40)

That the Scribes were a group who asserted considerable power is evident in the role assigned them by Mark in the downfall of Jesus. Again and again they are conjoined with the chief priests and elders in seeking means for the apprehension of Jesus and in playing a decisive role in his trial. Thus we read:

And he began to teach them that the Son of man must suffer many things, and be rejected by the elders and the chief priests and the scribes, and be killed, and after three days rise again. (Mark 8:31)

And the chief priests and the scribes heard it [that Jesus had driven the money changers out of the Temple and had charged that the "house of prayer" for all people had become a den of liars] and sought a way to destroy him; for they feared him, because all the multitude was astonished at his teaching. (11:18)

And they came again to Jerusalem. And as he was walking in the temple, the chief priests and the scribes and the elders came to him, and they said to him, "By what authority are you doing these things, or who gave you this authority to do them?" Jesus said to them, "I will ask you a question; answer me, and I will tell you by what authority I do these things. Was the baptism of John from heaven or from men? Answer me." And they argued with one another, "If we say, 'From heaven,' he will say, 'Why then did you not believe him?' But shall we say, 'From men'? "—they were afraid of the people, for all held that John was a real prophet. So they answered Jesus, "We do not know." And Jesus said to them, "Neither will I tell you by what authority I do these things." (11:27-33)

It was now two days before the Passover and the feast of Unleavened Bread. And the chief priests and the scribes were seeking how to arrest him by stealth, and kill him; for they said, "Not during the feast, lest there be a tumult of the people." (14:1-2)

And immediately, while he was still speaking, Judas came, one of the twelve, and with a crowd with swords and clubs, from the chief priests and the scribes and the elders. (14:43)

And they led Jesus to the high priest; and all the chief priests and the elders and the scribes were assembled. (14:53)

And as soon as it was morning the chief priests, with the elders and the scribes, and the whole council held a consultation; and they bound Jesus and led him away and delivered him to Pilate. (15:1)

So also the chief priests mocked him [on the cross] to one another with the scribes, saying, "He saved others; he cannot save himself. Let the Christ, the King of Israel, come down now from the cross, that we may see and believe." (15:31-32)

The Scribes are pictured in these passages as a significant element within the ruling class. They are allotted a role no less important than that of the chief priests and elders. They are participants in the sanhedrin, or council, that is convened by the High Priest to investigate Jesus, and they take part in the consultation of the sanhedrin that decided to turn Jesus over to Pilate. Mark leaves no doubt that the Scribes consorted freely and amiably with the ruling authorities.

The crucial problem, however, has not yet been solved. The passages in Mark analyzed thus far do not reveal any data that would enable us to differentiate the Scribes from other groupings on the basis of specific beliefs that they alone advocated. We see them as teachers who oppose Jesus' teachings, but this opposition does not necessarily carry with it a commitment to teachings that are specifically their own and bear their distinguishing hallmark. The chief priests and the elders and all the Jews, other than Jesus and his followers, presumably might have shared with the Scribes the doctrine that only God can forgive sins, that the Christ must be the son of David, that Jesus was an agent of Beelzebul, that his teachings about the Son of man were blasphemous. The denunciation of the Scribes for their swaggering and ostentatious display tells us nothing of the teachings that had enabled them to gain such prestige for themselves. Indeed, with the exception of their association with the synagogue, the Scribes could be assigned with impunity to the Pharisees or to the Sadducees or be considered a class *sui generis.* Certainly, no absolute identification with the Pharisees can be posited on the basis of the evidence thus far drawn from Mark. It is true that in other passages, not yet analyzed, the Scribes are joined with the Pharisees, but they are equally linked, as we have seen, with the chief priests and elders.

Fortunately, one passage in Mark makes a precise and unambiguous identification possible. This bit of evidence is precious, for it is uncontaminated by a link to either Pharisees or chief priests or elders. It stands forth as irrefutable proof that the Scribes as a class taught doctrines identical to those of the Pharisees, doctrines the Sadducees rejected. The text reads as follows:

And Sadducees came to him, who say that there is no resurrection; and they asked him a question, saying, "Teacher, Moses wrote for us that if a man's brother dies and leaves a wife, but leaves no child, the man must take the wife, and raise up children for his brother. There were seven brothers; the first took a wife, and when he died left no children; and the second took her, and died, leaving no children; and the third likewise; and the seven left no children. Last of all the woman also died. In the resurrection, whose wife will she be? For the seven had her as a wife."

Jesus said to them, "Is not this why you are wrong, that you know neither the scriptures nor the power of God? For when they rise from the dead, they neither marry nor are given in marriage, but are like angels in heaven. And as for the dead being raised, have you not read in the book of Moses, in the passage about the bush, how God said to him, 'I am the God of Abraham, and the God of Isaac, and the God of Jacob? He is not God of the dead, but of the living; you are quite wrong [in rejecting the belief in the resurrection of the dead."]

And one of the scribes came up and heard them disputing with one another, and *seeing that he answered them well,* asked him, "Which commandment is the first of all?" Jesus anwered, "The first is, 'Hear, O Israel: The Lord our God, the Lord is One; and you shall love the Lord your God with all your heart, and with all your soul, and with all your mind, and with all your strength.' The second is this, 'You shall love your neighbor as yourself.' There is no other commandment greater than these." And the scribe said to him, "You are right, Teacher; you have truly said that he is one, and there is no other but he; and to love him with all the heart, and with all the understanding, and with all the strength, and to love one's neighbor as oneself, is much more than all whole burnt offerings and sacrifices." And when Jesus saw that he answered wisely, he said to him, "You are not far from the kingdom of God." And after that no one dared to ask him any questions. (Mark 12:18-34; italics added)

The Scribes are opposed to the teachings of the

Sadducees. They believe not only in the resurrection of the dead but that resurrection can be proved from Scriptures. The Scribe is applauding Jesus as much for his exegesis as for his insistence that resurrection is an angelic state incompatible with the institution of marriage. Since the Scribes are juxtaposed to the Sadducees as opponents, and since this opposition involves an affirmation of the doctrine of resurrection, and since the belief in the resurrection was one of the fundamental dogmas that divided the Pharisees from the Sadducees, then a positive identification of Scribes and Pharisees inexorably follows. We have here no link between Scribes and chief priests, or between Scribes and elders, for the simple reason that the chief priests or elders may have included Sadducees who would perforce reject the belief in resurrection. The interlinkage between Scribes and chief priests and elders is exclusively limited to matters where joint activity was possible, i.e., where Jesus was threatening a doctrine common to both (as, for example, that only God can forgive sins or that prophecy had not been revived) or was threatening the established order (as, for example, when Jesus drove the money changers out of the Temple or excited the masses with the possibility that he might be the King of the Jews). Since the Scribes never express teachings either contrary to or incompatible with those of the Pharisees, and since they are shown to be in opposition to the Sadducees and in accord with the Pharisees in the one teaching that allows of a differential analysis, it may be affirmed that in Mark the Scribes and the Pharisees are one and the same.

And this very identification is confirmed in each of the Synoptic Gospels where the Scribes and the Pharisees are repeatedly joined together, not as distinct entities with either diverse teachings or diverse functions but as two words pointing to the same object. An analysis of the pertinent texts in Mark makes it difficult, if not impossible, to entertain a viable alternative.[2]

Let us look first at Mark 7:1, where we are informed

that "the Pharisees gathered together to him, with some of the scribes, who had come from Jerusalem." The Pharisees do here appear to be a group that is distinct from the Scribes. Yet an analysis of the entire section makes such a distinction untenable, for it confronts us with two groups of scholars, not only championing the very same position but upholding the binding authority of the *paradosis,* the Tradition of the elders. Particularly noteworthy is the fact that the Pharisees and Scribes speak with one voice and are challenged by Jesus as though they were one and the same. We find no distinction involving a higher status; the Scribes do not appear as spokesmen for the Pharisees, as might be expected if they were the scholars and the Pharisees the disciples. The Pharisees and the Scribes together ask Jesus why his disciples do not live in accordance with the Tradition of the elders but eat with hands defiled.

The question must be raised: Did the author of Mark conclude that since his sources used two terms they must be referring to two different groups? Is it possible that when the Gospel of Mark was written, the author knew of the Scribes only through his sources and thought that they must be a group distinct from the Pharisees? Yet his sources apparently contained no divergence in doctrine between the Scribes and Pharisees but, indeed, show them always to be in agreement and leave little doubt that the Pharisees were a scholar class (it will be recalled that Mark refers to the "disciples of the Pharisees" in 2:18). We are confronted with a single entity bearing two names, and not with two distinct entities that have only different names to differentiate them.

Matthew, like Mark, sometimes uses *Scribes* alone, sometimes combines them with the elders and the chief priests, and sometimes with the Pharisees. Although the usage in Matthew is frequently identical with that in Mark, there are several passages that are found only in Matthew. In one instance, a Scribe offers to follow Jesus (8:19) and in another Jesus is purported to have said,

"Therefore, every scribe who has been trained for the kingdom of heaven is like a householder who brings out of his treasure what is new and what is old" (13:52). These verses, however, communicate no information about who the Scribes were.

More significant is the fact that Matthew (22:34) portrays the Pharisees as approving the way in which Jesus had confuted the Sadducees on the issue of resurrection, whereas Mark (12:28) attributes this approval to a Scribe. Similarly, Matthew (22:34-40) attributes to a Pharisee the questioning of Jesus on what was the great commandment of the Law, while Mark (12:28-34) attributes this questioning to the selfsame Scribe.

Matthew likewise replaces the Scribes with the Pharisees when he has Jesus raise the question as to the lineage of the Christ:

Now while the Pharisees were gathered together, Jesus asked them a question, saying, "What do you think of the Christ? Whose son is he?" They said to him, "The son of David." He said to them, "How is it then that David, inspired by the Spirit, calls him Lord, saying,
> The Lord said to my Lord,
> Sit at my right hand,
> till I put my enemies under thy feet'
If David thus calls him Lord, how is he his son?" And no one was able to answer him a word, nor from that day did any dare to ask him any more questions. (Matt. 22:41-46)

For Matthew, the Pharisees are the authoritative teachers. It is to them that one turns for information on such matters as the identity of the Messiah. But in Mark (12:35-37) it was to the Scribes that Jesus turned for the authoritative doctrine. Are we then to believe that there were two separate and distinct scholar classes, each presiding over the identical teachings?

This question is even more sharply raised by Matthew 23 where the Scribes and Pharisees cannot be but one and the same. The Scribes *and* the Pharisees sit on Moses' seat; the Scribes *and* the Pharisees preach and do not practice; the Scribes *and* the Pharisees bind heavy burdens on men's shoulders, i.e., determine the Law; the Scribes *and* the Pharisees traverse land and sea for a proselyte; the Scribes *and* the Pharisees are hypocrites, whitewashed tombs, killers of prophets, persecutors of Christians—Matthew does not distinguish Scribes from Pharisees; he considers them to be one and the same.

Matthew's assumption that the Scribes and the Pharisees are identical is made manifest in his attributing to the Scribes and Pharisees those very characteristcs Mark had assigned to the Scribes. In Mark, Jesus had warned his disciples to "Beware of the scribes, who like to go about in long robes, and to have salutations in the market places and the best seats in the synagogues and the places of honor at feasts" (Mark 12:38-39). In Matthew, Jesus denounces the Scribes *and* the Pharisees for loving the "the place of honor at feasts and the best seats in the synagogues, and salutations in the market places (Matt. 23:6).

And in his affirming that the Scribes *and* the Pharisees loved to be called "rabbi" by men, Matthew is testifying that the Scribes and the Pharisees are one and the same and that they are authoritative teachers of the Law. That two distinct scholar classes would each regard the title "rabbi" as *its* hallmark stretches our credulity to the uttermost.

It is noteworthy that Matthew does not add "and the Pharisees" to the Scribes, nor does he replace *Scribes* with *Pharisees* in the Passion narrative. Here the Scribes are linked, as in Mark, to the chief priests and the elders, but not to the Pharisees. As such, they appear, as in Mark, as leaders of great importance who participate in the trial of Jesus. That these Scribes were other than the Scribes whom Matthew identifies with the Pharisees could be maintained only if the Gospel had differentiated them or if the Gospel had shown the Pharisees as partisans of Jesus. As for the first prerequisite, Matthew no more

114

differentiates than does Mark or Luke. As for the second, not only is Matthew very hostile to the Pharisees, but he introduces the Pharisees as maligners of Jesus *after* the crucifixion. Here the Pharisees appear without the Scribes, but clearly as leaders:

Next day, that is, after the day of Preparation, the chief priests and the Pharisees gathered before Pilate and said, "Sir, we remember how that imposter said, while he was still alive, 'After three days I will rise again.' Therefore order the sepulchre to be made secure until the third day, lest his disciples go and steal him away, and tell the people, 'He has risen from the dead,' and the last fraud will be worse than the first." Pilate said to them, 'You have a guard of soldiers; go, make it as secure as you can." So they went and made the sepulchre secure by sealing the stone and setting a guard. (Matt. 27:62-66)

The Pharisees *and not the Scribes* are joined together with the chief priests to thwart the resurrection of Jesus, whereas in the account of the trial and the crucifixion the Scribes are allied with the priests while the Pharisees are not mentioned at all. But whether Matthew uses "Scribes" or "Pharisees," he is referring to a class of respected and influential leaders.

In turning from Matthew to Luke, we are once again compelled either to recognize that the Scribes and the Pharisees are identical or to posit the existence of two scholar classes, undifferentiable except in name. Indeed, with Luke we are confronted with the choice of *three* scholar classes, all with identical teachings, or three names for the same class; for Luke frequently uses *nomikoi* ("lawyers") where Mark and Matthew use *Scribes* or *Pharisees*. Indeed, Luke conceivably may even offer us the choice of four classes, or four names; for he also uses the term *nomodidaskalos,* a teacher of the Law, which need not necessarily be synonymous with *nomikos,* "lawyer."

Luke's introduction of the terms *nomikos* and *nomodidaskalos* affords us striking evidence that *Scribes, Pharisees, lawyers,* and *teachers of the Law* must be synonymous, even though the author of the Gospel of Luke may not have recognized this synonymity. Otherwise how is one to account for Luke's usage of *nomodidaskalos* in the following passage?

On one of those days, as he was teaching, there were Pharisees and teachers of the law sitting by, who had come from every town of Galilee and Judea and from Jerusalem; and the power of the Lord was with him to heal. And behold, men were bringing on a bed a man who was paralyzed, and they sought to bring him in and lay him before Jesus; but finding no way to bring him in, because of the crowd, they went up on the roof and let him down with his bed through the tiles into the midst before Jesus. And when he saw their faith he said, "Man, your sins are forgiven you." And the scribes and the Pharisees began to question, saying, "Who is this that speaks blasphemies? Who can forgive sins but God only?" When Jesus perceived their questionings, he answered them, "Why do you question in your hearts? Which is easier, to say, 'Your sins are forgiven you,' or to say, 'Rise and walk'? But that you may know that the Son of man has authority on earth to forgive sins"—he said to the man who was paralyzed—"I say to you, rise, take up your bed and go home." And immediately he rose before them, and took up that on which he lay, and went home glorifying God. And amazement seized them all, and they glorified God and were filled with awe, saying, "We have seen strange things today." (Luke 5:17-26)

Luke is recording here an event that is found also in Mark (2:1-12) and Matthew (9:2-8); but whereas they have the Scribes denounce Jesus for blasphemy, Luke has the Scribes and the Pharisees make the blasphemy charge. But since Luke begins the story with the Pharisees and teachers of the Law, and then substitutes the Scribes for the teachers of the Law, it would seem that the author of Luke considered the Scribes and teachers of the Law to be synonymous. And in view of the fact that the Pharisees hold the identical views as the Scribes and the teachers of the Law, one wonders how two sets of authorities on the Law could be holding to a single position. This wonderment is compounded by the fact that neither Mark nor Matthew uses either *Pharisees* or *teachers of the Law*. Luke's use of the term *nomikoi*,

116

"lawyers," is equivalent to Mark's, Matthew's, and even his own use of *Scribes*. The *nomikoi* are always conjoined with the Pharisees and never put forth a position that is contrary to that of either the Scribes or the Pharisees. Thus when Luke had Jesus affirm that John was indeed a prophet, the Pharisees and the lawyers are linked together as having rejected John:

When they heard this all the people and the tax collectors justified God, having been baptized with the baptism of John; but the Pharisees and the lawyers rejected the purpose of God for themselves, not having been baptized by him. (Luke 7:29-30)

That the *nomikos*, "lawyer," is none other than the Scribe and Pharisee of Mark and Matthew is evident from the following passage:

And behold, a lawyer stood up to put him to the test, saying "Teacher, what shall I do to inherit eternal life?" He said to him, "What is written in the law? How do you read?" And he answered, "You shall love the Lord your God with all your heart, and with all your soul, and all your strength, and with all your mind; and your neighbor as yourself." And he said to him, "You have answered right; do this and you will live." (Luke 10:25-28)

In Mark, the questioner is a Scribe who has been impressed with Jesus' skillful refutation of the Sadducees (Mark 12:28-34), while in Matthew, as in Luke, it is a *nomikos* who is described as one of the Pharisees who does the questioning (Matt. 22:34-40). Luke, it is true, eliminates the Jesus-Sadducees debate, but preserves the Pharisaic identity of his *nomikos* by having him concerned with eternal life as a reality.

Luke's lawyers and Mark and Matthew's Pharisees appear as one and the same when the issue of healing the sick on sabbath is raised. Here is Luke's version:

One sabbath when he went to dine at the house of a leader who belonged to the Pharisees, they were watching him. And behold there was a man before him who had dropsy. And Jesus spoke to the lawyers and Pharisees saying, "Is it lawful to heal on the sabbath, or not?" But they were silent. Then he took him and healed him, and let him go. And he said to them, "Which of you having a son or an ox that has fallen into a well, will not immediately pull him out on a sabbath day?" And they could not reply to this. (Luke 14:1-6)

Yet in Mark (3:1-6) and Matthew (12:9-14) we find the Pharisees alone involved, and no laywers.

The synonymity of *Scribes, Pharisees,* and *lawyers* nowhere is more evident than in the following passages:

While he was speaking, a Pharisee asked him to dine with him; so he went and sat at table. The Pharisee was astonished that he did not first wash before dinner. And the Lord said to him, "Now you Pharisees cleanse the outside of the cup and of the dish, but inside you are full of extortion and wickedness. You fools! Did not he who made the outside make the inside also? But give for alms those things which are within; and behold everything is clean for you.

"But woe to you, Pharisees! For you tithe mint and rue and every herb, and neglect justice and the love of God; these you ought to have done, without neglecting the others. Woe to you, Pharisees! for you love the best seats in the synagogues and salutations in the market places. Woe to you! for you are like graves which are not seen, and men walk over them without knowing it." (Luke 11:37-44; contrast with Matt. 23:25-26, 23-24, 27-28, 2-3, 5*a*, 6-7)

Luke now drops *Pharisees* and introduces the *nomikoi,* "the lawyers":

One of the lawyers answered him, "Teacher, in saying this you reproach us also!" And he said, "Woe to you lawyers also! for you load men with burdens hard to bear, and you yourselves do not touch the burdens with one of your fingers. Woe to you! for you build the tombs of the prophets whom your fathers killed. So you are witnesses and consent to the deeds of your fathers; for they killed them, and you build their tombs. Therefore also the Wisdom of God said, 'I will send them prophets and apostles, some of whom they will kill and persecute,' that the blood of all the prophets, shed from the foundation of the world, may be required of this generation, from the blood of

118

The New Testament

Abel to the blood of Zechariah, who perished between the altar and the sanctuary. Yes, I tell you, it shall be required of this generation. Woe to you lawyers! for you have taken away the key to knowledge; you did not enter yourselves and you hindered those who were entering." (Luke 11:45-50; contrast Matt. 23:2a, 4, 29-36, 13)

Luke thereupon abandons *the lawyers* for *Scribes* and *Pharisees:*

As he went away from there, the scribes and the Pharisees began to press him hard, and to provoke him to speak of many things, lying in wait for him, to catch at something he might say. (Luke 11:53-54; contrast Mark 12:13)

And finally for Luke there are only the Pharisees:

In the meantime, when so many thousands of the multitude had gathered together that they trod upon one another, he began to say to his disciples first, "Beware of the leaven of Pharisees, which is hypocrisy." (Luke 12:1)

Gone are the Scribes; gone are the lawyers; only the Pharisees remain. But the leaven of the Pharisees is hypocrisy for Luke, and it is this hypocrisy Matthew attributes not only to the Pharisees but to the Scribes as well!

That Luke's choice now of Pharisees, now lawyers, now Scribes, is a random one, is proved by the parallel material in Matthew where the Scribes and Pharisees are welded together and lawyers are conspicuously mentioned. Luke has three names to assign to a single entity, and he does not hesitate to use these names singly or together. And probably for good reason! Finding in his sources *Scribes, Pharisees, lawyers,* and *teachers of the Law,* he may have thought they must be three or four different groups. He did not, however, find in his sources any differentiating criteria! He therefore treated the four names as though they denoted four identical objects. Luke has thus bequeathed us ambiguities that resolve, on analysis, into synonyms.

119

The ambiguity as well as the synonymity is forcefully brought forth in Acts in the person of Gamaliel:

> When they heard this they were enraged and wanted to kill them [the apostles]. But a *Pharisee* in the council named Gamaliel, [a *nomodidaskalos*] *a teacher of the law,* held in high honor by all the people, stood up and ordered the men to be put outside for a while. (Acts 5:33-34; italics added)

The two are indeed one. A Pharisee is a *nomodidaskalos,* and a *nomodidaskalos* is a Pharisee. Luke was unaware that he was saying, "But a *nomodidaskalos* in the council named Gamaliel, a *nomodidaskalos* held in high honor by all the people, stood up." Luke may very well have mistaken an explanation or translation for a separate and distinct group.[3]

The fact that the Gospel of Luke *indiscriminately* uses the four terms—*scribes, Pharisees, lawyers,* and *teachers of the law*—is rather decisive proof that at least this Gospel writer mistook synonyms for differentiations. And though the confusion is less evident in Mark and in Matthew than in Luke, it is a confusion nonetheless. The moment that Pharisees emerge out of these Gospels as a *scholar class* championing the concept of the twofold Law, the Written Law and the *paradosis,* "the Tradition," and differentiated from the Sadducees, then positing the existence of any other scholar class (be they called scribes, lawyers, or teachers of the Law)—holding and teaching the identical doctrines—becomes a virtual impossibility. Three or even four names for the same entity, however, is a frequent occurrence; three or four identical classes, free of *differentiae* but enjoying separate, distinct, and differential existence would be a miraculous phenomenon indeed!

One final word about the Gospel of John. In its own way, this Gospel confirms the analysis given above. The fact that Pharisees have completely replaced the Scribes, *even* in the account of the arrest, trial, and crucifixion, certainly points to synonymity, and not differentiation.

The problem with John does not lie here, but rather in the lack of specific data about the Pharisees. John is aware that the Pharisees had played an important role in Jesus' life, but seems to be unaware of who the Pharisees were. He uses a name, but he neither draws from his sources data that might clarify its meaning nor has a personal knowledge of living Pharisees to communicate. Only indirectly, through his reference to the Pharisees as those who controlled the synagogue and to Jesus as "Rabbi," does John offer a link to the Synoptics.

Before bringing to a close this analysis of the New Testament data relevant for a definition of the Pharisees, a brief analysis of the Synoptics' use of the term *hypocrites* is essential.

Matthew leaves little doubt that the hypocrites and the Pharisees must be one and the same. The "hypocrites" in Matthew have all the features that elsewhere in the Synoptics are associated with the Pharisees and the Scribes. This identification is forced upon us by the following diatribe against the hypocrites in the sixth chapter of Matthew:

Beware of practicing your piety [or righteousness, *dikaiosunen*] before men in order to be seen by them; for then you will have no reward from your Father who is in heaven.
[Cf. Matt. 23:2-5*a*. The scribes and the Pharisees sit on Moses' seat; . . . They do all their deeds to be seen by men."]
Thus, when you give alms, sound no trumpet before you, as the hypocrites do in the synagogues and in the streets, that they may be praised by men. Truly, I say to you, they have received their reward. But when you give alms, do not let your left hand know what your right hand is doing, so that your alms may be in secret; and your Father who sees in secret will reward you.
And when you pray, you must not be like the hypocrites; for they love to stand and pray in the synagogues and at the street corners, that they may be seen by men. Truly, I say to you, they have received their reward. But when you pray, go into your room and shut the door and pray to your Father who is in secret; and your Father who sees in secret will reward you. (Matt. 6:1-6)
[Cf. Mark 12:38-40. And in his teaching he said, "Beware of

the scribes, who like to go about in long robes, and to have salutations in the market places and the best seats in the synagogues and the places of honor at feasts, who devour widows' houses and for a pretense make long prayers. They will receive the greater condemnation." (See also Luke 20:45-47)]

And when you fast, do not look dismal, like the hypocrites, for they disfigure their faces that their fasting be seen by men. Truly, I say to you, they have received their reward. But when you fast, anoint your head and wash your face, that your fasting may not be seen by men but by our Father who is in secret; and your Father who sees in secret will reward you. (Matt. 6:16-18)
[Cf. Mark 2:18. Now John's disciples and the Pharisees were fasting; and people came and said to him, "Why do John's disciples and the disciples of the Pharisees fast, but your disciples do not fast?" (Matt. 9:14; Luke 5:33)]

That the "hypocrites" of Matthew 6 and the "scribes, Pharisees, hypocrites" of Matthew 33 are one and the same seems to be an inference not likely to be challenged. And that the "hypocrites" of Matthew 6 are none other than the Pharisee hypocrites who are denounced by Jesus for giving priority to the *paradosis* (Mark 7:5-8; Matt. 15:1-9) seems to be evident. And is not Luke referring to the Pharisees when he has Jesus heal an invalid woman on the sabbath day in the synagogue and then denounce the "hypocrites" for their indignation at his presumption?

But the ruler of the synagogue, indignant because Jesus had healed on the sabbath, said to the people, "There are six days on which work ought to be done; come on those days and be healed, and not on the sabbath day." Then the Lord answered him, "You hypocrites! Does not each one of you on the sabbath untie his ox or his ass from the manger, and lead it away to water it? . . . " (Luke 13:14-17)
[Cf. Luke 14:1-6: One sabbath when he went to dine at the house of a ruler who belonged to the Pharisees, they were watching him. And behold, there was a man before him who had dropsy. And Jesus spoke to the lawyers and Pharisees, saying, "Is it lawful to heal on the sabbath, or not?" but they were silent. The he took him and healed him, and let him go. And he said to them, "Which of you, having a son or an ox that

has fallen into a well, will not immediately pull him out on the sabbath day?" And they could not reply to this.]

And finally, Luke makes the identification of Pharisees and hypocrites absolute when he has Jesus warn his disciples: "Beware of the leaven of the Pharisees, which is hypocrisy" (12:1*b*).

CONCLUSION

In seeking a definition of the Pharisees derived from the New Testament alone—without recourse to either Josephus or the Tannaitic Literature—we have analyzed the pertinent texts where the term is used unambiguously. Adhering to our basic methodology, we began with Paul because his Epistles are the only writings in the New Testament whose authorship can be established with any certainty. His testimony, therefore, is to be accorded the highest value, since by his own admission he not only knew the Pharisees but had been one himself. And this definition derived from Paul is as follows: The Pharisees were those who had a distinctive approach to the Law and who held up righteousness under the Law as the highest ideal. Their distinctive approach was the affirmation that the *paradosis*, "the Tradition," was binding. The Pharisees were thus the exponents of the twofold Law.

Paul's definition, as we have seen, is confirmed by the Synoptics. Mark, Matthew and Luke portray the Pharisees as that scholar class which championed the authority of the twofold Law, the Written Law and the *paradosis*. The definition drawn from them enlarges that derived from Paul, since it neither contradicts it nor adds any data that would be incompatible with Paul's definition. The definition available in the Synoptics is an extension of Paul's. The Synoptics permit us to add to the basic definition the following: The Pharisees (1) were highly respected; (2) wielded great power; (3) had access to the ruling authorities, whether Roman (the procurator) or Jewish (the High Priest, the chief priests, and the

123

Herodians); (4) opposed Jesus' disregard for the *paradosis;* (5) persecuted the early Christians and expelled them from the synagogues.

The definition derived from John likewise neither contradicts that drawn from Paul and the Synoptics nor offers data incompatible with that definition. Although an analytical comparison between the Pharisees in John and the Pharisees in the Synoptics and in Paul leads one to suspect that John did not have any awareness of the Pharisees as a living phenomenon in Jesus' day—he mentions neither Scribes nor Sadducees but only Pharisees and Jews—he nonetheless conveys the idea that the Pharisees were a class of leaders who were well-versed in the Law, who controlled the synagogues, and who wielded great power.

The definition of the Pharisees derived from the New Testament is thus established as free of contradiction. This definition is not affected by the validity of the reasoning that would posit the absolute identity of Scribes, lawyers, teachers of the Law, and hypocrites with the Pharisees. Such an identification does not alter the definition derived from passages where the term *Pharisees* is used. Indeed, it does not even add to our knowledge of what differentiated the Pharisees from other groups. The Pharisees as a scholar class dedicated to the authority of the twofold Law is rooted in evidence that is self-sustaining. Nevertheless, the awareness that the terms *Pharisees, Scribes, lawyers, teachers of the Law,* and *hypocrites* are synonymous would eliminate the need for positing three or four different classes having identical characteristics, functions, doctrines, and teachings but enjoying separate and distinct embodiments.

Our definition drawn from the New Testament may now be concisely stated: The Pharisees were a scholar class committed to the authority of the Written Law and the *paradosis,* who enjoyed such prestige and who exercised such power that to all appearances they sat securely on Moses' seat.

Chapter III

The Tannaitic Literature

The Tannaitic Literature, like the writings of Josephus and the New Testament, gives internal evidence that it has a right to be heard in the construction of a definition of the Pharisees. The Hebrew term *Perushim,* which lies behind the Greek *Pharisaoi* and the English *Pharisees,* is found *only* in the Tannaitic Literature. So, too, the Hebrew term *Zedukim,* which underlies the Greek *Saddukoi* and the English *Sadducees,* is found only in the Tannaitic Literature. Indeed, scholars have always sensed that the Tannaitic Literature is the prime source for our knowledge of the Pharisees.

Yet, though the Tannaitic Literature is crucial, it is not easily exploited. Even more than the New Testament, this literature lends itself to arbitrary and subjective manipulation. Whereas the range of possible error for dating the New Testament texts is confined to 150 years or so, that for the Tannaitic Literature is *no less* than 350 years. Furthermore, whereas the books of the New Testament concentrate on Jesus and his message, the Tannaitic Literature is a repository of law and lore virtually unbounded in scope. Whereas the span of oral transmission of New Testament materials is reckoned in decades, that of the Tannaitic Literature is reckoned in centuries. Whereas the entire New Testament can be contained within a volume of five hundred pages or so, the Mishnah alone can barely be compressed into a volume of seven hundred pages. And in addition to the Mishnah there are the Tosefta, the Tannaitic Midrash, and the thousands of tannaitic passages strewn through the Palestinian and Babylonian Talmuds, a significant portion of which are communicated as anonymous dicta. The wonder is not that scholars have found support for arbitrary and subjective hypotheses in this complex literature but that they have been able to come up with any objective proposition at all.

If the Tannaitic Literature bristles with difficulties even when utilized for the solution of relatively simple problems, how compounded they become when one seeks to utilize this corpus to construct an objective definition of the Pharisees! The Pharisees were a product of historical processes, yet the Tannaitic Literature has no systematic, disciplined interest in history. Unlike the Bible, the Tannaitic Literature has no equivalent interest in the historical continuum. History as continuity or history as chronology or history as interconnected successive events is of no relevance. Single events, individual episodes, disconnected moments, yes; but sustained interconnections, interlinked chronology, interacting events, no.

It is literally true, however ironic, that if only the Tannaitic Literature had survived from the second pre-Christian century till the second century of the Common Era, we would be without any history of the Jews during the Intertestamental period. Imagine a literature embracing thousands of pages of law and lore, created during centuries marked by such tumultuous events as the Hasmonean Revolt, the collapse of the Zadokite priesthood, the rise and decline of the Hasmonean monarchy and priesthood, the penetration of Rome into the Near East, the rise and fall of the House of Herod, the disturbed era of the procurators, the birth of Christianity, the Great Rebellion against Rome and the destruction of the Second Temple, the Hadrianic persecutions and the Bar Kochba Revolt—and yet a literature either oblivious to these events or according them scant notice: an episode here, a personality there—*never* setting them in any historical continuum, never connecting them precisely in place or in time. Yet this is the literature that contains precious data about the Pharisees; that has within it deposits of the historical processes it deemed to be irrelevant; that bears witness to the march of time and the impact of events even though it pays them no heed. The Tannaitic Literature tantalizes the scholar with its hidden treasures yet offers only the barest clues as to where the locks may be found and only the most subtle hints of what keys might unlock them.

But before one can even hope to unravel the clues, one must make clear to the reader what exactly this Tannaitic Literature is. At the outset it must be emphasized that the Tannaitic Literature is an array, not a single collection, of highly diverse writings. The most authoritative corpus within this literature is the Mishnah, promulgated in the first decade or so of the second century by the head of the scholar class, Judah ha-Nasi (the Prince). The Mishnah is primarily a collection of laws arranged in six major divisions which are, in turn, subdivided into tractates. These, in turn, are subdivided into chapters and sections. Although most of the laws are set down anonymously, the opinions of individual scholars are frequently presented as well.

The Tosefta, like the Mishnah, is a collection of laws which differs from the Mishnah only in content—the laws included are sometimes different—though the form is not. It has the same six orders and the same division into tractates, chapters, and sections. Like the Mishnah, the Tosefta is almost exclusively a law book.

The Tannaitic Midrash (the Mekhilta, the Sifre, and the Sifra) differs radically in form from the Mishnah and the Tosefta; for although it contains law, this law is attached as a commentary to the Pentateuchal text. The laws are frequently derived from biblical verses by resort to logical-deductive methods, though no effort is made to arrange the laws so derived in any kind of logical or categorical order. The laws of the Mishnah and the Tosefta are *arranged,* for the most part, logically, whereas the laws of the Tannaitic Midrash are *derived,* for the most part, logically.

The Tannaitic Midrash also differs markedly from the Mishnah and the Tosefta in its inclusion of much nonlegal material. This nonlegal material, called *aggadah* (lore) in contrast to *halakhah* (law), likewise uses the Pentateuchal text as its point of departure and seeks to derive doctrinal teachings by hermeneutic methods.

Although like the Mishnah and the Tosefta, the Tannaitic Midrash contains much that is anonymous, it does cite the opinions of many individual scholars. The Tannaitic Midrash is thus a collective, exegetical-hermeneutical commentary to all the books of the Pentateuch with the exception of Genesis and the first eleven chapters of Exodus. This exclusion reveals that the propelling motive of the exegesis was the laws, for it is with Exodus 12 that the law begins to vie with narrative for primacy within the Pentateuch.

The Tannaitic Midrash never achieved the authority of the Mishnah, even though the laws may be the same and even though the exegetes are the very same scholars who are cited in the Mishnah.

The *beraitoth* (tannaitic teachings excluded from the Mishnah and the Tosefta) are sometimes law in the Mishnah form, sometimes law and lore *(aggadah)* in the tannaitic, midrashic, exegetical form, and sometimes lore *(aggadah)* unattached to biblical verses. These *beraitoth* are found strewn throughout the Palestinian and Babylonian Talmuds without any logical order and without any connection to contiguous verses in the Pentateuchal text. Rather they are cited by the *amoraic* scholars whenever a discussion of the laws of the Mishnah warrants, or whenever some clarification is needed, or whenever a subject is being discussed where it might be applicable. Frequently the *beraitoth* are anonymous, but as in the case of the Mishnah, Tosefta, and the Tannaitic Midrash, many are quoted which do make mention of the individual scholars.

These, then, are the tannaitic sources, diverse in form and unequal in authority.

Yet they possess in many respects an intrinsic unity that is missing in the Old and the New Testaments, for they are the handiwork of the same scholar class. The anonymity is the same anonymity; the scholars cited by name are the same scholars; the nonexegetical legal form, the same form; the exegetical principles, the same exegetical principles; the fundamental loyalties and presuppositions are likewise identical. The Tannaitic Literature, in short, refracts in *different* forms and on unequal levels of authority the activity of the *identical* scholar class, a scholar class that may have continuously changed its laws and continuously transformed its doctrines but a class that always remained steadfast to the fundamental principle upholding its authority, namely, the belief that God had revealed a twofold Law at Sinai: "Moses received the [written and unwritten] Torah from Sinai and transmitted it to Joshua, and Joshua transmitted it to the Elders, the Elders to the Prophets, and the Prophets to the Men of the Great Assembly *[Kenesset ha-Gedolah]*" (Ab. 1:1).

Both Christian and Jewish scholars have drawn on this literature for their image of the Pharisees. And the term *perushim* is indeed there for exploitation—and exploited it has been. The deceptive simplicity of the term seems to offer such reassuring clarity, and its preservation in the Tannaitic Literature such a pledge for its authenticity, that it is no wonder that scholars have pounced upon a seemingly unambiguous text in the Mishnah, Hag. 2:7, as an impeccable source for constructing a definition of the Pharisees. This text reads as follows:

The garments of an *am ha-aretz* count as suffering *midras*-uncleanness for *perushim;* the garments of *perushim* count as

129

suffering *midras*-uncleanness for them that eat Heave-offering; the clothes of them that eat Heave-offering are a source of *midras*-uncleanness for them that eat of Hallowed Things; the garments of those that eat of Hallowed Things count as *midras*-uncleanness for them that occupy themselves with the Sin-offering. Jose ben Joezer was the most pious in the priesthood, yet his apron counted as *midras*-uncleanness for them that ate Hallowed Things. Johannan ben Guggada always ate [his common food] in accordance with [the rules governing] the cleanness of Hallowed Things, yet his apron counted as suffering *midras*-uncleanness for them that occupied themselves with the Sin-offering.

This definition of the Pharisees, drawn from the Hagigah text, has been for most scholars *the* tannaitic definition. So much so, in fact, that the *perushim* of the Hagigah text have been regarded as synonymous with *haberim* since, like the *perushim,* the *haberim* are a sect-like grouping differentiated from the *am ha-aretz.*

The methodology followed by these scholars is clear: First the word *perushim* is detected and translated "Pharisees"; second, the context is read in the light of the translation of the word; third, the content of the text is utilized to define the word *perushim;* fourth, the definition having been secured via the word, it is then freely used to determine the word's meaning in other texts.

Is such a procedure legitimate? On what grounds do scholars determine that the word *perushim* must mean "Pharisees" in the Hagigah text? Is such a rendering a necessity or a choice? If necessity, then it can be invoked *only* if the word *perushim* is *never* used to mean anything else but Pharisees. If *perushim* is used, even in a single instance, to mean something other than Pharisees, then choice and not necessity is operative. Only possibility remains. And the moment possibility takes over, the scholar must justify his translation by stating his grounds. The appeal must be to something other than the word itself.

An adequate methodology must therefore abandon

the verbal approach to the definition of the Pharisees. It must determine the meaning of the word *perushim* by criteria that cannot be challenged, by a standard that remains fixed, firm, and independent of the individual scholar's wish, whim, or need. But such a standard and such criteria are not easily come by when the Tannaitic Literature is the source! This literature does not make its own demarcations. It never distinguishes explicitly between the term *perushim*—Pharisees—and the term *perushim*—not Pharisees. The spelling in all texts is identical; no explanatory glosses are provided. The Mishnah no more warns the reader that *Perushim* in Hagigah does *not* mean Pharisees than it reassures him that it does.

The method proposed in this study appeals to internal criteria and to an internal standard. It turns away from the word itself because it cannot be definitive. It seeks out, instead, some other measuring instrument for determining when *perushim* does, and when it does not, mean Pharisees. It begins with the assumption that only in those texts where the term *Perushim* is used in juxtaposition to *Zedukim* (Sadducees) does it *necessarily* mean Pharisees. These texts and only these texts can, at the outset, be called upon to furnish a definition. And only a definition so constructed can be regarded as the tannaitic image of the Pharisees. And the reason is simple: For whereas the Hebrew term *perushim* can be either a common or a proper noun, *Zedukim*, "Sadducees," can be a proper noun only. Consequently, whenever the *Perushim* are juxtaposed to *Zedukim*, the term *Perushim* must be translated "Pharisees" since the meaning of *Perushim* is guaranteed by the proper noun *Zedukim*, "Sadducees."

Those tannaitic texts in which the term *Perushim* is juxtaposed to *Zedukim* will be designated as the *unambiguous*, since the meaning of *Perushim* as "Pharisees" is assured by the usage of *Zedukim*, "Sadducees."

Those tannaitic texts in which the term *perushim* is used

in a context that precludes the meaning Pharisees will be designated as *control* texts, since they demonstrate that the term *perushim* need not mean Pharisees.

Those tannaitic texts in which the term *perushim* is (1) used, (2) not in juxtaposition to *Zedukim,* (3) but translated nevertheless as though the term meant Pharisees, will be designated the *ambiguous* texts, since the term *perushim* has been at times translated as "Pharisees" and at times not.

Having established these categories, we can now proceed to the comparison of the ambiguous with the unambiguous texts. If the definition derived from the ambiguous texts does not match the definition derived from the unambiguous texts, we shall then compare the ambiguous texts with the control texts. Should the definitions match, then we would be impelled to conclude that the meaning of *perushim* in the ambiguous texts is one and the same as those drawn from the control texts. Hence the term *perushim* in the ambiguous texts does not allow for the meaning "Pharisees"!

The texts that we are about to analyze are difficult texts, i.e., they deal with fine points of law and ritual. These texts presuppose a thorough knowledge of tannaitic law and doctrine. Some of these texts deal with such problems as to whether Holy Scriptures render the hands unclean, problems of great importance at the turn of the Christian era. Other texts deal with Temple rituals, the proper burning of the incense, the proper procedure to be carried out in the burning of the red heifer. For the purpose of establishing the definition of the term *Perushim*-Pharisees, however, the full and detailed understanding of these laws and rituals is *not* necessary. In fact, an attempt to explain the details adequately would divert the reader from the crucial issue: the determination of when *perushim* means Pharisees and when it does not.

Let us now collate the *unambiguous* texts and draw from them a definition of the Pharisees.

The first texts to be grouped into this category are those characterized by the formula: "The *Zedukim* [Sadducees] say, 'We complain against you *Perushim* because. . . .' The *Perushim* say, 'We complain against you *Zedukim* [Sadducees] because. . . .'"

These texts read as follows:

The *Zedukim* [Sadducees] say, "We complain against you *Perushim,* for you say that Holy Scriptures *[kitbe hakodesh]* render the hands unclean, but the writings of *homeros* [sic] do not render the hands unclean."

R. Johanan ben Zakkai said, "Have we nothing but this against the *Perushim*? For they [the Sadducees] say, 'The bones of an ass are clean, but the bones of Johanan the High Priest are unclean.'" They [the Sadducees] said to him, "As in our love for them so is their uncleanness, so that no man may make spoons of the bones of his father and his mother."

He [R. Johanan ben Zakkai] said to them, "Even so the Holy Scripture: as is our love for them so is their uncleanness; whereas the writings of *homeros* [sic] which we do not love, do not render the hands unclean." (Yad. 4:6)

The *Zedukim* [Sadducees] say, "We complain against you *Perushim* because you assert that the *nizzok* is clean. The *Perushim* say, "We complain against you *Zedukim* because you declare clean a stream of water that comes from a cemetery."

The *Zedukim* say, "We complain against you *Perushim* because you say that if my ox or ass has done damage, the owners are responsible, yet if my bondman or bondwoman have done damage, the owners are free of responsibility. If in the case of my ox and ass where I have no obligation of fulfilling divine commandments with respect to them, I nonetheless am responsible for the damage they do, how much more in the case of my bondman and bondwoman, concerning whom certain divine commandments are imposed upon me must I be responsible for the damage that they do." They [the *Perushim*] said to them, "No! Can you say concerning my ox and ass which have no understanding what you could say concerning my bondman and bondwoman who have understanding? If I anger them [i.e., the slaves], one [of them] may go and set fire to another's stack of corn, and it is I would have to make restitution." (Yad. 7)

These are the only controversies between the Sadducees and the Pharisees recorded in the Mishnah utilizing this dialogue formula. However, the Tosefta employs this formula but substitutes the Boethusians for the Sadducees. The term may nonetheless be considered synonymous, for the identical position taken by the Boethusians in the Tosefta texts is that attributed elsewhere in the Tannaitic Literature to the Sadducees. Furthermore, like the term *Sadducees, Boethusians* is a proper, not a common, noun. The text follows:

The Boethusians [Sadducees] say, "We complain against you *Perushim* [because you argue that] if the daughter of my son who comes from the strength of my son who came from my strength does indeed inherit me, is it then not logical that my daughter who comes directly from my own strength should inherit me?" The *Perushim* say, "Not at all. For if you refer to the daughter of the son, she takes a share with her brothers, whereas the daughter of the father does not share with her brothers. [You thus recognize that there are inheritance rights for the granddaughter, but not for the daughter]." (Tosef. Yad. 2:20)

The formula is likewise used in two other tannaitic texts. However, in these the *Perushim* appear, but their antagonists are not the Sadducees. These texts are nonetheless included, for they clearly portray the *Perushim* as holding a well-defined position on the Law. The Mishnah text reads:

Zadok of Galilee said, "I complain against you *Perushim* because you write [the name of] the [secular] ruler together with the name of Moses in a bill of divorce." The *Perushim* say, "We cry out against you, Zadok of Galilee, for you write the name of the [secular] ruler together with the name [of God] on the same page. Furthermore, you write the name of the [secular] ruler above, and the name [of God] below, for it is written in Holy Scriptures [Exod. 5:2], 'And Pharaoh said, "Who is the Lord that I should hearken unto his voice to let Israel go?"'' And when he smote him, what did he say? 'The Lord is the righteous one.'" (Yad. 4:8)

The other formula text is from the Tosefta:

The *toble shahar* [dawn immersionists] say, "We complain against you *Perushim* because you mention the name of God from the body which has impurity in it." (Tosef. Yad. 2:20)

An analysis of the formula texts now permits the following conclusions:

1. *Perushim* is a name assigned to a group that champions a definite position on the Law and is differentiable from the Sadducees, from Zadok of Galilee, and from the *toble shahar* who challenge the legal stance of the *Perushim*. It is to be noted the *Perushim* in these texts are not the subjects of a *law* differentiating them from their antagonists. We are not confronted with a legal demarcation of status or class. Rather do we witness groups contending with each other over legal principles as independent protagonists.

2. The *Perushim* hold to a differentiated position with respect to the Law in several areas: *(a)* the status of Holy Scripture and its relationship to "uncleanness of the hands"; *(b)* the purity status of the *nizzok;* *(c)* the responsibility of slaves for damage; *(d)* the laws of inheritance; *(e)* the status of the secular state with respect to the validity of a writ of divorce; *(f)* the spiritual evaluation of man's corporeal being.

3. The *Perushim* are not differentiated from the *am ha-aretz* but only from groups of individuals representing a contrasting approach to the Law.

4. The *Perushim* are not characterized by their adherence to the laws of ritual purity, even though these laws are at issue in two instances. What is revealed is a debate on the applicability of these laws, not on the greater or lesser purity of the antagonists. In one case, the *Perushim* seem to be more stringent—in the matter of

whether Holy Scriptures render the hands unclean—whereas in the other, the issue of *nizzok*, the Sadducees are. It is indeed evident that as far as the *toble shahar* were concerned, the *Perushim* seemed to be pictured as advocates of constant impurity.

To draw more far-reaching conclusions at this time would be premature, for they depend on texts as yet unanalyzed. The inferences drawn above do no more than make the texts explicit, and great care has been exercised lest any difference on interpretation of content contaminate the conclusions.

We now turn to a second group of texts that fall within the unambiguous corpus, because these record controversies between the *Perushim* and the Sadducees. Since, however, they do not make use of a formula, I shall group them separately:

Our rabbis have taught: "It is related of a Sadducee [High Priest] that he prepared [the incense] outside [the Holy of Holies] and then entered. When he came out he was extremely happy. His father met him and said to him, 'My son, although we are Sadducees we fear the *Perushim.*' He replied to him, 'My whole life I was troubled by the scriptural verse, "For in the cloud I shall appear on the *kaporet*" [Lev. 16:13]. I said, "When will I have the opportunity to fulfill the command of this verse?" And now that the opportunity arose, should I not fulfill the biblical verse?'"

They said, "Not many days went by before he died, and he was tossed in the refuse, and worms came forth from his nose." And some say that no sooner did he come forth [from the Holy of Holies] than he was stricken. For Rabbi Hiya taught, "A sort of voice was heard in the *azara* [outer court], for an angel came and beat him on his face, and his fellow priests entered and found something like the heel of a ram between his shoulders; for Scripture says [Ezek. 1:7], 'Their legs were straight and the soles of their feet were like the sole of a calf's foot.'" (Yom. 19*b*; cf. Y. Yom. 1:5)

One time [following the festival], they [the *Perushim*] purified the lamp, and the Sadducees said, "Come and see the *Perushim* immersing the orb of the sun." (Tosef. Hag. 3:35; cf. Y. Hag. 79:1)

These two texts convey the following data with respect to the *Perushim:*

1. They are a group concerned with the Law and hold to a view of the Law contrary to that of the Sadducees.

2. They demand that the Temple ritual be carried out in accordance with their prescriptions.

3. They exercise great power, striking fear in the hearts of the High Priestly families, and they are depicted as those who have control of the Temple.

4. They are antagonists of the Sadducees, not of the *am ha-aretz.*

A third category of texts belonging to the unambiguous corpus juxtaposes *Perushim* to Sadducees in part of the text, but employs a synonym for *Perushim* in another part.

Our Rabbis have taught: "It is related of a Sadducee who was speaking to the High Priest in the street and spittle fell on the garments of the High Priest. The face of the High Priest turned pale, and he came to his wife and told her what had happened. She said to him, 'The wives of the Sadducees are afraid of the *Perushim* and they therefore show their [menstrual] blood to the *Hakhamim* [the Sages], with the exception of one woman who was in our neighborhood who did not show the blood to the *Hakhamim* and she died. (Nid. 33*b*)

The synonym for *Perushim* in this text is *Hakhamim,* "Sages."

And why did they consider it necessary to make him [the High Priest] swear? For [the reason that] there had already occurred an instance involving a Boethusian [High Priest] who had prepared the incense on the outside [of the Holy of Holies] and the cloud of incense went forth and shook the entire Temple. [He had done this] because the Boethusians say, "He shall prepare the incense on the outside, for Scripture says: 'And the cloud of incense shall cover the *kaporet* which is above the ark so that he die not'" [Lev. 16:13]. The Sages said to them, "Is it not already stated in Scripture: 'And he shall put the incense on the fire before the Lord' [Lev. 16:4-5]? [The meaning is that] whoever prepares the incense is to prepare it only within [the

Holy of Holies]." If this be so, why is it stated in Scripture: "For in the cloud will I appear on the *kaporet*"? *This [verse] teaches that he put on it [the kaporet]* a pillar of cloud, but if he did not put on it a pillar of cloud he is subject to the death penalty.

When he [the Boethusian-Sadducean High Priest] went forth [from the Holy of Holies], he said to his father, "Your whole life you [and your fellow Boethusians-Sadduceans] used to interpret the verse [to mean that the High Priest prepares the incense outside the Holy of Holies], but you never followed through in action until I stood up and performed it [as the verse demands]." His father said to him, "Although we interpret, we do not carry out the interpretation in practice but we listen to words of the Sages. I would be truly amazed if you will live [much longer]." Three days had not gone by when they set him in his grave. (Tosef. Yom. 1:8)

In this text, too, *Hakhamim,* "Sages," is used as a synonym for *Perushim.*

We have now exhausted the unambiguous texts. They are, as is evident, very few in number. It is little less than astonishing that in the entire Tannaitic Literature no more than a half dozen or so texts utilize *Perushim* unambiguously to mean Pharisees; for all scholars concede that the Tannaitic Literature in some way reflects the teachings of the Pharisees themselves.

The sparse usage of *Perushim* to mean Pharisees may derive from the fact that some other term or terms are preferred. The clue for unravelling possible synonyms lies in the last grouping. These texts met the most rigorous standards for rendering *Perushim* as "Pharisees," for they utilize the word in juxtaposition to Sadducees. At the same time, *since these texts make use of a synonym for the Pharisees, the synonym could conceivably be used in other texts instead of Perushim.* The synonym thus far attested to is *Hakhamim,* or "Sages."

It is now proposed that we collate all texts in which *Hakhamim,* but not *Perushim,* is used in juxtaposition to the Sadducees.

False witnesses are not put to death until after judgment has been rendered; for the Sadducees used to say, "Only after he has been put to death [are the false witnesses to be executed], for it is written in Scripture: 'Life for life.'" The *Hakhamim* said to them, "Is it not written: 'Then you shall do to him, as he has thought to do to his brother?' Hence his brother must still be alive [when the false witness is executed]." [They objected,] "If so, why does Scripture say 'Life for life'?" [They replied,] "One might have thought that the false witness should be put to death as soon as they accepted their testimony. Scripture therefore teaches: 'Life for life'—the witnesses are not put to death until the judgment of death has been given [against the defendant who has been falsely accused]." (Mak. 1:6; cf. Sifre Shoftim 190)

The *Hakhamim* are here juxtaposed to the Sadducees. They engage in a controversy over the Law as it applies to testimony in a capital case. Indeed, the text differs from the formula texts only in the lack of the formula, though such a formula is nonetheless implied, namely, "The Sadducees say, 'We complain against you *Perushim* because. . . . The *Perushim* say we complain against you Sadducees because. . . .'" It is also to be noted that the Mishnah first states the law anonymously, i.e., as a *halakhah*, and then identifies this anonymous law with the *Hakhamim*. This usage opens up the possibility, to be discussed later, that the anonymous *halakhah*, wherever it occurs, presupposes the authority of the *Hakhamim*. And should it emerge that *Hakhamim* and *Perushim* are absolutely synonymous, then all anonymous laws recorded in the Mishnah could potentially be assignable to the Pharisees.

Judah ben Tabbai said, "May I never see consolation if I did not kill a single false witness in order to root out [a false notion] from the heart of the Boethusians [Sadducees]; for they [the Boethusians-Sadducees] used to say that the witness is not to be put to death until the convicted person has been executed."
Simon ben Shetah said to him, "May I never see consolation if you did not spill innocent blood; for Scripture says: 'By the testimony of two or three witnesses shall the guilty one be put to death' [Deut. 17:6]. Just as two witnesses [are required for the death penalty], so must both witnesses be proven false, before either can be executed."

139

At that moment Judah ben Tabbai took it upon himself not to teach the *halakhah* except in accordance with [the point of view] of Simon ben Shetah. (Tosef. Sanh. 6:6)

The following data may be extricated from this text: (1) Both Judah ben Tabbai and Simon ben Shetah support the *halakhah* cited in the Mishnah Makkoth. (2) Both would side with the *Hakhamim* against the Sadducees. (3) The Boethusians, as we would anticipate, hold the identical position as do the Sadducees on the issue of false witnesses. (4) The power to pronounce the death sentence by those following the *Hakhamim* is taken for granted. The law bearing on false witnesses is thus viewed as operative and not academic. (5) Both Judah ben Tabbai and Simon ben Shetah accept the authority of the *halakhah*. The only point at issue is which of the two *halakhic* points of view should be operative with respect to the putting to death of a *single* false witness. Judah ben Tabbai acknowledges the cogency of Simon ben Shetah's reasoning and recognizes the primacy of Simon ben Shetah in matters of *halakhah*. (6) The controversy between Judah ben Tabbai and Simon ben Shetah is of lesser gravity than the controversy between the *Hakhamim* (Judah ben Tabbai and Simon ben Shetah concurring) and the Sadducees-Boethusians. The latter dispute involved a basic irreconcilable principled conflict over the Law, whereas the former concerned merely a disagreement on the validity of a single *halakhah*, not of the *halakhah* system.

But we know more than this Tosefta records. Judah ben Tabbai and Simon ben Shetah appear elsewhere in Tannaitic Literature as the greatest legal authorities of their day, for one was the *Nasi* of the *Bet Din;* the other, of the *(Ab) Bet Din* (Hag. 2:2). As such, they were one of the so-called *Zugoth*, "Pairs," as those who held the title of *Nasi* and *(Ab) Bet Din* at that time were called. Since the total number of *Zugoth* from approximately 160 B.C. till Hillel and Shammai at the turn of the era was only six, and since during this century and a half only the names of the *Zugoth* are specifically associated with the *halakhah, it is apparent that Judah ben Tabbai and Simon ben Shetah were legal scholars of great renown and authority.*

At first [the Bet Din] would accept testimony concerning the New Moon from anyone. It once occurred that the Boesthusians [Sadducees] hired two witnesses to mislead the *Hakhamim;* for the Boethusians [Sadducees] do not admit that *'aseret* can fall after the Sabbath. (Tosef. R. H. 1:15)

The calendrical system and its operation through eyewitness testimony is rejected by the Boethusians, and they seek to thwart the *Hakhamim.* The latter appear in this text as the ultimate authorities for setting the dates of the festivals. They determine the *halakhah* and see to its proper administration. Are we to believe that alongside the *Hakhamim* was another class, the Pharisees, who were vested with the identical authority over the calendar and stirred up the same opposition from the Boethusians-Sadducees?

The following line of reasoning would thus seem to be legitimate: (1) The *Perushim* are Pharisees when juxtaposed to Sadducees. (2) The *Perushim* are identical with the *Hakhamim* in passages where such juxtaposition occurs. (3) *Hakhamim* in texts juxtaposed to Sadducees are identical with the *Perushim*-Pharisees. (4) The *Hakhamim*-Pharisees support the anonymous *halakhah.* (5) Judah ben Tabbai and Simon ben Shetah underwrite the anonymous *halakhah* and the principled opposition of the *Hakhamim* to the Sadducees. (6) Judah ben Tabbai and Simon ben Shetah advocate the *halakhah* of the *Hakhamim* in their controversy with the Boethusians. (7) They acknowledge the *halakhah* as the normative Law, binding on each of them. (8) They are known from the Tannaitic Literature to have been *Zugoth,* "Pairs," *Nasi* and *(Ab) Bet Din,* hence the authoritative teachers of the *halakhah.* (9) But the

141

halakhah is the Oral Law and not the literal Written Law. They are thus champions of the *halakhah* which the Sadducees-Boethusians negate. (10) The *Hakhamim-*Pharisees likewise recognize the authority of the *halakhah* in contradistinction to the Sadducees-Boethusians. (11) Judah ben Tabbai and Simon ben Shetah must therefore be individuals who are members of a larger class called *Hakhamim-*Pharisees. Indeed, as *Zugoth* they could have been none other than the leaders of the *Hakhamim-*Pharisees of their generation. (12) The *Hakhamim-*Pharisees are concerned with the Law. (13) The Law they are concerned with is the twofold Law, as is confirmed by *(a)* appeal to Scriptures as authoritative, *(b)* affirmation of the *halakhah,* the unwritten Law, as authoritatve, *(c)* rejection of the latter by the Sadducees-Boethusians. (14) The *Hakhamim-*Pharisees must be a scholar class, dedicated to the authority of the twofold Law and having as their spokesmen the *Nasi* and the *(Ab) Bet Din.* (15) The *Hakhamim-*Pharisees and the *Zug* Judah ben Tabbai and Simon ben Shetah are juxtaposed only to the Sadducees-Boethusians and not to the *am ha-aretz.* The controversies always involve law and never the degree of levitical purity of the contending groups. (16) The *Hakhamim-*Pharisees as well as Judah ben Tabbai and Simon ben Shetah assume the *halakhah* to be operative and not merely academic. The proof that it was operative is Judah ben Tabbai's boast that he had ordered the execution of a false witness to confute publicly the Boethusians.

Now that a connection between *Hakhamim* and *Perushim-*Pharisees has been established, and now that Simon ben Shetah's identification as one of the two major spokesmen of this class in his generation has been secured, we can include the following text into the corpus.

It was taught: "It once happened that King Yannai went to Kohalit in the wilderness and conquered sixty towns there.

When he returned he was extremely happy and he called all the *Hakme Yisrael* [Sages of Israel]. He said to them, 'Our forefathers used to eat salt plants when they were engaged in building the Temple; let us also eat salt plants in memory of our forefathers.' So they brought up salt plants [and set them] on golden tables and they ate.

"Now there was there a good-for-nothing evilhearted and worthless man named Eleazar ben Poirah. Eleazar ben Poirah said to King Yannai, 'O King Yannai, the hearts of the *Perushim* are against you.' 'Then what shall I do?' 'Make them swear by the front plate [the symbol of priestly authority] between your eyes.' So he made them swear by the front plate between his eyes.

"Now there was there an elder [*zaken*] named Judah son of Gedidyah. Judah the son of Gedidyah said to King Yannai, 'O King, the royal crown is enough for you. Let the priestly crown go to the seed of Aaron.' For they used to say that his mother had been taken captive in Modim [and therefore the legitimacy of his birth was in question]. Accordingly, the matter was investigated and found to be without substance. [Whereupon] the *Hakme Yisrael* separated in anger.

"Then Eleazar ben Poirah said to King Yannai, 'King Yannai, this is the law for even the most common [*hediot*] in Israel; but as to you, a king and a High Priest, shall that be your law, too?' 'Then what shall I do?' 'If you will listen to my advice, trample them down.' 'But what will happen to the Torah?' 'It is rolled up and lying in a corner; whoever wishes to study, let him go and study.'

"Said R. Nahman ben Isaac, 'Immediately the spirit of heresy was instilled into him, for he should have replied: "That is well for the Written Law, but what of the Oral Law?"'

"Immediately the evil burst forth through Eleazar ben Poirah, and all the Sages of Israel *(Hakme Yisrael)* were killed, and the world was desolate until Simon ben Shetah came and restored the Torah to its former glory." (Kid. 66*a*)

The account of King Yannai's break with the *Perushim-Hahkamim* may presuppose the Sadducees, but they are not specifically mentioned. The close resemblance of this account to that of Josephus' chronicle of the split between John Hyrcanus and the Pharisees must not be permitted to violate the methodological procedures that have been set up for the analysis of the tannaitic texts. Since the account of King Yannai's conflict with the *Perushim* quoted above does *not* specifically mention the Sadducees, it does not meet the criterion for inclusion into the corpus of unambiguous texts. This can be achieved only indirectly; for although the *Hakhamim* are identified with the *Perushim,* neither is placed in direct juxtaposition to the Sadducees. The link, therefore, in this instance must be Simon ben Shetah.

It has already been demonstrated that Simon ben Shetah held to the same legal position as did the *Hakhamim-Perushim* in their controversy with the Sadducees. Consequently, since Simon ben Shetah is identified with the *Hakhamim-Perushim* in the story of King Yannai's break with the Pharisees—indeed he is pictured as their chief—the *Hakhamim-Perushim* of this text must be identical with the *Hakhamim-Perushim* with whom Simon ben Shetah was linked in the Tosefta. The *Perushim,* therefore, of this passage must indeed be the Pharisees.

What data with respect to the *Hakhamim*-Pharisees does this story reveal?

(1) Simon ben Shetah is identified with the *Hakhamim.* (2) The *Hakhamim* are identified with the *Hakme* [Sages of] *Yisrael.* (3) The *Hakhamim* and the *Hakme Yisrael* are identified with the *Perushim.* (4) King Yannai was at first so favorably disposed to the *Hakhamim-Perushim-Hakme Yisrael* that he could think of no better way to celebrate his military victories than to throw a sumptuous party for the *Hakhamim-Perushim-Hakme Yisrael.* The latter must have been a distinguished and honorific scholar class to be accorded such recognition by the Hasmonean king. (5) The *Perushim-Hakhamim-Hakme Yisrael* are accused of disloyalty to the king in such a manner as to convey the notion that the king and everyone else had assumed the very opposite. (6) The *Hakhamim-Perushim-Hakme Yisrael* are recognized as having the Torah in their charge, for King Yannai sees a threat to the Torah if the *Perushim* are trampled. (7) The *Hakhamim-Perushim-Hakme Yisrael* must therefore have been a scholar class that possessed great power and influence, a class of legislators who deter-

mined the Law. Indeed, the nub of the story is that the Torah of the *Hakhamim-Perushim-Hakme Yisrael* had been operative and binding even on the king; he had broken with it; and it was restored to operation by Simon ben Shetah. Since we know that Simon ben Shetah was the champion of the *halakhah,* the Unwritten Law, and since we know that he opposed the Boethusians-Sadducees who rejected the *halakhah,* and since we know that Simon ben Shetah was one of the *Hakhamim-Perushim* who likewise affirmed the authority of the *halakhah* and opposed the Sadducees-Boethusians, the *Hakhamim-Perushim-Hakme Yisrael* of this text must have been likewise champions of the *halakhah* and opponents of the Sadducees. Hence in rejecting the *Hakhamim-Perushim-Hakme Yisrael* without abandoning concern for the Torah completely, King Yannai must have adopted the Sadducean concept of the single, written Law.

Still another link connects the unambiguous texts to those texts where the Pharisees are implied by synonymity. In the controversy between the *Perushim* and the Sadducees over whether Holy Scriptures render the hands unclean, Johanan ben Zakkai is found championing the view of the Pharisees. In the texts that follow, Johanan ben Zakkai confronts the Sadducees even though the *Perushim* are not mentioned:

It was taught in a *beraita* . . .:
From the eighth day [of Nisan] to the end of the holiday [of Passover] it is forbidden to mourn since [these days commemorate] the establishment of [the proper dating of] the festival of Shevuot. For the Boethusians [Sadducees] used to say that the festival is to be celebrated on a Sunday [and not on the forty-ninth day following the first day of Passover].
Rabbi Johanan ben Zakkai engaged them in discussion and said to them, "Fools, whence [your scriptural support]?" No one was able to answer him except an old man who babbled in opposition to him and said, "Moses our teacher was a lover of Israel and he knew that the festival [of Shevuot] is a single day. He therefore ordained that it should be on the day following the sabbath so that Israel might rejoice two days." He [R. Johanan

145

ben Zakkai] quoted the following verse [in rejoinder]: "'It is an eleven-day journey from Horeb by way of Seir' [Deut. 1:2]. If Moses our teacher was a lover of Israel, why did he cause them to tarry in the wilderness forty years?" He replied, "With such as this you brush me off?" He answered, "Fool! Is not our perfect Torah a match for your frivolous talk? One scriptural verse says: 'You shall count fifty days' [Lev. 23:16] while another scriptural verse says: 'Seven complete sabbaths shall be' [between Passover and Shevuot] [vs. 15]. How can these texts be [reconciled]? The first verse refers to the festival falling on the sabbath, while the other verse refers to the festival falling during the week." (Men. 65 *a-b*; see also Ta'an. 17*b*)

As it was taught: "On the 24th of Tebeth we returned to our Law, for the Sadducees used to say that a daughter should inherit with the daughter of the son. But R. Johanan ben Zakkai engaged them in discussion. He said to them, 'Fools, whence [your scriptural support]?' No one was able to answer him except an old man who babbled in opposition and said: 'If the daughter of his son who comes from the strength of his son inherits from him, how much more so his daughter who comes from his own strength?' He [R. Johanan ben Zakkai] brought the following verse [as refutation]: "'These are the sons of Seir the Horite, the inhabitants of the land: Lotan and Shobal and Zibeon and Anah" [Gen. 36:20], whereas [farther down] it is written: "And these are the children of Zibeon: Aiah and Anah"—which teaches that Zibeon had intercourse with his mother and begat Anah.' . . . He said unto him, 'Teacher, with such as this you brush me off?' He [R. Johanan ben Zakkai] said to him: 'Fool! Is not our perfect Torah a match for your frivolous talk? [Your reasoning is faulty, for one should argue as follows:] If the inheritance goes to the daughter of his son, it is because her claim is superior to that of his [surviving] brothers, whereas you must admit that the claim of his own daughter is inferior to that of his surviving brothers.'

"They [the Sadducees] were defeated. And they made that day a holiday." (B. B. 115*b*-16*a*)

Johanan ben Zakkai appears in both of these texts as the strident opponent of the Boethusians-Sadducees, even as in the controversy between the Sadducees and the Pharisees over Holy Scriptures rendering the hands unclean. His identity with the *Perushim* is thus confirmed, for he appears as the champion of the anti-Sadducean legal position in both sets of texts. This identity, however, is made even more secure when it is noted that he stoutly defends a principle that was espoused by the *Perushim,* namely, that the daughter of the son [of the deceased father] inherits along with her brothers, even though the daughter of the father does not inherit along with her brothers. We are thus justified in labeling Johanan ben Zakkai a Pharisee.

And Johanan ben Zakkai's orientation is shown to be identical with that of the Pharisees: (1) He is an opponent of the Boethusians-Sadducees. (2) He collides with them on legal issues. (3) He refutes their mode of exegesis. (4) His hallmark is not ritual purity but his approach to the Law. The two legal questions here have nothing whatever to do with ritual purity but with the proper date for the counting of the seven weeks to Pentecost and with the laws of inheritance. (5) He is juxtaposed to the Boethusians and Sadducees and not to the *am ha-aretz.*

Still another type of text confronts us, namely, where the Sadducees or Boethusians are found to be in opposition to the anonymous *halakhah.* Although neither the *Perushim* nor the *Hakhamim* are mentioned, the anonymous *halakhah* can be considered Pharisaic (1) because of the juxtaposition of the anonymous *halakhah* to the Sadducees-Boethusians, and (2) because the anonymous *halakhah* has proved to be identical with the Pharisaic position in those texts where *Perushim* occurs along with the anonymous *halakhah.* These texts are deemed Pharisaic by virtue of a synonymity derived from those texts wherein the anonymous *halakhah* and the *Perushim* are pitted against the Sadducees-Boethusians.

How did they used to do it [i.e., prepare for the cutting of the *omer*]? The messengers of the *Bet Din (shluhe Bet Din)* used to go out on the eve of the festival and make bunches while still attached to the soil, so that it would be easier to reap; and [all the inhabitants of] the towns nearby assembled there in order that it might be reaped in great pomp.

When it grew dark, he [the reaper] would say, "Is the sun

set?" They [the people] would reply, "Yes." "Is the sun set?" and they would again answer, "Yes." "With this sickle?" They would answer, "Yes." "With this sickle?" and they would answer, "Yes." "With this basket?" and they would answer, "Yes." "With this basket?" and they would answer, "Yes." On a sabbath he would say to them, "On this sabbath?" and they would [again] answer, "Yes." "On this sabbath?" and they would answer "Yes." "Shall I reap?" They would answer, "Reap." "Shall I reap?" and they would answer "Reap." He used to call out three times for each of these [questions] and they would [thrice] answer, "Yea! Yea! Yea!"

Why such concern? Because of the Boethusians [Sadducees], who used to say: "The cutting of the *omer* is not to take place on the day following the festival [but only on the morrow of the sabbath, i.e., on a Sunday]." (M. Men. 10:3)

The *halakhah* for the procedures to be followed in the cutting of the *omer* is pitted against the Boethusian claim that the *omer* is to be reaped only on a Sunday. The *halakhah,* in this instance, substitutes for the *Perushim*-Pharisees in the controversy, since the anonymous *halakhah* must have had authoritative exponents. The *halakhah,* after all, could not have been self-enunciating and self-promulgating. Behind the anonymous *halakhah* must have been the legal leadership that framed it, proclaimed it, and saw to its execution. Although anonymity testifies to the *halakhah's* claim to universal authority, it could have had its source only in a differentiated scholar class whose hallmark was the authority to determine the *halakhah.* The Boethusians, or Sadducees, are never the source of the anonymous *halakhah,* whereas the *Perushim*-Pharisees are identified with the anonymous *halakhah.* The Pharisees therefore must be the source of the *halakhah* here as well, for whereas the anonymous *halakhah* implies a source but does not articulate it, the *Perushim*-Pharisees are manifestly made up of individuals who could be, and often explicitly are, the source of the anonymous *halakhah.*

The text just cited not only transmits the anonymous *halakhah,* but reveals that the procedure it describes was

148

carried out in such a manner as to publicly expose the Boethusian-Sadducean error. The concrete nature of this Mishnah therefore permits the following conclusions, enriching the content of the tannaitic definition of the Pharisees:

1. The authority for the procedures and their execution rests with the *Bet Din.*

2. The *Bet Din* invests it authority in the emissaries of the *Bet Din* (the *shluhe Bet Din*).

3. The *shluhe Bet Din* do the actual preparation; they tied the unreaped corn in bunches so that the reaping would be easier.

4. Every effort was made to encourage broad public participation.

5. The *shluhe Bet Din* took charge of the ceremonies that called for public response to a series of questions calling attention to the deliberate act of cutting the sheaf on the second day of the Festival of Passover, even though this day was not a Sunday.

6. The crucial importance of the second day of Passover for the cutting of the sheaf was especially emphasized when the second day chanced to be on a sabbath. Not only was the authority of the *halakhah* proclaimed with respect to the proper day, but it was forcefully underwritten by the act of reaping on the sabbath—an act normally forbidden, on pain of death, to be carried out on the sabbath.

7. The *halakhah* testifies to the role of dramatization in underscoring its authority. It demanded a display of public approval annually for the *halakhah* and its promulgators, for the *Bet Din* and its emissaries. It called for a yearly rejection of the Boethusian-Sadducean approach to the Law. It triumphantly exposes the impotence of the literal Written Law which enjoins that the reaping of the *omer* shall take place "on the morrow of the sabbath," even as it highlighted the potency of an unwritten Law, the *halakhah*, which takes "sabbath" in

the text to mean the first day of the Festival of Passover, and not the seventh day of the week.

8. The *Perushim*-Pharisees as the living antagonists of the Boethusians-Sadducees must therefore have been the authorities for the anonymous *halakhah* that called for the public exposure of the Boethusians-Sadducees. They thus must have constituted the *Bet Din* that sent forth the emissaries who performed the concrete acts of public demonstration. The Boethusians-Sadducees could not have been members of the *Bet Din,* since the latter are committed to the public exposure of the Boethusians-Sadducees as falsifiers of the true meaning of the Law. The *Bet Din* must therefore be a body that consists of anti–Boethusian-Sadducees, hence of *Perushim*-Pharisees, i.e., *Hakhamim* (Sages) committed to the twofold Law.

9. Since the procedure was actually carried out, the *Bet Din* must have had the power to execute the laws it promulgated. But since the Pharisees-*Hakhamim* constituted the *Bet Din,* it is they who must have carried out the laws that they sanctioned. The Pharisees-*Hakhamim* therefore could not have been a passive class of academicians, but must have been active legislators with a flair for dramatizing their supremacy.

From the first of the month of Nisan until the eighth day [thereof] the *tamid* was instituted, and it is not permitted to mourn [on these days] because the Sadducees used to say that a single individual may donate and bring the *tamid.*
What were the grounds for their claims? Scripture states: "The one lamb which you [singular] shall offer in the morning, and the second lamb you shall offer at twilight" [Num. 38:4].
What did they [the Sages] reply to them? [They quoted the following scriptural verse:] "'My sacrifice, my food, for burnt offerings you [plural] shall observe' [Num. 38:2]. [The use of the plural indicates] that all [the cost of the sacrifice] are to come from the Temple treasury." (Men. 65*a*)

Here again we have the anonymous *halakhah* juxtaposed to the Sadducees. The anonymous *halakhah* must have had as its source scholars exercising legal authority. These scholars must have been opposed to the Sadducees. But the Pharisees-*Hakhamim* are known to have been champions of the anonymous *halakhah* against the Sadducees. The Pharisees must therefore be assumed to have been the scholars who authenticated the *halakhah* in this instance as well.

The issue in question is the proper functioning of the sacrificial cult; hence a concrete problem. In practice, both procedures could not have functioned simultaneously. Unless the question was merely academic, it involved the power to determine the procedures to be carried out daily in the Temple. If the *halakhah* did determine the practice, then its supremacy over the Sadducean claims was proclaimed daily. But behind the anonymous *halakhah* are the Pharisees-*Hakhamim*. Hence, the Pharisees-*Hakhamim* must have been a scholar class who sought the concrete implementation of the *halakhah* for the regulation of the cult and who benefited from the daily confirmation of authority assured by this procedure.

This text further reveals that the Sadducees were committed to a literal reading of the Pentateuchal law. They point to the unambiguous use of the singular pronoun with reference to the actual offer of the sacrifice: "The one lamb which you [singular] shall offer at twilight." By contrast, the anonymous *halakhah* cites a verse that can be linked to the morning and evening sacrifice only by resort to a complex line of reasoning since the verse "My sacrifice, my food which is presented to me for burnt offerings, you [plural] shall observe" does not specifically mention the morning and evening sacrifice. The anonymous *halakhah* thus presupposes the Oral Law as the authority for determining the meaning of the Written Law, in contrast to the Sadducees who appeal to the clear meaning of the literal text of the Pentateuch. The Pharisees-*Hakhamim* are thus once again, through an anonymous *halakhah*, opposing the

Sadducees, shown to be the protagonists of the twofold Law.

It is to be noted that neither in the text just cited nor in those texts where the Pharisees are identified with the *halakhah* do we find any juxtaposition to *am ha-aretz,* nor does it involve the rules of ritual purity.

The *lulab* takes precedence over the sabbath at the beginning [of the festival] while [the beating of] the willows [takes precedence over the Sabbath] at the conclusion of the festival.

It is related that the Boethusians [Sadducees] covered them [the willows] over with large stones on the eve of the Sabbath. The *am ha-aretz* found out about this and dug them out and removed them from under the stones on the sabbath because the Boethusians [Sadducees] do not admit that the beating of the willows takes precedence over the sabbath.

[The *halakhah* that the beating of] the willows [takes precedence over the sabbath] is a *halakhah* that goes back to Moses from Sinai. (Tosef. Suk. 3:1; cf. Suk. 43*b*)

Once again the anonymous *halakhah* confronts the legal position of the Boethusians-Sadducees. Once again we can link this *halakhah* to the Pharisees-*Hakhamim* by virtue of their antagonism to the Boethusians-Sadducees. But beyond this, these texts convey the following additional information:

1. The ruling that the beating of the willows takes precedence over the sabbath is specifically referred to as a *halakhah,* i.e., an unwritten law, that does not derive its authority from the Written Law, the Pentateuch, but from an orally transmitted law originating with Moses himself. The *Perushim-Hakhamim* thus underwrite the authority of the unwritten laws as ultimately derivative from the very same Moses who was responsible for revealing the Written Law.

2. The *am ha-aretz* are so loyal to the *halakhah*—hence to the Pharisees-*Hakhamim*—that they not only made provision on Friday eve for the beating of the willows on the sabbath, but they took pains to dig them out from under the stones where the Boethusians-Sadducees had

hidden them. The *am ha-aretz* are thus shown to be determined supporters of the *halakhah* and its champions, the Pharisees-*Hakhamim,* against the Boethusians-Sadducees.

3. The *halakhah* was operative, not academic.

The elders of Israel used to proceed on foot to the *har hamisha.* There was a place of immersion and they [the elders] used to render unclean the priest who was to burn the [red] heifer, because of the Sadducees, so that they should not be able to say, "It was performed [i.e., the red heifer was burnt] after sunset" [i.e., the priest burning the red heifer is regarded by the Sadducees as clean only if he has waited for the sun to set before immersing. If the sun has not set, then according to the Sadducees, immersion alone does not render him clean and he may not burn the red heifer]. (Par. 3:7)

It is related of a Sadducee [priest] that the sun set upon him and he came to burn the red heifer. R. Johanan ben Zakkai learned about this and he came and placed his two hands upon him and said, "My lord, the High Priest. How fit you are to be High Priest! Go down and immerse." Whereupon he went down and immersed himself [in accordance with the demand of R. Johanan ben Zakkai]. (Tosef. Par. 3:8; see also 3:6; M. Par. 3:5)

The anonymous *halakhah* sets hard and fast stipulations for the burning of the red heifer by the priest, stipulations which run contrary to those advocated by the Sadducees. The issue, be it noted, is not the act of burning but the ritual status of the priest who is to do the burning. Both the anonymous *halakhah* and the Sadducees are in agreement that the priest must be in a state of ritual purity. The Sadducees, however, demand two procedures before uncleanness is removed: immersion and the setting of the sun. One without the other is insufficient. They thus rely on a literal reading of Scripture, "And he [the priest] shall wash himself in water and shall become clean when the sun sets" (Lev. 22:6-7).

The anonymous *halakhah,* however, distinguishes between the two requirements: Immersion renders the individual clean with respect to everything but *terumah,* "heave offering." Only the permission to eat *terumah* must await the setting of the sun. The burning of the red heifer does not involve *terumah;* hence, the unclean priest need only immerse and not wait for the setting of the sun to be ritually fit to make the offering.

The significance attached to the difference in viewpoint between that of the *halakhah* and that of the Sadducees is confirmed by the public defiling of the priest, his immersion in a pool set aside for this purpose in the area where the burning is to take place, and his actual performing of the act of burning while the sun was still high in the sky—a dramatic exposure of Sadducean impotency and error.

The tenacity with which this *halakhah* was applied to life is thus manifest in these texts. In this instance Johanan ben Zakkai—already identified as a Pharisee—firmly insisted that the High Priest redo the ceremony since he had defied the *halakhah,* and the High Priest seemed to have no alternative but to knuckle under and conform to the *halakhah* after attempting to defy it.

That the Pharisees-*Hakhamim* are the authority for the anonymous *halakhah* pertaining to the red heifer follows from the same line of reasoning that has been adduced in other instances. The *halakhah* set rules rejected by the Sadducees. Behind the *halakhah* must be *halakhah* makers, legislators. The *halakhah* makers must have been opponents of the Sadducees. But the only opponents of the Sadducees who are not cloaked with anonymity are the Pharisees-*Hakhamim.* These Pharisees-*Hakhamim* have already been identified with the anonymous *halakhah* in other texts; hence they may be assumed to be the authorities who determined the procedures for burning the red heifer. This line of reasoning is confirmed by the specific mention of Johanan ben Zakkai whom we already know to be a champion of the Pharisaic *halakhah,* compelling the High Priest to redo the burning ceremony. To posit a scholar class who legislate the *halakhah,* functioning alongside the *Perushim-Hakhamim,* who likewise legislate the *halakhah* and who simultaneously share the identical antipathy toward the Sadducees, is to posit a healthy improbability—if not an impossibility. The information that can be gleaned from these last two texts for the tannaitic image of the Pharisees represents data hitherto unavailable. The Pharisees-*Hakhamim* are clearly involved in a dispute with the Sadducees involving ritual impurity. But it is to be noted that the anonymous *halakhah* takes a casual attitude toward uncleanness, not the Sadducees. The *halakhic* procedure demands that a clean priest deliberately be rendered unclean. This unclean priest is then compelled to immerse himself while the sun is still high in the sky to demonstrate that he becomes clean for the red heifer ceremony immediately following his immersion. The *halakhah* is thus seen to be ameliorating the laws of ritual purity, rather than making them more rigorous and demanding. The Sadducees, not the *halakhah* makers, emerge as the purists. It is the Sadducees who insist that uncleanness persists, even after immersion, until the sun has set. The *halakhah*, on the other hand, considers immersion alone to be sufficient to attain cleanness, unless the touching and the eating of *terumah*, "heave offering," which affects only the priests and their specific interests, is involved. Nonpriests as well as priests thus become ritually clean for all other purposes, including cultic events, by immersion alone. The *halakhah* thus sought to mitigate for nonpriests the rigorous purity laws of the Pentateuch. But behind the *halakhah* are the Pharisees-*Hakhamim*. Hence they must have framed the ameliorating *halakhah*. Their hallmark could scarcely have been the rigorous observance of the laws of purity when to all intents and purposes they were modifying these laws for nonpriests, who were not permitted to eat *terumah*, i.e., the rigorous features were applicable to the priests exclusively.

As for the other information revealed by these texts, it confirms what was extracted from the others: the

Pharisees-*Hakhamim,* presupposed by the *halakhah,* are a scholar class vitally involved in the functioning of society. They have a flair for dramatizing their authority at the expense of the Sadducean challengers. They bend Pentateuchal literality to their *halakhah.* They do not shrink from applying power when their authority is ignored; and once again, we miss the *am ha-aretz,* as their antagonists.

Thus far we have analyzed a series of texts that are linked to the Pharisees-*Hakhamim* by a common element, namely, juxtaposition in controversy with the Sadducees-Boethusians. One more linkage is yet to be demonstrated. It has been left for last because of its crucial and compelling character.

The basic methodological principle that has been invoked for determining when *Perushim* must mean Pharisees has been simple: juxtaposition and opposition to *Zedukim,* Sadducees, is prima facie evidence that *Perushim* in such a relationship can only mean Pharisees. The most decisive texts, therefore, are those which reveal most strikingly this juxtaposition, namely, the texts that utilize the formula "The Sadducees say. . . ;" "The *Perushim* say. . . ." If, then, one of the texts in the Mishnah utilizing this form contains a dictum found elsewhere in the Mishnah, not attributed to the *Perushim* but to the *Soferim,* are we to posit two distinct scholar classes or synonymity? Are we not confronted with the likelihood that the word *Perushim* was used only in juxtaposition to *Zedukim,* "Sadducees," because only in such confrontation was the term appropriate?

It will be recalled that one of the formula texts reads as follows: "The Sadducees say, 'We complain against you *Perushim*-Pharisees because you say that Holy Scriptures render the hands unclean.'" The dictum is clear: If Holy Scripture is touched by an individual, the latter's hands become unclean. The Pharisees thus enunciate here a law that has no literal basis in any scriptural text. If it is a law not explicitly spelled out in the Pentateuch, it must perforce be an unwritten law, a *halakhah.* The Pharisees thus appear as the spokesmen of an unwritten law.

Is this unwritten law of the Pharisees to be found elsewhere in Tannaitic Literature? Indeed, it is. It appears as an anonymous *halakhah:*

All Holy Scriptures render the hands unclean. The Song of Songs and Ecclesiastes render the hands unclean. R. Judah says, "The Song of Songs renders the hands unclean, but with respect to Ecclesiastes there is controversy." R. Jose says, "Ecclesiastes does not render the hands unclean, but it is with respect to the Song of Songs that there is controversy." R. Simon says, "Ecclesiastes [as to rendering the hands unclean] is one of the instances where the school of Shammai was more lenient and the school of Hillel more rigorous." R. Simon ben Azzai says, "I have received a tradition from the seventy-two elders on the day that they elevated R. Eleazar ben Azariah [to the position of *Nasi*] in the academy that both the Song of Songs and Ecclesiastes render the hands unclean." R. Akiba says, "God forbid! No one of Israel ever quarreled over whether the Song of Songs renders the hands unclean. . . . If they quarreled at all, it could only have been over Ecclesiastes." (Yad. 3:5)

I have quoted this passage at length so as to preclude any doubt that the anonymous *halakhah* affirms that Holy Scriptures render the hands unclean. Four distinguished sages debated whether Ecclesiastes or the Song of Songs render the hands unclean, but they are in complete agreement that Holy Scriptures render the hands unclean.

A dictum of the *Perushim*-Pharisees thus appears as an anonymous *halakhah* when the Sadducees are not involved. The *Perushim*-Pharisees must therefore have been the authorities responsible for this *halakhah.* Yet we find this very same anonymous *halakhah* attributed to a class who are not called *Perushim.*

"Everything which renders *terumah* unfit renders the hands unclean so as to be in the second degree of uncleanness. One hand can render the other hand unclean"—these are the words of R. Joshua. The *Hakhamim,* however, say, "That which is in the second degree of uncleanness cannot make anything else unclean in the second degree." He [R. Joshua] said to them, "But do not Holy Scriptures which are [unclean] in the second degree render the hands unclean?" They said to him: "We do not deduce the words of the Torah from the words of the *Soferim* [the Scribes]; nor the words of the *Soferim* from the words of the Torah; nor the words of the *Soferim* from the words of the *Soferim.*" (Yad. 3:2)

The anonymous *halakhah* "Holy Scriptures render the hands unclean" thus turns out to be "the words of the *Soferim.*" But this very same *halakhah* is identified as a dictum that distinguished the Pharisees from the Sadducees in Yad. 4:6. Hence the *Perushim* must be identical with the *Soferim!* If identical with the *Soferim,* then entitled to all the rights and privileges pertaining to that honorific class. And these are considerable: The *Soferim* have the right to make law that is not deducible from Scripture; they can make law that is not dependent on a logical connection with any other law that they themselves have made; they can make law that has no connection with Scriptures whatsoever. The Pharisees-*Soferim* are thus the source of the unwritten laws, irrespective of whether or not they are scripturally grounded. But these unwritten laws are the *halakhah*. The Pharisees-*Soferim* must therefore be the legislators of the *halakhah*.

But the *Hakhamim* are also the source of the *halakhah*. They have also been found to be synonymous with the *Perushim*-Pharisees; and these, in turn, are now seen to be identical with the *Soferim*. The *Soferim* therefore must be identical with the *Hakhamim*. Hence, *Perushim*-Pharisees, *Hakhamim,* and *Soferim* are one and the same, with only this distinction: *whereas Hakhamim and Soferim appear in the Tannaitic Literature without the Sadducees, the Perushim-Pharisees never do.* We may therefore conclude that there must have been a deliberate avoidance of the term *Perushim* as the normal or preferred usage. Such avoidance may have its roots in a negative resonance inherent in the term *Perushim* ("separatists," "deviants," "heretics") as a denial of the right to the honorifics *Soferim* and *Hakhamim*. Hence *Perushim* was appropriate in the mouth of the Sadducees but inappropriate as the name for the legislators of the *halakhah*.

The identification of the Pharisees with the *Soferim* thus gives us a scholar class whose hallmark is the championship of the authority of the twofold Law, the Written and the Oral. But this hallmark is not dependent on an identification with the *Soferim*. It exists implicitly in every single text where the *Perushim* are juxtaposed to *Zedukim*, for the controversies have meaning only insofar as a basic cleavage existed on the relationship of the Pentateuch to the Oral Law.

The identification with the *Soferim* does, however, permit an elaboration of content and an explicit support for the assumption that the Pharisees exercised hegemony over the Law. For in tractate Sanhedrin, we find the following testimony to the authority of the *Soferim:*

There is a greater rigor applied to the words of the *Soferim* than to the words of the Pentateuch. One who says "There is no need to wear phylacteries" in order to transgress the words of the Pentateuch is free of guilt. [One, however, who says,] "Five *totafot* are required rather than four" in order to transgress by adding to the number prescribed by the words of *Soferim*, is guilty. (San. 11:3)

The *Soferim*-Pharisees are thus accorded ultimate authority, for their unwritten laws carry more weight than the Written Law. But are not these unwritten laws, the *halakhoth*, the very ones which are recorded anonymously throughout the Tannaitic Literature? Are we then not bound to acknowledge that every anonymous *halakhah* antedating A.D. 70 must have been the legislation of the *Soferim-Hakhamim-Perushim* (Pharisees)? And are we not to assume, on the basis of the documented instances, that the *halakhah* was operative in all realms: cultus, festivals, property, ritual purity, calendar, criminal and civil law, etc.? It is regrettably true that we cannot date every *halakhah* with precision. In most instances, the anonymous *halakhah* is unrevealing as to when it was introduced. Yet the principle that the *halakhah* system was operative, and that the architects of this system were the *Soferim-Hakhamim-Perushim,* a scholar class of legislators of the Unwritten Law and upholders of the twofold Law concept, is in no way affected by our limitations.

And now a word about ritual purity. The *Soferim-*Pharisees affirm that Holy Scriptures render the hands unclean. They thus show concern over matters of ritual purity. But what is striking in this instance is not their efforts to avoid ritual uncleanness but the effort to make it inescapable for *terumah*-eating priests. The Holy Scriptures which the *Soferim-*Pharisees recognize as divinely revealed becomes the source of uncleanness in the second degree. This would mean that whenever Holy Scriptures, the Pentateuch included, were so much as touched, uncleanness in the second degree, i.e., uncleanness of the hands, was the inevitable consequence. The only exception (Kel. 15:6) was made for the scroll of the Torah that was kept in the inner part of the Temple from which the High Priest had to read on the Day of Atonement. But even this scroll generated second-degree uncleanness when taken out of the inner sanctum (Tosef. Kel. 2:5, 8).* The Pharisees-*Soferim* by this *halakhah,* to which they attached great significance, reveal that they welcomed uncleanness and were not at all affrighted by the prospect of uncleanness every time they touched the Pentateuch.

The reasons for this *halakhah* need to be dealt with only briefly, for they presuppose knowledge not explicitly set forth in the text. Nevertheless, it can be pointed out that the uncleanness of hands was a pseudouncleanness, i.e.,

---

* Although the Tosefta reads *"Ezra,"* the context makes it clear that the issue centers on the removal of the scroll from the sanctuary.

it had no practical consequences for the individual unless he were a priest. It did not interfere with his comings and goings and involved no inconvenience. Uncleanness of the hands had one, and only one, generative effect: it rendered *terumah,* "heave offering," unfit for consumption. Thus a priest who had come into contact with Holy Scriptures could not touch or eat *terumah* until after he had undergone immersion and after the sun had set. The *Soferim*-Pharisees were thus, it seems, using the technicalities of the laws of ritual purity to discourage priestly handling of Holy Scriptures; for such handling carried with it stringent penalties. *The Pharisees thus did not make the laws of ritual purity rigorous for themselves but for the priests.* They were seeking, so it seems, to exclude priestly control of the Law and not devising a means for separating themselves from the *am ha-aretz.*

The building of the corpus of unambiguous texts is now complete. It consists of the following categories: (1) texts where the term *Perushim* is juxtaposed to the term *Sadducees*; (2) texts where synonymity is established by virtue of juxtaposition of the *Hakhamim,* individual sages, or anonymous *halakhah* to the Sadducees-Boethusians; (3) texts where synonymity is established by virtue of a dictum affirmed by the *Perushim* yet attributed either to the anonymous *halakhah* or to the *Soferim* in texts where the Sadducees-Boethusians do not appear. Each of these categories is not only separable from the others, but the subdivisions in each can be clearly distinguished. The tannaitic image of the Pharisees may thus, in the interests of the most rigorous criteria, be restricted to the first grouping of texts, or it may draw on all subdivisions or on all the other categories and subdivisions. Whatever the decision, the outcome is identical: The image that emerges from the most rigorously determined corpus is identical with that drawn from the other subdivisions and categories. The Pharisees are in all texts the champions of the twofold Law, the Oral and the Written, and are the opponents of the Sadducees-Boethusians who adhere to the Written Law alone. Indeed, if only the controversy over Holy Scriptures' rendering the hands unclean had remained extant, this conclusion would follow from the structure and content of the text, for nowhere in Scriptures is there even a hint of such a concept as Holy Scriptures' rendering the hands unclean. *It is thus unscriptural law.* Hence the Pharisees must be the proponents of the authority of the twofold Law. The other subdivisions and categories thus merely confirm that which can be deduced from the most rigorously constructed category. They provide content; they permit elaboration; they do not, however, affect the core definition but merely reiterate it. The other categories thus appear as extensions of the first; indeed, they are hypothetically deducible from it, as it, in turn, follows directly from them.

Let us now collate the control texts. These texts, it will be recalled, are those in which the term *perushim* occurs, but where scholars do not translate *perushim* as "Pharisees."

Our Rabbis taught: When the Temple was destroyed for the second time, *perushim* multiplied in Israel who took it upon themselves not to eat meat and drink wine.
R. Joshua engaged them in discussion. He said to them, "My sons, why do you not eat meat nor drink wine?" They replied, "Shall we eat flesh from which one used to offer sacrifices on the altar, but now is done away with? Shall we drink wine which one used to pour as a libation on the altar, but now is done away with?" He said to them, "If so, we should not eat bread, for the meal offering has been done away with." [They answered him,] "It is possible to survive on fruits." [He said unto them,] "We should not eat fruits either because the offering of the first fruits is no more." [They replied,] "We can get along with other fruits." [He then said,] "We should not drink water, because the libation of water is no more. . . ." They were silent.
He said to them, "My sons, come and I shall tell you [what to do]. Not to mourn at all is impossible, because the decree is irrevocable. To mourn overmuch is also impossible, because we do not impose a decree on the community unless the majority

are able to endure it; for it is written: 'You are cursed with a curse, yet you rob me [of the tithe], even this whole nation' [Mal. 3:9]. The Sages have therefore said as follows: 'A man may stucco his house, but leave a little bare. . . .'" (Tosef. Sot. 15:11-12, B. B. 60*b*)

Perushim in this passage has been given the following renderings: (1) Marcus Jastrow (in *A Dictionary of the Targum, the Talmud Babli and Yerushalmi and the Midrashic Literature,* 1926, *s.v. parush*), "abstemious"; (2) Eliezer Ben Yehuda (in *A Complete Dictionary of Ancient and Modern Hebrew,* 1943, *s.v. parush*), "one who separates himself and keeps himself away, especially from the sensual desires and transgressions" (my rendering of the Hebrew definition); (3) Krupnik and Silberman (in *A Dictionary of the Talmud, the Midrash and the Targum,* 1927, *s.v. parush*), "ascetic"; (4) Lazarus Goldschmidt (in *Der Babylonische Talmud,* 1912, *ad loc.*), *"enthaltsam"*; (5) the Soncino translation of the Talmud, *ad loc.,* "ascetics."

Nor do Schürer, Herford, Moore, Finkelstein, or others cite the above text in building their definition of the Pharisees.

Before leaving this text, however, let us note some of its other characteristics. (1) The *perushim* here are not juxtaposed to the Sadducees. (2) They do not seem to be scholars; indeed, they seem to be grieving individuals seeking some form of penance for the destruction of the Temple. (3) They deviate from the ordinance of the *Hakhamim,* "Sages"; yet they do not offer alternate legislation, but merely choose to be "abstemious" for themselves.

It was taught: Judah the son of Durtai *piresh* from the *Hakhamim,* both he and his son Durtai, and they went and dwelt in the south. He said, "If Elijah should come and say to Israel, 'Why did you not sacrifice the *Hagigah* on the sabbath?' what can they answer him? I am amazed at the two outstanding men of the generation, Shemaiah and Abtalion, who are great *Hakhamim* and great interpreters of the Torah *(darshanim),* and yet have not said to Israel that the *Hagigah* overrides the sabbath."

Rav said, "What is the reason of the son of Dutai?" [There then follows an attempt by Rav to give exegetical reasons.] Said Rav Ashi, "And are we to vindicate and explain the reasons of *perushim*?" (Pes. 70*b*)

Scholars agree that *perushim* here does not mean Pharisees: (1) Jastrow, "seceders"; (2) Krupnick and Silberman, "seceders"; (3) the Soncino translation of the Talmud, "schismatics"; (4) Goldschmidt, *"die sich absondern."*

The text is instructive. *Perushim* is used to designate those who separated themselves from the *Hakhamim.* Both Durtai and his son had been associated with the *Hakhamim,* until the issue of the *Hagigah* sacrifice taking precedence over the sabbath arose. In rejecting the decision of the *Hakhamim,* he and his son became *perushim,* i.e., "deviants," "heretics," "separatists," and *not* Pharisees. We are thus confronted with the stark paradox that the word *perushim* not only need not mean Pharisees but may even mean "those who separate themselves from the Pharisees." The word *perushim* thus emerges as a word used indiscriminately to designate a deviant, irrespective of what he might be deviating from. The substance of his heresy can be determined only by its usage in context.

Note also that this text shows no affinities to the texts of the authentic corpus. There is no controversy with Sadducees-Boethusians. The *perushim* Durtai and his son do not advocate the anonymous *halakhah.* They are not interchangeable with either the *Hakhamim* or the *Soferim.* They mention by name two *Hakhamim,* Shemaiah and Abtalion, who are known from other tannaitic sources to have been the *nasi* and the *Ab Bet Din,* respectively, and it is from the *halakhic* decision of the latter that they are separating themselves, i.e., becoming *perushim.* Indeed, they are viewed with such contempt by an outstanding amoraic sage that he would not even give their exegesis a hearing, dismissing them with the epithet *perushim.*

The eighteen benedictions referred to by the *Hakhamim* correspond to the eighteen *azkarot* of the Psalm that begins, "Ascribe unto the Lord, O sons of might" [Ps. 29:1]. The blessing which pertains to the *minim* ["heretics"] includes that against the *perushim;* that of the *gerim* includes the *zekenim* ["elders"], and that of David includes Jerusalem. If one said these. . . , he has fulfilled his obligation. (Tosef. Ber. 3:25)

The word *perushim* is here a synonym for *minim,* "heretics"; the text affirms this explicitly, and the scholars echo this affirmation: Jastrow, "renegades"; Ben Yehuda, and S. Lieberman (*Tosefta Kifshuta* I, [New York, 1955] p. 54), "people who are accustomed to separate from the ways of the collective group" (author's translation).

This text thus confirms the paradox: *Perushim* not only need not mean Pharisees but can actually mean anti-Pharisees, i.e., heretics who have challenged the Pharisees. The *Hakhamim* are specifically referred to as the authorities responsible for the eighteen benedictions; and yet the benediction they formulated against the *minim,* calling on God to annihilate them, is deemed valid if *"perushim"* is substituted for *"minim."* But the *perushim* in the authentic texts are synonymous with *Hakhamim* and with the anonymous *halakhah.* Are then the *Hakhamim* calling down curses upon themselves in the guise of *minim* and *perushim*?

"Perushim" therefore was used by the Sages to denote "heretics." But this is not so shocking when it is recalled that *perushim* meant Pharisees in the authentic texts only when juxtaposed to Sadducees, who, no doubt, looked upon the *Hakhamim-Soferim* as *perushim,* "heretics." In texts where no Sadducees-Boethusians are found, the very same dictum is uttered by *Hakhamim-Soferim* or by the anonymous *halakhah* or by individual sages—never by *perushim.* Precisely because the *Hakhamim-Soferim* did not consider themselves to be "heretics," they were scrupulous in proscribing this usage, except when

appropriate, i.e., in controversy with the Sadducees. Indeed, so free were they from an attachment to this name that they used it without hesitancy to denounce those who deviated from the *halakhah* and who challenged their authority. Those bearing the honorific title *Hakhamim-Soferim* presumably had no fear that their use of the term *perushim* would be ambiguous. Their fearlessness is boldly evident in the Tosefta text where *minim* and *perushim* are treated as synonyms.

These then are the control texts. That they are only three in number is irrelevant. What is crucial is that scholars who translate *perushim* as "Pharisees" in the Hagigah text do not translate *perushim* as "Pharisees" in the control texts just cited. In making this choice, they undercut any claim that *perushim* must mean Pharisees. If, then, *perushim* can mean anti-Pharisees, anti-*Hakhamim,* anti-*halakhah,* anti-Shemaiah and Abtalion, indeed "heretics" rejected by the Sages, how can the term *perushim* be self-defining? If it means both Pharisees and anti-Pharisees, the term *perushim* surely leaves us in the lurch!

And, if by their own reasoning, scholars have seen the necessity of translating *perushim* as "ascetics," why do they hesitate to translate *perushim* as "ascetics" in the Hagigah texts?

The existence of these controls thus precludes an invariable, single meaning for *perushim.* The meaning of *perushim* can be determined only by contextual criteria and not by the word itself. Surely if the same word can mean A, non-A, and anti-A, it cannot be self-defining.

Let us now collate the ambiguous texts. These are the texts where *perushim* is not juxtaposed to *Zedukim,* "Sadducees." Yet most scholars translate the term *perushim* in these texts as Pharisees.

The garments of an *am ha-aretz* are a source of *midras*-uncleanness for *perushim;* the garments of *perushim* are a source of

midras-uncleanness for those who eat *teruma* [i.e., the priests];
the garments of those who eat *teruma* are a source of
midras-uncleanness for [those who eat of] *kodashim*; the
garments of those that eat of *kodashim* are a source of
midras-uncleanness for those [who are in charge of] the water of
purification. Joseph ben Joezer was the most pious in the
priesthood, yet his apron was a source of *midras*-uncleanness
for those who eat of *kodashim*. Johanan son of Gudgada all his
life used to eat [common food] as though it were *kodashim*, yet
his apron was a source of *midras*-uncleanness for [those who
were in charge of the waters of purification]. (Hag. 2:7)

We have already become familiar with this text as the
proof text par excellence for the definition of the
Pharisees as scrupulous observers of the laws of ritual
purity who separate themselves from the *am ha-aretz*. The
scholars who translate the word *perushim* as "Pharisees"
in this text are legion. Virtually every translator of this
Mishnah, be it Danby or Goldschmidt or the translators
for the Soncino Talmud, renders *perushim* as "Pharisees";
every lexicographer, be it Jastrow, Ben Yehuda, or
Krupnick-Silberman, does likewise; virtually every student of the Pharisees, be it Schürer, Finkelstein, or
Herford, echoes this rendering.

And the grounds? Clearly not the juxtaposition of
perushim to *Zedukim*, "Sadducees," nor a legal controversy with some other grouping, nor the affirming by the
Perushim of a *halakhah*, nor synonymity with *Hakhamim-
Soferim* or some individual sage. The unambiguous texts,
without exception, have the *Perushim* stating a legal
position; they are never themselves the subject of the
law. In this text, however, the *perushim* are a grouping
separated from other groupings by virtue of the *halakhah*,
and not, as in the authentic texts, the source of the
halakhah itself. In this Hagigah text the *perushim* are
distinguished from (1) the *am ha-aretz*, (2) the eaters of
terumah, (3) those who engage in certain cultic activities,
indeed even (4) the sage, Joseph ben Joezer—known
from other tannaitic sources to have been one of the

so-called *Zugoth,* "Pairs," and hence the leader of the *Hakhamim* in his day. The *perushim* in this text, however, are not distinguished from these others by virtue of a legal controversy, as in the authentic texts, but by degrees of ritual purity.

Why then the compulsion to identify these *perushim* with the Pharisees? The word itself? But since these very same scholars agree that the word can also mean "heretic" or "ascetic," why the rendering of *perushim* here as "Pharisees"? Perhaps because heretics would violate the context? Indeed it would! But would "ascetics"? The latter meaning surely is interchangeable with the *perushim* in this text.

R. Joshua used to say, "A foolish saint and a cunning knave and an *isha perusha* and *makkot perushim*—these wear out the world." (Sot. 3:4)

Scholars with almost one accord render *isha perusha* as "Pharisaic woman" and *makkot perushim* as "Pharisaic plagues." The Soncino translation is "a female Pharisee," "the plague of Pharisees"; Goldschmidt, *"Eine pharisäische Frau"*, *"die Schläge der Pharisäer"*; Danby, "a hypocritical woman" but "the wounds of the Pharisees"; Jastrow, "sanctimonious woman" but "the wounds inflicted by the Pharisees."

Our Rabbis have taught: "There are seven types of *perushim:* the *shikmi parush,* the *nikpi parush,* the *gizai parush,* the *mhukia parush,* the *parush* [who constantly exclaims,] 'What is my duty that I may perform it?', the *parush* out of love, and the *parush* out of fear." (Sot. 22*b*; cf. J. Sot. 5:7-8)

All seven types of *perushim* as viewed by this *beraita* display a negative attitude toward these *perushim.* They are not exemplars held up for emulation. This is clear from the discussion which follows in the Talmud. Thus the *shikmi parush* is one who performs the action of Shechem; the *nikpi parush* is one who knocks his feet

168

together; the *kizai parush* is one who in his ultra asceticism dashes his face against the wall; the *medukia parush* is one whose head is bowed like a pestle in a mortar; the *parush* who constantly exclaims, 'What is my duty that I may perform it?' is one who gives the impression that he had already fulfilled all the commandments and is looking for more; the *parush* from love is one who loves the rewards of the commandments; the *parush* from fear is one who is afraid of the punishments that he may receive if he is not overscrupulous.

What does an analysis of these ambiguous texts reveal? A complete lack of affinity to the authentic texts! (1) There are no Sadducees or Boethusians. (2) The *perushim* are not the source of the *halakhah* but are subsumed under it. (3) The *perushim* are evaluated negatively, not honorifically. (4) The term is not interchangeable with *Hakhamim-Soferim*. (5) The singular form is used for the *perusha* woman and for the labeling of each of the seven classes of *perushim*; in the authentic texts *Perushim* is used *only* in the plural.

A careful examination of the dictum of R. Joshua throws light on what he meant by a *perusha* woman and the *makkot perushim*. He is listing those who deviate from the norm. Thus a foolish pietist is one who strays from the path of true piety; a cunning rogue, one who forsakes the roguish mean. Similarly a *perusha* woman must be analogous—hence, a woman who is "ascetic" or "celibate," one who abandons the *res media* of the *halakhah*. *Makkot perushim* represent some kind of a non-*halakhic* practice, such as flagellation carried out for ascetic purposes. The term would mean "the lashings, or stripes, or flagellations of ascetics." Surely a devotee of the *halakhah,* such as R. Joshua, would not attribute the wasting away of the world to a Pharisaic woman, if the synonym *Hakham* or *Sofer* were in his mind. Nor would he be likely to have said "the plagues of *Hakhamim* or *Soferim* waste the world away."

Similarly with the seven types of *perushim.* Every one represents a deviant from the *halakhic* norm. Is one to believe that the *perushim* of the authentic texts, the stalwart opponents of the Sadducees, the legislators of the *halakhah,* the champions of the twofold Law fall into seven classes of pious fools straying from the *halakhic* norm that they themselves had established, and that they are typed by themselves so negatively? But why even raise such a question? All that one need do is substitute *Hakhamim-Soferim* for *perushim* to see how ludicrous it all becomes.

What then prompted scholars to render *perushim* as "Pharisees" in these texts? Presumably the word. Yet these very same scholars did not translate *perushim* as "Pharisees" when they found it in the control texts. Did not the translator of the Soncino Talmud translate it "ascetics" when confronted with the *perushim* who multiplied following the destruction of the Second Temple? Did not Godschmidt utilize an equivalent German word, *"Enthaltsame"*? Did not Jastrow forgo Pharisees as the translation for *perushim* and did he not render it "ascetic" when confronted with the fact that the context precluded any other intelligible rendering? It is thus evident that since the word *perushim* in and of itself need not mean Pharisees, there is no compelling reason for translating it as such in this Hagigah text where the *perushim* are juxtaposed, not to the Sadducees, but to the *am ha-aretz;* where the *perushim* are the subjects of the *halakhah,* not its source; where "ascetics," not the authoritative teachers of the twofold Law, are implied.

The Hagigah text when set alongside the authentic texts shows itself to be incongrous. By contrast, when it is set alongside the control texts, it displays absolute congruence.

Other texts containing the words *parush* or *perushim* have likewise been drawn upon by scholars for a definition of the Pharisees, despite the fact that they have nothing to offer as credentials other than a word that can mean Pharisees, non-Pharisees, or anti-Pharisees.

> Bet Shammai says, "A *zav* who is a *parush* should not eat with an *am ha-aretz,*" but Bet Hillel permits him. (Tosef. Shab. 1:15)

The *parush* here is the same sort of individual we found, in the plural, in the Hagigah text. He is no more a Pharisee here than he is there. He is juxtaposed to the *am ha-aretz,* not to the Sadducees-Boethusians. He is being regulated by the *halakhah,* not framing it. He is in the singular, not the plural. He is a man who has undertaken a vow to maintain a certain state of ritual purity which carries with it the separation from the *am ha-aretz.* He thus falls under the provisions of the *halakhah* because he has undertaken a voluntary obligation. No *halakhah* exists anywhere that either defends or advocates becoming a *parush.* He is someone who has undertaken to separate himself from others, just as individuals separated themselves from the majority when they took it upon themselves to mourn for the loss of the Temple by refraining from eating meat and drinking wine. This text is thus to be assimilated with the control texts, for it uses the term *parush* in an analogous fashion. It can lay no claim for inclusion into the authentic corpus, since it displays none of the credentials necessary for entry.

> "For I am the Lord your God. Hallow yourselves and be holy, for I the Lord your God am holy." As I am holy so be you also holy; as I am *parush,* so be you also *perushim.* (Sifra to Lev. 11:44)

> "You shall be holy, for I, the Lord your God, am holy." Be you *perushim.* (Sifra to Lev. 19:2)

> "You shall be unto me a kingdom of priests and a holy nation." Holy, holy, hallowed, *perushim* from the people of the world and their detestable things. (Mekhilta to Exod. 19:6)

Many scholars, such as Moore and Baeck, have not

only translated *perushim* here as "Pharisees" but have contended that the essential meaning of the term is derived from its usage here.* *Perushim* is used as a synonym for *kedosim,* "holy ones." The Pharisees thus called themselves the *perushim,* or "holy ones."

But what are the grounds for insisting that *perushim* means Pharisees here? Do we find any Sadducees-Boethusians in controversy with them? Is *perushim,* "holy," interchangeable with *Hakhamim-Soferim*? Do the *perushim* in these texts propound dicta or legislate *halakhah*? Are the Israelites being called upon to be lawmakers or to lead a holy life in accordance with the *halakhah*? Is God calling for the people to imitate him as lawmaker or as the model of holiness? Surely, when the people are enjoined to be a holy nation by separating from the peoples of the world and their detestable things, they are being called upon to keep the *halakhah,* not formulate it.

The word *perushim* need not mean Pharisees; this has already been demonstrated. But neither must its meaning be circumscribed to "ascetics" or "heretics." The root *parosh,* "to separate," can breed substantives that run the whole gamut of possible separations, including "holiness." The evidence for such a usage is not difficult to find in the Tannaitic Literature. That it is not synonymous with Pharisaism the following texts will demonstrate:

A woman prefers one *kab* and lechery to nine *kabim* and *perishut.* (Sot. 3:4)

Perishut here surely means "abstinence," "continence," and not "Pharisaism"!

R. Phineas ben Jair used to say, . . . purity leads to *perishut* and *perishut* leads to holiness. (Sot. 9:15)

---

*George Foot Moore, *Judaism* (Cambridge, Mass., 1927), I:61; Leo Baeck, *The Pharisees and Other Essays* (New York, 1947), pp. 3, 50, especially pp. 5-12.

The categories enumerated are gradations of purity, not religious groupings or schools of thought. No *halakhah* confronts us here; only stages on the path to holiness. *Perishut,* i.e., "abstinence, restraint, continence, separation from sensuality," is a prerequisite for attaining holiness, not the quality of being a Pharisee.

When Rabban Gamaliel the Elder died the glory of the Law ceased and purity and *perishut* died. (Sot. 9:15)

Are we to believe that the Mishnah is informing us that with the death of Rabban Gamaliel the Elder, Pharisaism died? Is it not obvious that a personal attribute of an individual is being referred to? Yet this seemingly unambiguous non-Pharisaic meaning of *perishut* did not restrain Danby from translating it "the cleanness practiced by the Pharisees," although the text reads: "A condition of doubt about *hulin* concerns the cleanness of *perishut* " (Teharot 4:12).

Why should not *perishut* here mean simply "self-restraint, abstinence, a state of separation from uncleanness"? Does it not, here as elsewhere, refer to a self-limitation, permitted and regulated by the *halakhah* but not required by it?

All the tannaitic texts utilizing *perushim* have now been collated. But before the tannaitic definition of the Pharisees can be spelled out, an additional group of texts involving the *haberim* must be analyzed, because most scholars consider the term *haberim,* or "Associates," to be synonymous with, or inseparable from, *perushim,* "Pharisees." Their reasoning is based on the fact that in the Hagigah passage as well as in the text dealing with a *zav* who is a *parush,* the *perushim* are juxtaposed to the *am ha-aretz* as being more rigorous in matters of ritual purity. Since in the tractate of Demai, the *haberim* are likewise distinguished from the *am ha-aretz* because they do not eat even common food in a state of ritual purity, it is postulated that the *perushim* and *haberim* are intimately interrelated. The *haberim* thus look very much like the *perushim* of the ambiguous texts. By assuming synonymity, scholars draw on the more detailed information about the *haberim* to fill in the lacunae with respect to the *perushim.* We have no alternative therefore but to include the *haberim* texts in the ambiguous corpus.

If a man has taken upon himself to become a *haber,* he may not sell to an *am ha-aretz* either moist or dry [produce]; nor may he buy from him moist [produce]. He may not be a guest of an *am ha-aretz,* nor may he receive as guest an *am ha-aretz* who is wearing his own garment. (Dem. 2:3)

It was taught: "One who pledges himself to accept *dibre haberut* must do so in the presence of three *haberim.* His children and household need not pledge before three *haberim.* . . ."
    It was taught: ". . . Even a *talmid hakham* must pledge himself before three *haberim.* . . ." (Bek. 30*b*; see also Tosef. Dem. 2:2-3)

These two texts will suffice for analytical purposes. The other references to the *haberim* need not be cited, for their status differs in no wise from the two passages set forth above. If the *haberim* in the above texts fail to meet the criteria for identification with the *Perushim*-Pharisees of the unambiguous corpus, they can gain no access through the texts that have not been cited in full. The *haberim,* unlike *perushim,* leave little doubt as to who they are in whatever text they may be found.

A close analysis of the *haberim* texts reveals that the *haberim* bear no resemblance to the *Perushim*-Pharisees of the unambiguous texts. The *haberim* are juxtaposed to the *am ha-aretz,* not to the Sadducees-Boethusians. They are the subjects of *halakhah,* not its formulators. They utter no dicta, offer no legal opinion. The *haberim* are not one and the same as the *Hakhamim* or *Soferim.* Rather they are individuals who have voluntarily undertaken to tithe doubtful produce. A scholar may choose to become a *haber,* but he is not required by the *halakhah* to become one. The eating of *demai* (doubtful-if-tithed) produce is not a breach of the *halakhah,* as eating pork would be; indeed, we learn that it may be freely given to the poor and to passing guests: Rabban Gamaliel even gave it to his laborers (M. Dmay 3:1). The *halakhah* spells out the *halakhic* consequences of becoming a *haber,* not its *halakhic* necessity.

But the Pharisees of the unambiguous texts are the very *Hakhamim* responsible for the legislation regulating the *haberim.* They determined the status of the *haber,* just as they determined the status of the nazirite, the priest, the levite. They do not separate themselves as a class by making laws applicable to themselves alone. There was not one *halakhah* for the Pharisees-*Hakhamim-Soferim* and another for the people at large. The *halakhah* was deemed to be universal, though as in the case of a priest, bound by the *halakhah* applicable only to priests. One might choose to become a nazirite and thereby find oneself regulated by the appropriate *halakhah.* One might take a vow and thus come under the provision of the *halakhah* spelling out its implications. Similarly, one might choose to become a *haber* and find oneself bound by the *halakhah* regulating this freely chosen status. As a Pharisee-*Hakham-Sofer,* he was an *halakhah* maker and an authoritative spokesman for the twofold Law. One's *bête noire* were the Sadducees, not the *am ha-aretz;* one's hallmark, mastery of the twofold Law, not ritual purity.

The *haberim* are not Pharisees. They do not match the *Perushim-Hakhamim-Soferim* of the unambiguous texts. However, they do bear some resemblance to the *perushim* of the ambiguous texts, a fact that is even more disqualifying. And finally we find that an *amoraic* teacher, Abaye, in attempting to overcome a difficulty, explains that the individual in question was a Sadducean *haber* (Nid. 33*b*)! A Sadducean-Pharisee perhaps?!

Since all the tannaitic texts utilizing the term *perushim* have now been collated and, in addition, other texts pertaining to the problem have been investigated, we are now ready to construct a tannaitic definition of the Pharisees from the texts that have met the criteria of authenticity. Only those that have found their way into

175

the authentic corpus can legitimately communicate information about the Pharisees. All other texts are excluded because they fail to meet the objective criteria. The word *perushim* is no longer sufficient. It has been disqualified because it was found in the control texts to mean both "ascetics" and "heretics," i.e., to mean non-Pharisees and anti-Pharisees. Its usage in the ambiguous texts offered no affinity to the unambiguous corpus, at the same time that it typed out with the ambiguous texts and analogous derivatives. The Hagigah proof text thus collapses as a source for the Pharisees, and with it all the *haberim* passages that were assimilated to it. We are left with the unambiguous texts alone, and from these the definition of the Pharisees must be constructed.

The image of the Pharisees thus derived will come, however, as no surprise. It has been prefigured in the analytical discussions of the texts themselves. Nevertheless, it must now be set down for the record, so that it can be compared with that drawn from Josephus and the New Testament.

The Pharisees were a scholar class dedicated to the supremacy of the twofold Law, the Written and the Unwritten. They actively opposed the Sadducees who recognized only the Written Law as authoritative, and they sought dramatic means for proclaiming their overriding authority. Their unwritten laws, the *halakhah*, were operative in all realms: cultus, property, judicial procedures, festivals, etc. The Pharisees were active leaders who carried out their laws with vigor and determination. They set the date for the cutting of the *omer*. They set up the procedures for the burning of the red heifer and compelled priestly conformance. They insisted that the High Priest carry through his most sacred act of the year in accordance with their regulations. They determined judicial procedures, the rightful heirs to property, the responsibility of slaves for damages, the purity status of Holy Scriptures.

The Pharisees utilized this name only in controversies with the Sadducees. In all other texts, they appear as the *Hakhamim,* "Sages"; as the *Soferim,* "Scribes"; as the scholar class legislating the anonymous *halakhah;* as individual spokesmen for this class; as the scholars who sit in the *Bet Din,* "Legislature." The shying away from the name "Pharisees" is thus clearly no accident, for never once does it find its way into a text without the Sadducees. They therefore must have viewed it as lacking in the honorific implications of such titles as *Hakhamim* and *Soferim;* indeed, it must have been a term that was not meant to be complimentary at all. Since the word has "heretics" as one of its meanings, and since it is used in the tannaitic literature only in juxtaposition to the Sadducees, who would have viewed the concept of the twofold Law as heretical, it would seem that it must have been originally hurled at the *Hakhamim-Soferim* as a denial of their claim to authority over the Law. In the eyes of the Sadducees, the *Hakhamim-Soferim* were indeed *perushim,* "heretics."

The scrupulous avoidance of the name *perushim* by the *Hakhamim-Soferim* thus accounts for the paradox that the very literature that would be expected to give us the most information about the Pharisees hardly ever mentions them by this name at all. Little information is given about the Pharisees because only a few of the controversies with the Sadducees have been recorded. But the Tannaitic Literature is a vast repository of information concerning the *Hakhamim-Soferim,* and their *halakhah-*making activity. Scarcely a paragraph of the Mishnah or the Tosefta or the *beraitoth* or the Tannaitic Midrash is without some reference to the *Hakhamim.* Every anonymous *halakhah* that antedates the destruction of the Temple is their handiwork. And do not the distinguished leaders of the *Hakhamim-Soferim*—Simon ben Shetah, Shemaiah and Abtalion, Hillel and Shammai, Johanan ben Zakkai, Rabban Gamaliel—fill the pages of this literature? The Pharisees, once liberated from the limited, circumscribed, and rare usage of *perushim* and identified as the *Hakhamim-Soferim,* can reclaim their identity as that scholar class that created the concept of the twofold Law, carried it to triumphant victory over the Sadducees, and made it operative in society.

This definition of the Pharisees is not unfamiliar. It is identical with that set forth by Josephus in *Ant.* XIII:297, 408b:

For the present I wish merely to explain that the Pharisees had transmitted to the people certain laws handed down from the Fathers *[paredosan . . . ek pateron]* which are not written down in the laws of Moses, and for this reason are rejected by the group of Sadducees, who say only the written laws are to be taught, whereas those handed down from the Fathers *[ek paradoseos ton pateron]* are not to be observed. And concerning these matters they came to have controversies and serious differences, the Sadducees having only the confidence of the wealthy, whereas the Pharisees had the support of the masses.

. . . and whatever of the laws introduced by the Pharisees in accordance with traditions of their Fathers *[kata ten patroan paradosin]* had been abrogated by Hyrcanus her [i.e., Salome Alexandra's] father-in-law, these she again restored.

It also resonates in Paul:

As to the Law a Pharisee . . . as to righteousness under the law blameless. (Phil. 3:5-6)

And I advanced in Judaism beyond many of my own age among my people, so extremely zealous was I for the traditions of my fathers *[ton patrikon mou paradoseon].* (Gal. 1:14)

Likewise in the Gospels:

The scribes and the Pharisees sit in Moses' seat; so practice and observe whatever they tell you. (Matt. 23:2)

And the Pharisees and the scribes asked him, "Why do your disciples not live according to the tradition *[paradosis]* of the elders? . . . And he [Jesus] said to them, "You have a fine way

178

of rejecting the commandment of God in order to keep your tradition *[paradosis]*." (Mark 7:5-9)

The hitherto discordant sources are now seen to be in agreement. Josephus, Paul, the Gospels, and the Tannaitic Literature are in accord that the Pharisees were the scholar class of the twofold Law—nothing more, nothing less.

Part II

Historical
Reconstruction

Chapter IV

From Definition to Historical Reconstruction

The sources have yielded a viable definition of the Pharisees. Josephus, the New Testament, and the Tannaitic Literature, though focusing on the Pharisees with different lenses, were looking at the identical object. The Pharisees in all the sources are a scholar class championing the twofold Law and enjoying great power and prestige. Josephus and the Tannaitic Literature may have applauded this leadership while the New Testament resented it, but all the sources agree that it was there, active, and centered on the twofold Law.

This definition of the Pharisees thus offers a secure foundation for embarking on the hazardous task of historical reconstruction. It serves as a compass, assuring the scholar of his bearings; a fixed point of reference for his hypotheses; a known destination, determining the roads he may take; a touchstone for the genuineness of his speculations. If the Pharisees are truly known, then their history cannot belie their identity. Their history must be not only compatible with the definition, but it must make intelligible how the Pharisees could have come into existence from nonexistence. There was a time, whenever it may have been, when there were no Pharisees; then there is a time when there are Pharisees, sitting on Moses' seat. And since the Pharisees have now been defined by a rigorous methodology as a scholar class dedicated to the twofold Law, their origins must be traced back to that historical juncture when the concept of the twofold Law came into being. But such a historical juncture could not have taken place at just any time, or under just any circumstances. It could have occurred once and once only; for with the birth of the concept of the twofold Law, a process was unleashed that is still ongoing. To be sure, the Pharisees and their twofold Law may have undergone change at certain times and in certain places, but since their origin, and to our day, they and their direct descendents have exerted a definitive role as authoritative spokesman for Judaism.

To pinpoint precisely this historical juncture is no easy task. Indeed, it is even more difficult than the construction of a viable definition; for *no* source *explicitly* reveals either the time or the circumstances that gave rise to the Pharisees and the concept of the twofold Law. Josephus has preserved no ancient source; the Tannaitic Literature is even less helpful; the New Testament, of no help at all. Our method, therefore, for solving the problem of origins must safeguard against misuse of the sources at the same time that it exploits them to the full.

Such a method must concentrate on setting up a system of controls. The first of these controls would be the definition itself; for any historical reconstruction that undercuts the definition or dissolves it must *ipso facto* be rejected. The second control is to establish a point in time when neither the Pharisees nor the twofold Law existed. The third control is to establish a point in time when the existence of the Pharisees and the twofold Law is explicitly affirmed. The fourth control is to determine whether a conjuncture of historical circumstances occurred of sufficient magnitude to make intelligible so revolutionary a phenomenon. In short, we must look for the emergence of the Pharisees during the interval between their *nonexistence* and their *existence*. Somewhere in the chasm between periods of nonexistence and existence, the Pharisees and their twofold Law were born.

The definition has already been established. The first explicit reference to the Pharisees is likewise known: Josephus affirms that the three *haereseis*—those of the Pharisees, the Sadducees, and Essenes—were flourishing in the time of Jonathan the Hasmonean (*Ant.* XIII:171-73). What we must now determine is the point in time at which there were *no* Pharisees and *no* twofold Law and analyze the structure of Jewish society then prevailing.

To pinpoint that time when the Pharisees did not yet exist and when the twofold Law was not yet operative is a desideratum not easily come by. Scholars have recognized few barriers restricting their postulations on origins of the Pharisees to a specific point in time. Speculation has moved freely within hundreds of years. Some scholars insist that the Pharisees as such did not make their appearance till the Hasmonean period, even though their forerunners, the Scribes, or *Soferim,* date back to Ezra or even earlier. Other scholars do not shrink from assigning the origins of the Pharisees to the early years of the Restoration, to the struggle between Zerubbabel, a scion of David, and the High Priest Joshua. Still others favor other datings.

As for the twofold Law, even greater scholarly divergence exists. The consensus of scholarly opinion insists that the unwritten laws had a provenance even prior to the crystallization of a specific class named the Pharisees. It is argued that the logic of the situation leaves no alternative. No society can exist, it is argued, with fixed, immutable laws, however divine they may be deemd to be. No sooner was the Pentateuch canonized than exegesis inevitably followed. The divine Law had to be studied with great care so that law might keep peace with life. A class of *Soferim,* Scribes or exegetes, thus sprang up as a necessary consequence of the canonization of the Pentateuch. This class, which looked to Ezra as their prototype, made the study of the Pentateuch their special concern and soon attained such mastery and skill that they replaced the priests as the caretakers of the Law. These *Soferim* were the forerunners, it is alleged, of the Pharisees. Long before the Hasmonean Revolt, so it is reasoned, they had pondered the Pentateuch, wrestled with the text, and drawn inferences that were not explicitly set forth therein.

How, then, can one affirm a point of time at which there were no Pharisees or proto-Pharisees or twofold Law? How could such a claim defend itself against the charge of subjectivity or of the wish to favor a particular hypothesis? The answer must be: Build safeguards into the method of dating;—procedures necessarily binding because they are logical imperatives.

Such a method would operate with the following principle: No data can be admitted as evidence for solving a historical unknown unless such data explicitly reveal knowledge of the unknown, i.e., if a scholar is to affirm the existence of anything, he must cite sources that make explicit reference to the object or the idea as indeed existent. Thus, if one were to assert that Jesus had been crucified in Athens in the days of Socrates, one would have to offer explicit evidence that this indeed had occurred. The fact that the sources do not affirmatively deny such an event does not serve as evidence that the event indeed occurred. The principle, then, is simple: Silence cannot be cited in support of the positive existence of anything.

This principle is fully applicable to the problem of the emergence of the Pharisees and the twofold Law. To claim that the Pharisees existed by X date, one must point to a source that mentions them *explicitly* as existing at that time. The same holds true for the twofold Law. If its existence is posited, then *explicit* proof must be forthcoming that it was indeed there. Thus whereas we do have Josephus as the source for the existence of the Pharisees in the time of Jonathan, *we have no sources for the* existence of the Pharisees or the twofold Law prior to the *Hasmonean Revolt.* The Pharisees and the twofold Law can therefore be assigned to a pre-Hasmonean date only if *silence* is allowable for affirming the existence of something.

But what of the logic of the situation? Did not the canonization of the Pentateuch necessitate interpretation, exegesis, and is this not equivalent to the twofold Law? Surely this is an argument that cannot be brushed aside. Yet the answer is given by Josephus:

> For the present I wish merely to explain that the Pharisees had passed on to the people certain regulations handed down by the fathers and *not* recorded in the laws of Moses, *for which reason they are rejected by the Sadducees,* who hold that only those laws *[nomina]* should be considered valid which were written down [in the laws of Moses] and those which were handed down from the Fathers must not be observed.
>
> And concerning these matters, they [the Pharisees and the Sadducees] came to have controversies and differences, the Sadducees having the confidence of the wealthy alone but no following among the masses, while the Pharisees have the support of the populace. (*Ant.* XIII: 27-98; italics added)

Although Josephus was writing in the first Christian century, he had no compunction in stating, *as a matter of course,* that the Pentateuch could not only be taken literally, *but that the Sadducees made such literality the touchstone of their* haeresis. Unwritten laws were not only considered unnecessary by them but positively unlawful. If, then, even after the Pharisees and the twofold Law had long been in existence, the Sadducees could still engage the Pharisees in controversy on the grounds that the literal Pentateuch was sufficient and adequate, how can the viability of such a position be denied for a period when neither the Pharisees nor the twofold Law is mentioned in any source whatsoever? This sufficiency was defended by the Sadducees for several hundred years *following* the known existence of the Pharisees and the twofold Law! On the basis of this passage in

Josephus, the existence of the Pharisees and the twofold Law prior to the Hasmonean Revolt must be proven by *explicit* references in the sources; otherwise, each scholar is free to construct whatever existences his imagination spins off as credible to that scholar.

Adhering to this principle, can we establish a time after the promulgation of the Pentateuch when there were no Pharisees and no twofold Law? Does a source exist which can be dated with some certainty, and which is, at one and the same time, *silent* with reference to the Pharisees and the twofold Law, and yet *articulate* with respect to the literal Pentateuch? Such a source does indeed exist. It is Ecclesiasticus, the Wisdom of Ben Sira. Unlike other pre-Hasmonean sources, the author acknowledges his authorship and describes a specific High Priest, Simon. In addition, the book has a Prologue written by Ben Sira's grandson, and referring to a specific Ptolemaic king, Euergetes. The possibility for precise dating—specifically, 280 or 180 B.C.—thus exists.*

But equally important is the kind of book Ecclesiasticus happens to be. Ecclesiasticus is neither a chronicle nor a story; it is neither psalmody nor prophecy. It is rather the thoughtful musings of a lover of Wisdom as he contemplates the society in which he lives. As such, no aspect of the scene about him is overlooked. His maxims, proverbs, and sententious remarks are framed in response to the conduct of the rich and poor, master and slave, parent and child. His religious loyalties spur him to express his feelings toward God, Torah, the cultus, the priests, the Scribes, and the spiritul heroes of yesteryear. He has pithy comments touching on every class and every kind of virtue and foible. Ben Sira roams through all the world that surrounds him, considering nothing too low for a well-turned proverb nor too exalted for an

---

*On the problem of dating Ben Sira, *see* E. Rivkin, "Ben Sira and the Non-existence of the Synagogue," in *In the Time of Harvest*, ed. Daniel Jeremy Silver (New York, 1963), pp. 350-54.

exhortatory maxim. And since everything was raw material for his Wisdom, Ben Sira can be assumed to have been silent only when there was *nothing* of significance to communicate. This holds especially with respect to religious life and institutions, the very leitmotiv of his discourses. For though Ben Sira rambles through all of society and its vagaries, he lavishes his greatest love on the cultus, the Aaronide priesthood and the Written Law.

Because Ben Sira's book is the kind of book it is, we can begin our analysis by constructing the Pharisee-free society he describes. This society will be one built on articulated data, not eloquent silence. Whatever Ben Sira does not mention specifically has no objective claim to existence. Contrariwise, whatever he describes as existent may not be altered by imagined phenomena grounded in unbroken silence. And once we have reconstructed Ben Sira's society from his explicit testimony, we will have set up a barrier blocking any intrusion by the Pharisees and their twofold Law into the Aaronide priestly system. Such a barrier will compel us to look for the birth of the Pharisees at a time beyond this barrier.

But Ben Sira offers an additional service. In permitting us to determine how a Pentateuchal society functioned, he throws light on how such a society must have developed. It will enable us to extract from the Pentateuch those elements that had been decisive in making Ben Sira's society the one he describes.

Ben Sira's book is thus a sentinel source. It stands guard over a pre-Pharisaic and pre–twofold Law society. It protects a society constructed by Aaronide priests on the foundation of a single Written Law, the Pentateuch, from encroachment by scholars who, armed with silent sources, would alter its salient features. It is a book that compels scholars to turn away from Ben Sira's time and to look toward the Hasmonean Revolt for the birth of the Pharisees and the twofold Law. And having found the pre-Hasmonean society to have been constructed on a literal reading of the Pentateuch, scholars must confront the possibility that the Pharisees were a revolutionary scholar class, and the twofold Law a novel revelation.

But before the necessity of such a choice can be proven, we first must construct the society of Ben Sira's day from Ecclesiasticus. We must then analyze the Pentateuchal foundation upon which this society was built. And finally we shall be able to unveil a revolution which heretofore has remained hidden. Armed with a viable definition of the Pharisees, we shall see how this scholar class restructured the system of authority Ben Sira so lovingly described.

Chapter V

Ben Sira and Aaronide Hegemony

Ben Sira spreads before us a hierocratic society. A priesthood consisting exclusively of "the sons of Aaron" formed its ruling class, and a High Priest, a direct descendent of Aaron, Eleazar, Phinehas, and Zadok, exercised ultimate authority. This priesthood presided over an elaborate cultic system designed to expiate the sins of the people through the medium of divinely ordained sacrifices so that Israel might enjoy peace, tranquility, prosperity, and long life. Undergirding this system was the Pentateuch, which (so it was believed) had been revealed by God to Moses, and which spelled out in elaborate detail the central role of the cultus and the hegemony of the Aaronide priesthood.

Although critical scholars of our age have demonstrated the composite nature of the Pentateuch, and have separated the so called P sources from the other sources of the Pentateuch, Ben Sira and his contemporaries had no such notions. For them the Pentateuch was a single book written by Moses in which the priestly legislation of Exodus, Leviticus, and Numbers was the core of Mosaic legislation. For them, the supremacy of the Aaronides was the leitmotiv of the Mosaic Law. Indeed, although Ben Sira pictures God as choosing Moses to reveal the Law, it is Aaron whom he considers to be the revelation!

191

From his [Jacob's] descendents the Lord
    brought forth a man of mercy,
    Who found favor in the sight of all flesh
And was beloved of God and man,
    Moses, whose memory is blessed.
He made him equal in glory to the holy ones,
    and made him great in the fears of his enemies. (45:1-2)

And [he] gave him the commandments face to face,
    the law of life and knowledge,
to teach Jacob the covenant,
    and Israel his judgments.

    He exalted Aaron, the brother of Moses,
        a holy man like him, of the tribe of Levi.
    He made an everlasting covenant with him,
        and gave him the priesthood of the people.
    He blessed him with splendid vestments,
        and put a glorious robe upon him (45:5*b*-7)

God makes an eternal covenant with Aaron, not
Moses. Aaron's sons are to enjoy the priesthood forever,
not Moses'! Moses reveals Aaron to Israel and then
passes on, while Aaron and his progeny exercise
hegemony over the Law unto all generations:

Before his time there never were such beautiful things.
    No outsider ever put them on, but only his sons
    and his descendants perpetually.
His sacrifices shall be wholly burned
    twice every day continually.
Moses ordained him,
    and anointed him with holy oil;
it was an everlasting covenant for him
    and for his descendants all the days of heaven,
to minister to the Lord and serve as a priest
    and bless his people in his name.
He chose him out of all the living
    to offer sacrifice to the Lord,
incense and a pleasing odor as a memorial portion,
    to make atonement for the people.
In his commandments he gave him authority
    in statutes and judgments,
to teach Jacob the testimonies,
    and to enlighten Israel with his law.

Outsiders conspired against him,
    and envied him in the wilderness,
Dathan and Abiram and their men
    and the company of Korah, in wrath and anger.
The Lord saw it and was not pleased,
    and in the wrath of his anger they were destroyed;
he wrought wonders against them
    to consume them in flaming fire.
He added glory to Aaron
    and gave him a heritage;
he allotted to him the first of the first fruits,
    he prepared bread of first fruits in abundance;
for they eat the sacrifices to the Lord,
    which he gave to him and his descendants.
But in the land of the people he has no inheritance,
    and he has no portion among the people;
for the Lord himself is his portion and
    inheritance. (45:13-22)

The High Priestly line is also to remain sacrosanct. It is to belong to the descendents of Eleazar and Phinehas:

Phinehas the son of Eleazar is the third in glory,
    for he was zealous in the fear of the Lord,
and stood fast, when the people turned away,
    in the ready goodness of his soul,
    and made atonement for Israel.
Therefore a covenant of peace was established with him,
    that he should be the leader of the sanctuary and
    of his people,
that he and his descendants should have
    the dignity of the priesthood forever. (45:23-24)

But this glory and power of Aaron was no nostalgic memory of years gone by. It was as luminous in Ben Sira's day as he believed it to have been when the Israelites wandered in the wilderness. Simon, the High Priest in Ben Sira's day, was no less resplendent than his forefather Aaron was thought to have been; indeed, he is Aaron's mirror image.

The leader of his brethren and the pride of his people
    was Simon the high priest, son of Onias,

who in his life repaired the house,
    and in his time fortified the temple. . . .
How glorious he was when the people gathered round
    him as he came out of the inner sanctuary!
Like the morning star among the clouds,
    like the moon when it is full; . . .
When he put on his glorious robe
    and clothed himself with superb perfection
and went up to the holy altar,
    he made the court of the sanctuary glorious.
And when he received the portions from the hands of
      the priests,
    as he stood by the hearth of the altar
with a garland of brethren around him,
    he was like a young cedar on Lebanon;
and they surrounded him like the trunks of palm trees,
    all the sons of Aaron in their splendor
with the Lord's offering in their hands,
    before the whole congregation of Israel.
Finishing the service of the altars
    and arranging the offering to the Most High,
      the Almighty,
he reached out his hand to the cup
    and poured a libation of the blood of the grape;
he poured it at the foot of the altar,
    a pleasing odor to the Most High, the King of all.
Then the sons of Aaron shouted,
    they sounded the trumpets of hammered work,
they made a great noise to be heard
    for remembrance before the Most High.
Then all the people together made haste
    and fell to the ground upon their faces
to worship their Lord,
    the Almighty, God Most High.
And the singers praised him with their voices
    in sweet and full-toned melody.
And the people besought the Lord Most High
    in prayer before him who is merciful,
till the order of worship of the Lord was ended;
    so they completed his service.
Then Simon came down, and lifted up his hands
    over the whole congregation of the sons of Israel,
to pronounce the blessing of the Lord with his lips,
    and to glory in his name;
and they bowed down in worship a second time,
    to receive the blessing from the Most High. (50:1-21)

With Ben Sira's adulation of the Aaronides spread before us, we can scrutinize with special care those passages that bear directly on problems of power and authority.

The source of all power and authority is clearly God who made known his Law through Moses in a direct revelation:

> He made him [Moses] hear his voice,
>   and led him into the thick darkness,
> and gave him the commandments face to face,
>   the Law of life and knowledge,
> to teach Jacob the covenant,
>   and Israel his judgments. (45:5)

Moses, in turn, bestowed upon Aaron and his descendents not only an everlasting priesthood but also the *ongoing authority over the Law:*

> Moses ordained him,
>   and anointed him with holy oil;
> it was an everlasting covenant for him
>   and for his descendents all the days of heaven,
> to minister to the Lord and serve as priest
>   and bless his people in his name. . . .
> to make atonement for the people.
> In his commandments he gave his authority
>   *in statute and judgments,*
> *to teach Jacob the testimonies,*
> *and to enlighten Israel with his law.* (45:15; italics added)

Aaron is to have a monopoly not only of altar rights but of the administration and the teaching of the Law as well. He alone is clothed with authority, and he alone presides over its meaning. The Aaronides are to share this monopoly with no one, least of all the Levites. For in contrast to Deut. 33:8-11, which assigned the Law to the entire tribe of Levi, Ben Sira asserts that it is the exclusive prerogative of Aaron and his sons, threatening interlopers with the fate of Dathan, Abiram, Korah and his fellow Levites who had dared to challenge Aaron's monopoly (45:18-19).

Aaron is the salt of the earth, the Lord's terrestrial favorite:

He added glory to Aaron
and gave him a heritage;
he allotted to him the first of the first fruits,
he prepared bread of first fruits in abundance;
for they eat the sacrifices to the Lord,
which he gave him and his descendants. (45:20-22)

Ben Sira is also careful to associate Phinehas not only with Aaron but with Moses. Only one legitimate High Priestly line is recognized, and that is through Phinehas. The Pentateuchal promise to Phinehas (Num. 25:10-13) is echoed by Ben Sira (45:23-24).

The significance of this covenant with Phinehas must be stressed, for the line of Phinehas in Ben Sira's day was traced through Zadok down to the contemporary High Priest Simon (cf. I Chron. 24:1-3; Ezra 7:1-5; 6:50-53). Ben Sira upholds this High Priestly line, sees it as a rightful monopoly of altar and Law originally invested in Aaron, and prays that it prove to be everlasting. Ben Sira is thus a fervid and loyal Zadokite who grounds his loyalty in the *literal* commands of the Pentateuch. This Pentateuch was hardly ambiguous in its consignment of Korah and his fellow Levites and anti-Aaronides to Sheol (Num. 16); when it threatened death to any non-Aaronide who approached the altar (Num. 18); when it allowed only the High Priest to enter the Holy of Holies (Lev. 16); when it promised the High Priesthood to the descendents of Phinehas only (Num. 25:12-13). Neither the High Priest Simon nor Ben Sira needed unwritten laws to clarify the Pentateuchal text insofar as Aaronide prerogatives were concerned.

The Law that Ben Sira upholds is no twofold Law. Nowhere do we find a term for law which requires a nonscriptural rendering. Aaron is charged with authority over and the teaching of commandments *(mitzwoth),* judgments *(mishpatim), testimonies (edoth),* statutes *(hukkim)*, laws *(torot)* (45:17)—all biblical terms. Moses gives the people the Law of life *(torat hayyim)* which contains commandments and judgments (45:5). Indeed, whenever Ben Sira has occasion to refer to the laws, and this is not infrequently, he *always* uses the terminology of the Pentateuch. Never does he use a Greek word which would necessitate the Hebrew *halakhah* or *gezerah* or *takkanah,* terms coined to designate the unwritten laws.

Equally striking is the fact that Ben Sira accords to the Aaronide priests, and to them exclusively, the control of the Law. No other class has any authority over the Law, *not even* the *Soferim*-Scribes. Loyalty to the Law was demanded of all classes; the right to determine this Law rested solely in the hands of the Aaronides.

What, then, was the role of the Scribes-*Soferim* who are nowhere mentioned in the Pentateuch? Are they to be identified with the Pharisees-*Hakhamim-Soferim* simply because Ben Sira describes them as an honorific class dedicated to the study of the Law? And what of Ezra, the *Sofer*-Scribe who was so venerated by the Pharisees-*Hakhamim-Soferim?*

The answer to these questions is given in all innocency by Ben Sira himself. The *Soferim*-Scribes whom he knew and whose company he kept were Pentateuchalists, hierocratic intellectuals, Aaronide supremacists, and lovers and seekers of Wisdom. They were the devotees of the *onefold* Law, the Written Law, and of its authoritative spokesmen, the Aaronide priests. These *Soferim* share only a name with the Pharisees-*Hakhamim-Soferim,* not an essence.

Ben Sira is our only source that gives us a detailed description of the pre-Hasmonean *Soferim*-Scribes. In all other biblical books, the class is either not mentioned at all or is referred to by name only. In most instances the word *soferim* means either literally "a scribe" or "secretary" and does not convey any special honorific status. In others, it suggests elevated status, but does not make clear precisely what this status is. Thus Ezra is called a *Sofer,* who is agile in the Law (Ezra 7:6), but he is also a priest whose genealogy is traced to Zadok, Phinehas, Eleazar, and Aaron (7:1-5). His leadership and authority thus stemmed far more from his status as a descendent of Aaron, Eleazar, Phinehas, Zadok, than from his status as *Sofer,* whatever the term may have meant.

Ben Sira does, however, give us a full description of the *Soferim* of his day. He etches their image sharply by contrasting it to that of the peasant and artisan:

> The wisdom of the scribe depends on the opportunity
>> for leisure;
>> and he who has little business may become wise.
> How can he become wise who handles the plow,
>> and who glories in the shaft of a goad, . . .
> So too is every craftsman and master workman
>> who labors by night as well as by day; . . .
> All these rely upon their hands
>> and each is skillful in his own work.
> Without them a city cannot be established,
>> and men can neither sojourn nor live there. (38:24-31)

Ben Sira clearly has observed the farmer behind the plow, the artisan in his workshop (v. 27), the smith at his anvil (vv. 28-29), the potter at his wheel (vv. 29-30). He is appreciative not only of their skills but of their concern with the form and quality of their efforts. Ben Sira is thus not depreciating their worth when he bluntly states that it does not give them a voice in running society:

> Yet they are not sought out for the council of the people,
>> nor do they attain eminence in the public assembly.
> They do not sit in the judge's seat,
>> nor do they understand the sentence of judgment;
> they cannot expound discipline or judgment,
>> and they are not found using proverbs.
> But they keep stable the fabric of the world,
>> and their prayer is the practice of their trade. (38:33-34)

By implication, the *Sofer* can and does do what the farmer and the artisan cannot—namely, participate in the council of the people, attain eminence in the public assembly, serve as judge, expound discipline and judgment and toss off proverbs.

Ben Sira, however, is not content with a *Soferic* image drawn by implication. He paints it with bold strokes:

> On the other hand he who devotes himself to the study
>   of the law of the Most High
> will seek out the wisdom of the ancients,
>   and will be concerned with prophecies;
> he will preserve the discourse of notable men
>   and penetrate the subtleties of parables; . . .
> He will serve among great men
>   and appear before rulers;
> he will travel through the land of foreign nations,
>   for he tests the good and the evil among men.
> He will set his heart to rise early
>   to seek the Lord who made him,
> And will make supplication before the Most High;
> he will open his mouth in prayer
>   and make supplication for his sins.
> If the great Lord is willing,
>   he will be filled with the spirit of understanding;
> he will pour forth words of wisdom
>   and give thanks to the Lord in prayer.
> He will direct his counsel and knowledge aright
>   and meditate on his secrets.
> He will reveal instruction in his teaching,
>   and will glory in the Lord's covenant. (39:1-8)

The *Sofer* is a student of the Law of the Most High, a master of its contents. This Law is the Written Law, the onefold Law, the very same Law that had, according to Ben Sira, betowed upon the Aaronides, and the Aaronides alone, absolute authority over its meaning (45:17). The *Sofer* prides himself on *knowing* the Petateuch, a knowledge that could only reinforce his veneration of the Aaronides and their divinely ordained power, since the Pentateuch is the source of their hegemony. The *Sofer* knows nothing, however, of a twofold Law, of the *halakhah;* nor is he aware of himself as a law*maker*. He certainly does not sit in Moses' seat. He seeks out the wisdom of the ancients, but not their legislation; he concerns himself with prophecies, but not with *halakhoth, takkanoth,* or *gezeroth;* he preserves the discourses of notable men, but he does not preserve unwritten laws; he delights in proverbs and parables, but not in the Oral Law; he prays, but not in a synagogue; he acknowledges the profundity and the glory of the Lord's Law, but not because it was a twofold Law. No matter how the verses are twisted, the *Sofer* is *not* a legislator; he does not arrogate to himself authority over the Law; he does not challenge Aaronide supremacy. He is merely following the command of the Pentateuch that had admonished: "And these words which I command you this day shall be upon your heart; and you shall teach them diligently to your children, and shall talk of them . . . when you lie down, and when you rise" (Deut. 6:5-7). To meditate on the Law is precisely what the Law enjoins, since it reveals the absolute power assigned to the Aaronides (cf. Num. 16–18).

The *Sofer* was not free to interpret the Law or to tamper with its meaning. If there was a problem about the Law, then only the Aaronides could give an authoritative answer. The *Sofer's* provenance was not the Law but Wisdom. His role in society was to contemplate, to think, to muse. No restriction was placed either by the Law or by the Aaronides on his pursuit of Wisdom; his polishing of a well-turned proverb; his pride in a subtle parable; his propounding of a striking riddle; his acute observation of some glaring paradox. Such intellectual activity was welcomed by the Aaronides, for it did not challenge their power or undermine their authority. Wisdom, proverbs, maxims, parables, were an intellectual dimension the Pentateuch had not prohibited. Its silence thus gave assent to the musings of the *Soferim;* for to the extent that Wisdom is alluded to in the Pentateuch, it is held in high regard. The *Soferim* thus had a free hand, upheld by the Aaronides themselves, to articulate Wisdom, so long as this Wisdom admonished total and absolute obedience to the Law and the Aaronide supremacy it undergirded. Indeed, for Ben Sira, since Wisdom is the very foundation and mainstay of the Law, it upholds Aaronide supremacy. The Lord who created Wisdom is the very one who gave the Law:

Whoever keeps the law controls his thoughts,
and wisdom is the fulfillment of the fear of the Lord. (21:11)

If you desire wisdom, keep the commandments,
and the Lord will supply it for you.
For the fear of the Lord is wisdom and instruction,
and he delights in fidelity and meekness.
Do not disobey the fear of the Lord;
do not approach him with a divided mind. (1:26-28; cf. 14:11, 20–15:8; 17:11-15)

Wisdom is God's handiwork and therefore takes up residence in Zion and the holy Tabernacle:

In the holy tabernacle I ministered before him,
and so I was established in Zion. (24:10)

The Pentateuch is the repository of all this glory and beauty:

All this is the book of the covenant of the Most High God,
the law which Moses commanded us
as an inheritance for the congregation of Jacob.
It fills men with wisdom, like the Pishon,
and like the Tigris at the time of the first fruits.
It makes them full of understanding, like the Euphrates,
and like the Jordan at harvest time.
It makes instruction shine forth like light,
like the Gihon at the time of vintage. (24:23-27)

The *Sofer*'s realm thus does not collide with the Pentateuch or Aaronide supremacy. It is contiguous and coexists harmoniously. Its autonomy is taken as a matter of course and is *not* erected on an exegetical foundation. Not once does Ben Sira cite a biblical verse in support of Wisdom's claim. We have here no exegetical enterprise, no close scrutiny of the text, no hermeneutics, no

201

midrash. Ben Sira simply affirms that the Lord created Wisdom; that the Lord chose Jacob for its habitation; that Wisdom and the fear of the Lord go hand in hand; that the pursuer of Wisdom is a devotee of the Law and an enthusiastic supporter of the cultus. Like the psalmist, the *Sofer* offers praise; sings hymns; reflects on God's majesty and power; exalts the Law, the priesthood, and the Temple; ponders the mystery of life and God's providence. The *Sofer* needs no exegetical, midrashic support for elaborating upon Pentateuchal themes, for reiterating Pentateuchal motifs, for subsuming under Pentateuchal monotheism the varieties of human experience. There was no need for exegesis. The Aaronide rendering of the Pentateuch was adequate, satisfactory, even elevating, to the *Soferic* class; it was not regarded as a barrier or obstacle.

The *Soferim* of Ben Sira are thus *not* assimilable to the *Soferim-Hakhamim*-Pharisees, even though the name *Soferim* is shared. The differentiae preclude identity:

1. The Pharisees-*Soferim* are a ruling class. They determine the meaning of the Pentateuch in the light of their concept of the twofold Law. They and not the Aaronides are the authorities who decide how the cultus is to be conducted. It is they, and not the Aaronides, who have authority in statutes and judgments, and who teach Jacob the testimonies and enlighten Israel with the Law. Ben Sira's *Soferim,* by contrast, are hierocratic, Aaronide centralists, who reign over proverbs, parables, and Wisdom, but not over the Law.

2. The Pharisees-*Soferim* are the champions of the oral, unwritten mode. They transmit unwritten laws and they teach oral lore. They are a nonwriting scholar class. We know of no Pharisee-*Sofer* who *wrote* a book, a psalm, a proverb, or a poem. Indeed, the Pharisees-*Soferim,* as we shall see, abandoned the poetic form altogether, not even using it in the composition of prayers. Though nurtured on the prophets and the Psalms, and freely quoting them, the Pharisees-*Soferim* never utilize, even in oral

discourse, the parallelism characterizing these writings. Instead, they developed the *maaseh* form, the anecdotal, episodic, pericopal form which is absent from the Scriptures. And even when they offer a parable, it is encased in a form alien to biblical writ.

Not so Ben Sira and his *Soferim*. He is a writer. He adheres closely to the biblical literary forms: his proverbs are *formally* no different from those in Proverbs and Ecclesiastes; his prayers and hymns are not unlike the Psalms; his literary style is throughout characterized by parallelism. Not once does he resort to the *maaseh* form; not once to the formula "And to what is this to be compared?"; not once to an exegetical aside.

3. The style and the mode of the Pharisees have no counterpart in the Bible. Ben Sira and his fellow *Soferim*, by contrast, show themselves to have taken the Bible as their model and guide. Unlike the Pharisees-*Soferim*, they found the Pentateuch eminently satisfying without the need for supplanting it by unwritten laws and unwritten doctrines.

Ben Sira's *Soferim* and the *Soferim*-Pharisees are thus two distinctly different classes—the former flourishing in the pre-Hasmonean epoch, the latter only subsequently. The former are an honorific but powerless class; the latter honorific *and* ruling. The former are Pentateuchal literalists; the latter, upholders of the twofold Law. The former pursue Wisdom; the latter the twofold Law.

The evidence for the two separate and distinct classes is decisive. Ben Sira describes the hierocratic, Aaronide *Soferim* of the pre-Hasmonean period; Josephus, the new Testament, and the Tannaitic Literature, the Pharisees-*Soferim* of a later day. A comparison between the two shows no identity; only the name is the same.

This sharing of a name by two or more differentiated classes is by no means uncommon. We have numerous examples of identical names which not only bespeak different notions but conjure up opposites. Thus, "scholar" is used to designate both those who study the

Bible dogmatically and those who study it critically. A "sage" in one culture may be antithetical to the "sage" in a contrasting culture. The name "rabbi" is applied in our own day to spiritual leaders whether they are Orthodox or Reform, even though the Orthodox rabbi insists that the Law is both binding and Mosaic, while the Reform rabbi denies that the Law is either binding or Mosaic. The term *kohen,* "priest," at one time was used to designate an individual who offered sacrifices, then to a Levite, then to an Aaronide, and finally to an Aaronide who no longer offers sacrifices. Similarly, the name "prophet" has been used to refer to Elijah, to Amos, to Ezekiel, and to Balaam, not to mention Jesus and his disciples.

Soferim is a name of this type. Like other names, it has so generalized a meaning that it can be freely applied to classes that have in common only a nondifferentiating quality. Anyone engaged in some kind of study and learning may be called a scholar; anyone claiming to speak the word of God may be called a prophet; anyone linked to a cultic function may be called a priest; anyone assuming spiritual leadership within Judaism may be called a rabbi. So with the word *Soferim:* the hierocratic, Aaronide *Soferim* were intellectual devotees exclusively of the *literal* Pentateuch, while the Pharisees-*Soferim* were intellectuals who were loyal to the Pentateuch *and* the Oral Law. The former alone were in existence in the time of Ben Sira, while the latter superseded them during the Hasmonean period.

Ben Sira and his fellow *Soferim* must therefore be identified as Pentateuchal literalists and Aaronide centralists, even though the term *Soferim* itself does not occur within the Pentateuch. Unlike the Aaronides, the Levites, the *Zekenim* ("Elders"), and the *Nesiim* ("Princes"), the *Soferim* do not figure in the wilderness experience. Neither do we find them mentioned as other than secretaries or copyists in exilic or postexilic prophets. Nor are they to be found in Psalms, Proverbs, Ecclesiastes, or Job. The only biblical books that mention

them as possibly other than secretaries are I Chron. 2:55;
II Chron. 34:13; Ezra 7:6, 11; and Neh. 8:1, 4, 9; 12:13, 26,
36; 13:13, with all but two of these references involving
Ezra alone. The class of *Soferim* is thus a new class which
must have emerged subsequent to the canonization of
the Pentateuch, but a class which did not challenge
Aaronide supremacy. Yet for a new class to emerge,
some change in the structure of society must have
occurred, even though this change may have served to
make a stronger, not weaker, Aaronide structure. Since
Ben Sira's *Soferim* were Pentateuchalists and Aaronides,
they were evidently a creation of a triumphant,
flourishing, and confident hierocratic society, a society
which, as is evident from the books of Nehemiah and
Ezra, had had its beginnings in trepidation and
uncertainty. The canonization of the Pentateuch may
have launched the Aaronides, but the emergence of
Soferim reveals how successful these priests had been.
Ben Sira is reflecting on an Aaronide society that has
attained such stability and such affluence that there is
room for a class of intellectuals who are free to pursue
Wisdom and serve in positions of honor so long as
authority over the Law is securely in Aaronide hands.

Ben Sira's society was one far more urbanized and
complex than the predominantly agricultural society that
had originally bound itself by the Pentateuch. It was a
society that not only had grown in wealth and prosperity
but had developed a class of intellectuals, *Soferim,* who
were impressed with the compatibility of the Wisdom
emanating from the Hellenistic world with the Law of
Moses. They were not as yet threatened by aggressive
Hellenistic intrusions. They were still living in a society
responsive to Aaronide leadership. Urbanization had not
yet undermined the relevance of the Pentateuch or
confidence in the capacity of the Aaronide priesthood to
govern. Consequently, the *Soferim* were the darlings of
the Aaronides, not their nemesis, for the paths of

Wisdom which they trod all led to the Temple Mount and to the holy altar of divine expiation.

This harmonious relationship between the Aaronides and the *Soferim* was abetted by the policies of the Ptolemies who ruled over Palestine from Alexander's death in 323 B.C. until Antiochus III (242-187 B.C.) wrested it from their hands in 197 B.C. The Ptolemies were not Hellenizers. With the exception of Alexandria and one or two other cities, the Ptolemies did not look to the proliferation of *poleis*, with their wide range of privileges and broad autonomy, as the means for consolidating and securing their Empire. They thus foreclosed any hope on the part of Jews living in Jerusalem, no matter how Hellenized they might become, that Jerusalem would be made a *polis*, by reaffirming the hegemony of the Aaronide High Priest. Since Hellenization was not encouraged, Hellenistic thought could flourish among the *Soferim* without endangering the Aaronide system. Indeed, to press for *polis* rights was to arouse the concern of the Ptolemies, not their support.

The takeover by the Seleucids undercut this symbiosis. By contrast to the Ptolemies, the Seleucids had from the outset encouraged the spread of *poleis* as the most effetive means for governing a widespread empire. Hellenization was encouraged as a unifying force. Hence, when Antiochus III took over Palestine, hopes were bound to arise among many upper-class Jews that Jerusalem might indeed be transformed into a *polis*. Although this group was a minority, it had its supporters within the High Priestly family itself. As such, the Seleucid takeover proved to be unsettling.

And no less unsettling was the fact that in the decades following Ben Sira's death, the ongoing process of urbanization had so altered the structure of experience of merchant, shopkeeper, artisan, and peasant alike that the Pentateuch no longer resonated with their deepest needs and their innermost yearnings. For the Pentateuch had been designed for a relatively simple agricultural-priestly society and not a highly complex urban-agricultural society embedded within a world of *poleis*—a world in which each individual was stirred on the one hand by feelings of loneliness, alienation, and insignificance, and on the other by intimations of personhood, self-worth, and immortality.

When, therefore, a crisis of leadership occurred with first Jason and then Meneleus violating the Law by buying the High Priestly office from Antiochus IV, the people were ripe, not merely for rebellion, but for revolution.

Part III

Pharisaism:
An Internal Revolution

Chapter VI

The Hidden Revolution

The history of humankind has been punctuated by certain recurrent processes that have radically altered the shape, character, and direction of the historical continuum. These phenomena which involve profound and radical transformation of the course of historical development are referred to as revolutions. Revolutions are occasions of heightened social interaction; of decisive decision making; of disintegrative and reintegrative processes; of the displacement of previously dominant forms of social organization and principles of authority by those which are new; of the transfer of power from one class to another and from one type of leadership to another. Revolutions are the culmination of changes and developments that have been long in the making and which have gradually built up into situations breeding conflict and demanding decisive resolution. Revolutions mark the end of one dominant mode of social organization and the inauguration of some novel form of social cohesiveness. A revolution, in essence, is that process by which one system of authority is replaced by another; one set of overriding loyalties, by those of another kind.

Revolutions do not occur gratuitously. They are set in motion by a pattern of change; they are not mechanically induced by any single thought or a single event. Revolutions can occur only when the processes of change have altered the perceptions of those who are experiencing the impact and pressure. Such alteration necessarily carries with it both emotional and intellectual assessments. But these in turn are severely limited and restricted by the thought tools and the emotional tools at hand, the degree and extent to which they can be modified, and the range of possible innovation. Thus whereas Luther could deal with the problems of ecclesiastical power only by recourse to Scripture, Robespierre could freely launch his critique by an appeal to Reason.

A prerequisite for a revolution, therefore, is not only dissatisfaction but a heightened awareness that frustration is both unnecessary and susceptible to remedy. These are occasions when the ties that bind restless classes to the old order become so taut with strain that *any* increase in tension must snap the connection. But in addition, for a revolution to transform society, there must be individuals who are capable of forging other ties and of working out novel modes of cohesion.

Judea had undergone certain major structural changes during the third century which had made it a far more complex society than the one that had functioned in the days of Nehemiah or that which had flourished when Alexander the Great gained hegemony over Judea. New classes had come into existence; old classes had undergone modification. The simple congruence between the Pentateuchal-Aaronide ideology and the needs, thoughts, and aspirations of multiple classes no longer existed. The structural disintegration underlying all revolutions had clearly evolved by 198 B.C. when the Seleucids wrested sovereignty from the Ptolemies. All that was necessary for a deepgoing and radical revolution was a set of abrasive events that would compel a reassessment of the claims to absolute authority which had for more than two centuries allowed the Aaronides to rule by divine right.

What was needed was a situation involving a catastrophic loss of confidence in the ability of the theocratic system to function effectively in a crisis threatening to extinguish the community itself—a situation jarring every individual out of his reliance on normal expectancies, forcing decision making of a most radical sort on every Jew, prying open the mind to the necessity for contemplating daring and frightening goals. It had to be the kind of situation to bring into question the very principles that underwrote the existing institutions of authority, power, and sanctity and to allow for the formulation of principles justifying novel institutions, elevating new and radical leaders into the positions of authority and power.

Such a situation occurred when Antiochus IV (175-163 B.C.) imposed forced Hellenization upon the Jews. It was a situation that was rooted in a set of incidents set in motion when the Seleucids had gained control of Judea. Unfortunately, the exact details of these events may not be recoverable, and those details which are known may lend themselves to variant interpretations. Nevertheless there can be no doubt that almost immediately following the consolidation of Seleucidian hegemony, a severe struggle for power broke out for the High Priesthood. Those elements that challenged the legitimate incumbent sought the support of the Seleucids. Jason, a theocratic Hellenist, had the legitimate High Priest Onias III (*ca.* 185-170 B.C.) removed from office and introduced Hellenistic reforms which did not undermine the authority of the theocracy. The cultus and the privileged Aaronide priesthood were preserved, and the Pentateuchal authority of the theocracy reaffirmed. Meneleus, on the other hand, was presumably willing, in the interests of achieving full Hellenistic *polis* rights, to abandon the very ground of theocratic power, the Pentateuch. The use of swine's flesh on the altar and the dedication of the cultus to Zeus represented a mortal blow to a theocratic system that had derived its authority from the Mosaic law.

Thus in the short span of less than thirty years, the

Jewish population had been witness to the inner bankruptcy of the theocratic structure. Those clothed with authority and those venerated for their holy ministrations had shown themselves unworthy of the power they wielded. Jason, though a brother of the High Priest, had bought the office for himself and openly introduced Hellenistic practices. Meneleus, too, though belonging to the influential and respected family of the Tobiads, went even further when he flaunted law and tradition by usurping the High Priesthood for himself and when he used the High Priestly office to destroy the very source of theocratic power, the belief in a single God.

These struggles for power could leave no element in Jewish society unaffected. Each class and each individual had no choice but to make some response to such disturbing stimuli. Some assessment had to be made of the situation and some decision reached as to what should and could be done. The disintegration of unified theocratic leadership compelled a reevaluation of the entire theocratic system.

Confronted with the internal collapse of the constituted system of authority, the new classes that had been maturing during the past century were propelled into innovating activity. The cords of loyalty to the theocratic system had been severed by leaders within the system itself. The alliance of the usurping High Priest Meneleus with the Hellenizing Antiochus raised to the fore the most crucial issue of authority, institutions, leadership, and direction. The revolution, the structural prerequisites for which had been long in preparation, broke forth with all the destructive and creative power that is a distinguishing feature of the most momentous revolutions in humankind's history. The old theocratic-Pentateuchal system was shorn of its authority; its most powerful institutions were radically modified; its autocratic priestly leadership was replaced. A new system of authority emerged; novel institutions were created; fresh concepts were generated, and a new leadership gave direction.

This revolution which so dramatically altered the shape and course of Judaism has been obscured by the sound and fury of the Hasmonean Revolt. Our sources I and II Maccabees focus almost exclusively on the heroic leadership of the Hasmoneans. They give us the vivid impression that the Hasmoneans and their followers were concerned with restoration, not transformation. The role of the Pharisees is acknowledged in no way. They are given no credit for stirring the people with the good news that God had given two Laws, not one, and that he had promised to each and every individual who obeyed his twofold Law, eternal life.

The Pharisaic Revolution has remained a hidden revolution, but it was a revolution nonetheless. The sources may have obscured it, but they did not totally erase all its markings. Telltale data have seeped through the cracks and crevices of silence—data that presuppose the revolution not explicity mentioned.

The first decisive datum of this sort is to be found in I Macc. 14:25-44. It is the record preserved for posterity on bronze tablets and put on pillars on Mount Zion (I Macc. 14:27-48):

On the eighteenth day of Elul, in the one hundred and seventy-second year, which is the third year of Simon the great high priest, in Asaramel [exact meaning unknown], in the great assembly [or, Great Synagogue *(synagoge megale)]* of *the priests* and the *people* and the rulers of the nation and the elders of the country, the following was proclaimed to us:

"Since wars often occurred in the country, Simon the son of Mattathias, *a priest of the sons of Joarib,* and his brothers, exposed themselves to danger and resisted the enemies of their nation, in order that their *sanctuary and law* might be preserved; and they brought great glory to their nation. Jonathan rallied the nation, *and became their high priest,* and was gathered to his people. And when their enemies decided to invade their country and lay hands on their sanctuary, then Simon rose up and fought for his nation. . . .

"The people saw Simon's faithfulness and the glory which he

had resolved to win for his nation, *and they made him their leader [hegoumenon] and high priest,* because he had done all these things and because of the justice and loyalty which he had maintained toward his nation. He sought in every way to exalt his people. And in his days things prospered in his hands, so that the Gentiles were put out of the country, as were also the men in the city of David in Jerusalem, who had built themselves a citadel from which they used to sally forth and defile the environs of the sanctuary and do great damage to its purity. He settled Jews in it and fortified it for the safety of the country and of the city, and built the walls of Jerusalem higher.

"In view of these things King Demetrius confirmed him in the high priesthood, and he made him one of the king's friends and paid him high honors. For he heard that the Jews were addressed by the Romans as friends and allies and brethren, and that the Romans had received the envoys of Simon with honor.

"And the Jews and their priests decided that Simon should be their leader *[hegoumenon]* and high priest for ever, until a trustworthy prophet should arise *[eis ton aiona heos tou anastenai propheten piston],* and that he should be governor *[strategon]* over them and that he should take charge of the sanctuary and appoint men over its tasks and over the country and the weapons and the strongholds, and that he should take charge over the sanctuary, and that he should be obeyed by all, and that all contracts in the country should be written in his name, and that he should be clothed in purple and wear gold.

"And none of the people or priests shall be permitted to nullify any of these decisions or to oppose what he says, or to convene an assembly in the country without his permission, or to be clothed in purple or put on a gold buckle. Whoever acts contrary to these decisions or nullifies any of them shall be liable to punishment."

And all the people agreed to grant Simon the right to act in accord with these decisions. So Simon *accepted* and *agreed* to be high priest, to be commander and ethnarch *[strategos kai ethnarches]* of the Jews and priests, and to be protector of them all. And *they* [the people] gave orders to inscribe this decree upon bronze tablets, to put them up in a conspicuous place in the precincts of the sanctuary, and to deposit copies of them in the treasury, so Simon and his sons might have them. (Italics added)

The author of I Maccabees has recorded here a truly revolutionary act. A Great Synagogue *(synagoge megale)* of the priests, the people, the rulers of the nation *(archonton*

216

ethnous), and the elders of the country *(kai ton presbuteron tes choras)* proclaimed that Simon the son of Mattathias of the family of Joarib was to be the leader and High Priest of the Jews forever, until a true prophet arose. For this proclamation there is absolutely no Pentateuchal warrant. The Pentateuch is clear and explicit that Phinehas the son of Eleazar the son of Aaron is to have for himself and his seed after him a covenant of an everlasting priesthood (Num. 25:13). This covenant is subsequently confirmed when Phinehas does indeed function as *the* priest (Joshua 22:13-34) on the occasion of the distribution of the land among the tribes. Likewise, the genealogies as given in I Chronicles (6:1-15, 49-53) and in Ezra (7:1-5) trace the High Priestly lineage through Aaron-Eleazar-Phinehas through Zadok in an unbroken line. And as for the High Priests who administered in the Temple after the promulgation of the Pentateuch, they considered themselves to be the direct descendents from Zadok, Phinehas, Eleazar, and Aaron. Indeed, the line was broken only when first Jason and then Meneleus flagrantly violated the sacred order of High Priestly succession.

The family of Joarib was a priestly family, but not a High Priestly family. Hence, neither Jonathan, who had been serving as High Priest, or Simon, who was now invested with the High Priesthood, had a right to be the High Priest, since they were not the direct descendents of Zadok, Phinehas, Eleazar, and Aaron. As far as the Pentateuchal Law was concerned, and as far as all previous precedent was concerned, they were usurpers. The High Priesthood belonged, as of right, only to Zadokites.

Declaring that Simon and his sons were to enjoy the High Priestly office until a true prophet would arise was in and of itself an audacious revolutionary act. To have this investiture carried through by a *synagoge megale* was to compound the audacity. God had commanded Moses to single out Aaron and Eleazar and Phinehas for the

High Priesthood. This investiture was to be an eternal one. No provision was made for its abrogation or alteration. Only God, through a true prophet, had the right to change the order of succession. Certainly a *synagoge megale* is nowhere mentioned in all of Scripture, much less in the Pentateuch. Indeed, the Pentateuch assigns to no assembly or institution the right to alter, abrogate, or legislate any divine law! And as for a *synagoge megale* exercising such unwarranted prerogatives, only the Tannaitic Literature bespeaks of such a body when it recalls the *Kennesset ha-Gedolah.*

And if we look more closely, there are other revolutionary markings. The Pentateuch displays two calendrical systems. The first of these is an extremely loose one, which sets no fixed days for the festivals, and which is not spelled out. It is only alluded to when Abib is mentioned as the month of the Exodus (Exod. 13:4). The second of these is the Aaronide calendar. This calendar is characterized by numbered, not named, months, and by the spelling out with precision the exact day of the exact numbered months the festivals and holy days are to be celebrated, with the exception of Pentecost (Lev. 23:4-44). Of the two calendars, it was the Aaronide calendar which functioned following on the promulgation of the Pentateuch. This is evident from the fact that the books written following the canonization of the Pentateuch and prior to the Hasmonean Revolt use numbered months. Even a book as late as Daniel uses only numbered months. Yet the proclamation of the *synagoge megale* begins with "On the eighteenth day of Elul" without even designating it as the "sixth month." Now the only source we have of a *sacred* calendar that uses named months exclusively and includes Elul, is the Mishnah, as tractate Rosh ha-Shanah so boldly reveals. There is thus here another radical break with Pentateuchal precedent: a calendar that does not even acknowledge the Aaronide calendar by so much as the expression "Elul, which is the sixth month," or the "sixth month, which is Elul"! This is all the more remarkable in view of the fact that the author of I Maccabees himself frequently uses numbered months (4:52; 9:3, 54; 10:21; 14:27; 16:14).

This proclamation, inscribed on bronze tablets and set upon pillars on Mount Zion, publicly testified that a revolution had occurred and that it was to be regarded as legitimate because it had the imprimatur of the Great Synagogue, the *synagoge megale.* The High Priesthood was no longer the prerogative of the Aaron-Eleazar-Phinehas-Zadok line. It was now vested in the Hasmonean family until a true prophet would arise in Israel. A priestly dynasty which had exercised unbroken hegemony from the time of the promulgation of the Pentateuch until the ousting of Onias III was dissolved. The commands of the Pentateuch had been superseded by the decision of a Great Synagogue which God had not mandated and Moses had not ordained. It was a body whose authority to depose and seat High Priests is nowhere written down in the Law of Moses. Its authority was self-generated. It derived, consequently, from revolutionary, not Pentateuchal, right.

This transfer of power from the Zadokite line to the Hasmonean line was carried through and legitimatized by an authority elevated above them both. Simon does not proclaim himself as the High Priest. The right of Simon and his sons to be High Priests is bestowed upon them by a Great Synagogue, a *synagoge megale.* A Great Synagogue is thus the ultimate authority, elevated above the High Priesthood and over the written Law of Moses. But whence this hegemony? If it is not from Moses, and if it is not from the champions of the Zadokite line, and if it is not avowed as a revolutionary usurpation pure and simple, whence the grounds; whence the rationale? The answer is to be found in that class which was rejected by the Zadokites/Sadducees because it did not recognize the binding character of the *written* Law of Moses exclusively. It was a class which felt free to legitimate a new High Priest line on the basis of *laws not written down in the laws of Moses.* In a word, the Scribes-Pharisees was such a class. They could convoke a Great Synagogue, *synagoge megale,* to serve as a constituent assembly to formalize the transfer of the High Priesthood from the Zadokite family to the Hasmonean family and from the Aaronides to themselves. They had this right because they affirmed that the laws *not* written down in the laws of Moses were binding laws.

And among the laws not written down was that law which allowed the scholar class to convoke a Great Synagogue, a *synagoge megale,* with the full divine right to transfer authority from one High Priestly family to another.

Underwriting this assumption is the fact that the Pharisees are umbilically related to the Sadducees (the Zadokites), whose historical origins are indelibly impressed in their name. They came to be called Sadducees because of their insistence that only a descendent of the Aaron-Eleazar-Phinehas-Zadok line could minister as High Priest. And the only time this right was challenged by Jews utterly loyal to God and his revelation and not Hellenists at all was when Jonathan took over the High Priesthood and when a Great Synagogue, *synagoge megale,* publicly proclaimed this transfer of power sacrosanct. The rejection of this act by the Zadokites-Sadducees set them in opposition to those who had legitimated this transfer of power on the basis of an authority *not* written down in the Law of Moses. These must have been the champions of the laws not written down, the *paradosis,* the *Soferim* of the twofold Law, in contradistinction to the Aaronide-*Soferim* of Ben Sira's day. And it was these *Soferim* whom the Zadokites-Sadducees, in their wrath, denounced as *perushim,* "separatists," "heretics." The umbilical cord from which neither would be sundered was thus tightly tied. And undergirding the Great Synagogue, the *synagoge megale,* as a creation of *Soferim*-Pharisees is the fact that while the term *Kenesset ha-Gedolah* is nowhere found in the Bible, it is recalled in the tannaitic texts as a body of supreme importance which was so endowed with authority that it canonized the prophets and the Hagiographa (cf. B.B. 14b).

The facts, then, are clear: a revolution had occurred. A body not authorized by the Pentateuch, a Great Synagogue, had legitimatized the transfer of power from a Pentateuchally ordained High Priesthood to one not authorized in the written Law of Moses. Whoever sanctioned the legality of the transfer must have been a class whose authority was acknowledged by both the Hasmoneans and the people at large as legitimate. It had to be a class that affirmed that right of a Great Synagogue to do what it did, even though it had no Pentateuchal warrant. This class could not have been the Zadokites-Sadducees. The only other class attested to by Josephus as functioning at this time, which was also a class continuously clashing with the Sadducees, were the Pharisees. According to Josephus, the Pharisees, along with the Sadducees and Essenes, were functioning in the time of Jonathan—the first Hasmonean to serve as High Priest and, hence, the first to have provoked the opposition of the Zadokites-Sadducees. *Josephus mentions the Pharisees and the Sadducees for the first time in his writings at that very moment when the issue of who should be High Priest once the hostilities came to any end emerged.*

We should also have anticipated that if the Pharisees had indeed been responsible for legitimizing Simon and his sons as High Priests through a Great Synagogue *not* authorized by the Pentateuch, they would have enjoyed the favor of Simon and his son John Hyrcanus. Indeed, as the legitimatizers of the Hasmoneans, we would expect them to be teachers of Simon and John, and we would assume that the *paradosis*, the laws not written down in the Law of Moses, would be the laws of the land. Such would be the inexorable logic following on a revolution and a transfer of power made possible and legitimatized by the Pharisees.

Josephus confirms explicitly this anticipation when he

tells us that John Hyrcanus regarded himself as a disciple of the Pharisees and looked to them for assurances that he was indeed comporting himself as a righteous person. Josephus also informs us that the Sadducees had enjoyed no such relationship with John when he became High Priest. When, however, a fall-out occurred between John Hyrcanus and the Pharisees and John broke with the Pharisees and took up with the Sadducees, John abrogated the laws of the Pharisees—laws which hitherto had been operative with John's sanction and laws which, as Josephus points out, had been handed down from the Fathers and had not been written down in the Law of Moses. Josephus also stresses that the Sadducees rejected the *paradosis,* acknowledging only the laws written down by Moses as binding. And it was because of this fundamental cleavage, Josephus assures us, that the Sadducees and the Pharisees were embroiled in controversies with each other. He also notes that the majority of the people were adherents of the Pharisees, hence, devotees of the *paradosis (Ant.* XIII:293-98).

Josephus goes farther. He points out that John's break with the Pharisees and his abrogation of the *paradosis* stirred the people to insurrection (*Ant.* XIII:299; *War* I:67). Although he succeeded in putting down the rebellion, his son Alexander Jannaeus was not so fortunate. A bitter civil war raged throughout his entire reign—a war carried on so resolutely by the Pharisees and their followers that Alexander was unable to carry through to victory. Indeed, peace was restored only after Salome Alexandra had become "a disciple" of the Pharisees, gave them a free hand to dispose of their Sadducean enemies, *and had the* paradosis *reinstituted,* which her father-in-law had abrogated (*Ant.* XIII:408).

Josephus' testimony to the Pharisaic Revolution is thus stark indeed:

1. Prior to the Hasmonean Revolt, Josephus knows nothing of Sadducees, Pharisees, or Essenes; yet they are very much around in the time of Jonathan. Sometime

between the infamous decrees of Antiochus IV and the victories of Judah and Jonathan, three schools of thought, highly differentiated from each other, have emerged among the Jews.

2. Jonathan, Simon, and John Hyrcanus function as High Priests although not of the family of Zadok.

3. During the first years of John Hyrcanus' High Priesthood, the Pharisees are his teachers and their *paradosis* is observed by the people with his sanction.

Whence this phenomenon: a system of laws adhered to tenaciously by the majority of Jewish people, not written down in the Law of Moses, rejected on that account by the Sadducees, and championed by a nonpriestly class utterly unknown to Josephus until the time of Jonathan? Whence but a revolution?

The Mishnah, like I Maccabees and Josephus, presupposes the Pharisaic Revolution. It is the most enduring achievement of this revolution, even though it nowhere acknowledges that a revolution had occurred. Indeed, the Mishnah takes for granted that the Oral Law was no less revealed to Moses on Sinai than the Written Law and that the scholar class were no less the spokesmen of God's will than the prophets had been. Nevertheless, the Mishnah, when set alongside the Pentateuch, starkly reveals not a logical progression, but a quantum jump.

By any measure, the Mishnah is incongruent with the Pentateuch. The Pentateuch is framed in historical narrative. It makes a clear distinction between the various phases of the history of humankind and of the people of Israel. The patriarchal age is sharply distinguished from the Exodus and the wilderness wanderings. The laws are throughout embedded in events and in the ebb and flow of time. God reveals his laws in thunder and lightning, in the Tent of Meeting, and on this or that occasion.

Not so the Mishnah. Here there is no narrative at all. The laws are simply set down as laws. God does not thunder them forth, nor does he spell them out. Yet these laws are set down as binding and as definitive. They take precedence over any Pentateuchal formulation when there is a clash between a *halakhah* and a literal reading of the Law. At no time does the Mishnah allow for the Pentateuch to speak out unmediated by the scholar class.

And if we compare the Mishnah with the Prophets and the Hagiographa, the discontinuity is no less striking. "Thus saith the Lord" is nowhere to be found in the Mishnah, even though the laws are as binding as if the formula had been used. Nor is poetry anywhere to be found in the Mishnah; nor is the proverb or maxim after the manner of Proverbs or Ecclesiastes.

The Mishnah does not even follow the Pentateuch in the arrangement of the laws. The first tractate of the Mishnah deals with the reciting of the Shema, with prayer and benedictions, and not with the Passover. The Pentateuchal sequence is nowhere adhered to in the Mishnah. It has its own logic and not that of the Pentateuch.

Not only are the macroforms incongruent, but the microforms as well. The formulas for the laws in the Mishnah are nowhere to be found in the Pentateuch. Whereas the Pentateuch articulates laws either as a direct command ("Thou shalt not" or "Thou shalt") or as a contingent statement ("If a man . . . then" or "When you come into the land, then"), the Mishnah makes use of none of these. Instead we find questions ("From what time do we read the *Shema*?" "How does one make the blessing over fruit?" "Which place is the proper place for the sacrifices?" "With what do we kindle the Sabbath light?"); or categories ("There are four principal kinds of damage"); or flat affirmations ("The morning prayer may be said until noonday"; "Three who have eaten together are obligated to . . ."; "These are the things which have no limit").

The formulas for nonlaw in the Mishnah are likewise non-Pentateuchal. Thus when in the Mishnah an episode is reported, it is introduced by the term *maaseh* ("it is related")—never by the Pentateuchal "And it came to pass." And most significantly, the *maaseh* is always an exemplum or a paradigm, never an incident within a continuous, ongoing narrative.

Not only are the forms discontinuous but the language as well. The Mishnah is replete with nonbiblical vocabulary set within a nonbiblical syntax. Most striking is the rich coinage of technical terms: *halakhah,* "oral law"; *takannah,* "ordinance"; *gezerah,* "decree"; *bet din,* "law house"; *bet ha-kenesset,* "synagogue"; *Makom,* "the All-Present"; *Shekhinah,* "the indwelling Presence"; *ha-Kadosh Barukh Hu,* "the Holy one Blessed be He"; *hayab,* "obligated"; *mutar,* "permitted"; *asur,* "prohibited"; *shetar,* "legal document"; *olam ha-ba,* "the world to come," etc. None of these expressions are to be found in the Pentateuch, the Prophets, or the Hagiographa. And as for syntax, the Mishnah is terse, unadorned, elliptical, and stripped of narrative overlays.

One of the most striking formal differences between the Mishnah and the whole body of Scripture is the use of proof-texting. Nowhere in the Pentateuch, the historical books, the prophets, or the Hagiographa is there to be found the formula *she-neemar,* "as it is stated in Scripture." The biblical books require no proof-texting, since each book is written as though God himself had revealed its contents to the writer. The most one finds is an occasional allusion to the fact that one should abide by all that is written in the Torah. But one looks in vain for any proof text where a biblical verse is called upon to support some law or doctrine.

Indeed, proof-texting is nowhere to be found in the Wisdom of Ben Sira. As pointed out above, Ben Sira appeals to no Scriptural verses to uphold his assertion that Wisdom, like the Torah, comes directly from the Lord. Nor does he draw on proof texts to confirm any of his maxims, proverbs, and paradoxes.

The proof-texting mode is thus a radical innovation.

Yet it is used throughout the Mishnah as though it were the most traditional of modes. There is never any sign of awareness of its novelty, nor any apologia for its ubiquitous use. Indeed, there is no tractate of the Mishnah that does not bristle with proof texts.

The proof-texting mode of the Mishnah is very revealing of certain fundamental assumptions underlying its usage. Although the Pentateuch was accorded a special status elevating it above the Prophets and the Hagiographa, this status did not carry with it any downgrading of the divine revelation incorporated in these books. God's revelation was identical wherever vouchsafed to Moses or to Joshua or to David or to Solomon or to Isaiah. This is evident throughout the Mishnah. Scriptural support for oral laws or for oral doctrines are freely drawn from all three sources of divine revelation. Priority is *not* given the Pentateuch, as the following examples reveal:

They [the scholars] ordained that a man should inquire of the welfare of his neighbor by mentioning the name [of God], as it is said (Ruth 2:4), "And behold Boaz came from Bethlehem and he said to the reapers, "The Lord be with you." And they said to him, "May the Lord bless you." And it further states (Judges 6:12), "The Lord be with you, O man of valor." And it further states (Proverbs 23:22), "Do not despise thy mother when she is old"; and it says further (Psalms 119:126), "It is time to do something for the Lord; they have made void your Law." (Ber. 9:5)

In this instance, the Pentateuch is not cited at all!

The Mishnah is no less incongruent with the Pentateuch on substantive issues. This is most blatantly revealed in the large number of tractates dealing with whole categories of laws that are *not* in the Pentateuch at all. Tractate *Berakoth,* "Blessings," prescribes when the *Shema* should be read, though there is no command in the Pentateuch that it be read at all. It likewise lays down precise laws as to when the *Tefillah,* the prayer par excellence, is to be said, even though nowhere in the

226

Pentateuch is any prayer made mandatory. It also enjoins the saying of blessings for a wide variety of occasions, despite the absence in the Pentateuch of any provision for mandatory blessings.

Tractate Kethuboth deals with the marriage contract, though the Pentateuch acknowledges no such instrument. Tractate Sanhedrin concerns itself with the prerogatives and functions of the *Bet Din,* a non-Pentateuchal institution. Tractate Ta'anith, "Fasts," deals exclusively with non-Pentateuchal fasts, while Tractate Megillah lays down the law for reading the scroll of Esther and for the reading of the Pentateuch and the Prophets—a reading nowhere prescribed in the Pentateuch as a weekly procedure. Tractate Yadayim, "Hands," is concerned with a state of uncleanness which is not explicated in the Pentateuch.

Other tractates, though *nominally* related to the Pentateuch, contain laws which are unknown to the Pentateuch. Tractate Rosh ha-Shanah begins with the assertion that there are four New Years, even though the expression *Rosh ha-Shanah,* "New Year," is not to be found in the Pentateuch. Nor does the Pentateuch know of a New Year, even indirectly, for kings or the tithing of cattle or the reckoning of years or of the trees. And totally absent from the Pentateuch is any provision for a calendrical system based on the *observation* of the new moon as spelled out in the tractate. The Pentateuch knows nothing of witnesses to the birth of the moon; of their obligation to violate the sabbath, if need be, to reach Jerusalem in time to bear valid witness; or of a *bet din* which, after interrogating the witnesses, proclaimed the New Moon.

Nor is there any Pentateuchal warrant for much that is in Tractate Yoma, "Yom Kippur." Where, for example, is one to find in the Pentateuch any provision for the briefing of the High Priest by the emissaries of the *Bet Din,* an institution utterly unknown to the Pentateuch?

Or where is there in the Pentateuch any such procedure as that set down in tractate Yoma 7:1?

The High Priest then came to read [from the Torah] . . . The *Hazan ha-Kenesset* takes the book of the Torah and gives it to the *Rosh ha-Kenesset,* and the *Rosh ha-Kenesset* gives it to the *Segan,* and the *Segan* gives it to the High Priest, and the High Priest stands and receives it, reading it standing. He reads [the section beginning] "After the death . . ." (Leviticus 16) . . . "And on the tenth day . . ." (Leviticus 23:26-32), and he rolls up the scroll and places it in his bosom and says, "More than what I have read before you is written here."

"And on the tenth" . . . which is in the book of Numbers [literally: which is in that fifth of the Pentateuch dealing with the census] (29:7-11), he would say by heart. He would then recite over it the eight blessings: for the Law, for the Temple service, for the Thanksgiving, for the Forgiveness of Sin, and for the Sanctuary for itself, and for the Israelites for themselves, and for Jerusalem for itself, and for the priests for themselves; and for the rest, the prayer.

Likewise, we look in vain in the Pentateuch for the ceremony the High Priest is to perform when he enters the Holy of Holies on Yom Kippur:

They brought out to him the ladle and the fire-pan and he took his two hands full [of incense] and put it in the ladle, which was large according to the largeness [of his hand], or small according to the smallness [of his hand]; and such [alone] was the prescribed measure of the ladle. He took the fire-pan in his right hand and the ladle in his left. He went through the Sanctuary until he came to the space between the two curtains separating the Sanctuary from the Holy of Holies. And there was a cubit's space between them. R. Jose says: Only one curtain was there, for it is written, *And the veil shall divide for you between the holy place and the most holy.* The outer curtain was looped up on the south side and the inner one on the north side. He went along between them until he reached the north side; when he reached the north he turned round to the south and went on with the curtain on his left hand until he reached the Ark. When he reached the Ark he put the fire-pan between the two bars. *He heaped up the incense on the coals and the whole place became filled with smoke.* He came out by the way he went in, and in the outer space he prayed a short prayer. But he did not prolong his prayer lest he put Israel in terror. (Yom. 5:1; italics added)

This procedure is of especial significance, since we know from several tannaitic texts (Yom. 19*b*; Y. Yom. 1:5, Tosef. Yom. 1:8) that the Sadducees/Boethusians affirmed that the High Priest was to light the incense before entering the Holy of Holies and not within the Holy of Holies as set forth in the above-cited Mishnah. (See chapter 3, "The Tannaitic Literature," for the full texts.)

An analysis of the Mishnah thus reveals that it consists of (1) categories of law that have no Pentateuchal counterpart, (2) categories that have nominal, but not substantive, counterparts, (3) categories that have both nominal and substantive counterparts in the Pentateuch. These categories are succinctly confirmed in a precious Mishnaic text:

The [laws pertaining to] absolution of vows hover in the air, for they have nothing in Scripture on which to support themselves. The *halakhoth* dealing with the Sabbath, Festal offerings, Sacrilege are like mountains hanging by a hair, for whereas there is very little in Scripture, there are abundant *halakhoth*. [The *halakhoth* pertaining to] civil cases, and the [Temple] procedures, and cleanness, and uncleanness, and forbidden degrees [of consanguinity]—these do have [Scriptural verses] on which they can support themselves. But those [*halakhoth* having little or no support in Scripture] and those [which do have] are [equally] the essentials of the Law. (Hag. 1:8)

No less hovering in the air without Pentateuchal support is the Mishnaic affirmation of belief in the world to come and the resurrection of the dead—the ultimate reward for obeying the *halakhoth*. Yet this belief is stated starkly and without equivocation in the Mishnah: "All Israel has a share in the world to come, as it is said (Isaiah 60:21), 'And your people shall all be righteous, for ever they shall inherit the land. The branch of my planting, the work of my hands that I may be glorified'" (Sanh. 10:1).

There is no embarrassment here with the fact that the text says nothing of the world to come but only of the world that is. If Israel is righteous, then the people of Israel shall inherit the land forever. There is nothing in this verse which even remotely implies *eternal* life for the individual—only eternal life for the people of Israel as a whole. Yet the Mishnah does not hesitate to hang this dogma on a scriptural "hair."

Nor does the Mishnah hesitate to exclude from the world to come anyone who says that the resurrection of the dead is not derivable from the Torah (Sanh. 10:1). This, in effect, put the Sadducees, who rejected this belief because it was not articulated by Moses, on the same plane with those who asserted that the Torah was not from Heaven. The Written Law is thus made utterly dependent on the Unwritten Law! God had revealed a twofold, not a onefold, Law. Those who, like the Sadducees, rejected this concept were not included within "all Israel," even though they believed that the Torah was from Heaven. Their flesh may have been the flesh of Israel, but their spirit was the spirit of unbelief.

This non-Pentateuchal dogma of the world to come and resurrection is a core teaching of the Mishnah. Indeed, this belief is the cornerstone of the entire *halakhah* system. It was only because the true believer and true devotee of the twofold Law could hope for the immortality of his soul and the resurrection of his body that he was ready, willing, and able to yoke himself to the twofold Law and abide by its discipline.

The centrality of this belief is evident in several Mishnaic texts. Thus in tractate Peah 1:1 we read:

These are the things which a person eats the fruits thereof in this world, while the principle remains enduring for him in the world to come: Honoring father and mother, the doing of gracious acts, and the bringing about peace between man and his neighbor, but the study of the [twofold] Torah outranks them all.

Similarly, a person condemned to death is urged to make confession so that he might even at this last moment earn for himself a share in the world to come:

When the [condemned] was about ten cubits away from the stoning chamber, they would say unto him, "Confess," since it was the custom of those condemned to death to confess; for *whoever confesses has a share in the world to come.* For we have found that in the case of Achan that Joshua said to him, "My son, give glory unto the Lord God of Israel and give praise unto him *[we-ten lo todah].*" And Achan answered Joshua and said, "Of a truth, I have sinned against the Lord and this is what I did" (Joshua 7:20).

And how do we know that his confession expiated his sin? For it is said (Joshua 7:25), "And Joshua said, 'Why did you bring trouble on us? The Lord brings trouble on you this day.'" [The meaning is] *This* day you are troubled, but you are not to be troubled in the world to come.

If the convicted one does not know how to confess, they say to him, "Say [the following]: 'May my death be an expiation for all my transgressions.'" (Sanh. 6:2; italics added)

The belief in the resurrection of the dead was, in fact, so central that it was incorporated in the essential blessings of the *Tefillah,* the prayer par excellence, which came to be called the *amidah* or the *shemoneh esrae* (the eighteen benedictions). Thus we read in tractate Berakoth 5:2: "We make mention of the power of the rains in the blessing pertaining to the resurrection of the dead."

And as for the concomitant belief in the world to come, the formula uttered at the conclusion of the blessings said in the Temple was altered so as to allow for no ambiguity:

All those who used to conclude blessings in the Temple used to say, "From everlasting *[min ho-olam]*." But when the heretics perverted the truth and said there is one world only, they [the scholars] ordained that they should say "from everlasting to everlasting *[min ho-olam we-ad ha-olam]*." (Ber. 9:5)

Underlying all these discontinuities separating the Mishnah system from the Pentateuchal system is the fact that a scholar class is sitting in Moses' seat even though

Moses had never bestowed upon a scholar class any authority over God's Law. Such authority had been vouchsafed prophets and priests, but not scholars. Yet nowhere in the Mishnah do we find the *halakhah* expounded by either a prophetic or a priestly class. No *halakhah* is ever introduced with the formula "And the Lord spoke unto Shemaiah [or Abtalion or Hillel or Shammai] these words, saying . . ." or with the prophetic formula "Thus says the Lord. . . ." Nor do we find anywhere in the Mishnah the priesthood, as a class, exercising any authority, even in the Temple, that is not on sufferance of the scholar class.

The Mishnah is thus a repository exclusively of the teachings of a scholar class. And since these teachings are set forth as authoritative and binding, and since they are teachings which, for the most part, are not written down in the Pentateuch, they testify to a system of authority that is self-assumed, self-asserted, and self-validated. Such a self-generated, self-validating system—a system nowhere acknowledged or mandated in Scripture—could have emerged only in the wake of a deep and profound revolution, a revolution that transferred ultimate authority over the Law from the Aaronide-Zadokite priesthood to the scholar class of the twofold Law.

The Mishnah thus bears living witness to a revolutionary transformation by virtue of the chasm which separates its system of Law from the Pentateuchal system of Law, and its scholar class from the Prophets and Priests of Scriptures. *These discontinuities are so fundamental that they cannot be attributed to a slow, evolutionary process.* There was no inner logic within the Pentateuch that the sons of Aaron whom God had given authority over his statutes and judgments unto all eternity should make way for a scholar class whom God at no time acknowledges as even existing, much less as exercising power over his Law. Nor was there any inner logic that the Written Law, explicitly proclaimed by God himself as immutable, should be supplanted by whole categories of law not even mentioned in the Pentateuch.

The Mishnah testifies to a revolution simply by its existence, even though it never acknowledges that such a revolution occurred or indicates the moment in time when the scholar class with their twofold Law supplanted the Aaronide-Zadokite priesthood. So much of the Mishnah consists of anonymous teachings allowing for no precise dating that it would be rash to claim that one anonymous *halakhah* is early, another late. Yet the Mishnah testifies to a revolution led by a scholar class, proclaiming the twofold Law as the true and authentic revelation, and it also testifies to the fact that this scholar class was none other than the Pharisees.

As we have seen above (chapter 3, "The Tannaitic Literature"), the Mishnah has preserved several controversies between the Sadducees and the Pharisees. For our present purposes, we need focus our attention on only one of these, that dealing with whether or not Holy Scriptures render the hands unclean. The Sadducees, it will be recalled, rejected this dictum, while the Pharisees affirmed it.

Now what is striking is that this Pharisaic dictum is nowhere written down in the Pentateuch. Not only does the Pentateuch not acknowledge a category of "uncleanness" of hands, but it nowhere even remotely implies that the Law could in any way be the source of uncleanness. The Sadducees are thus simply reaffirming Scripture in rejecting the Pharisaic dictum that Holy Scriptures render the hands unclean. The Pharisees, for their part, affirm that a law not written down in the Law of Moses is nonetheless binding law. The Sadducees and Pharisees in the Mishnah are thus juxtaposed on the issue of the Written Law and the Unwritten Law, even as they are so juxtaposed by Josephus in *Antiquities.*

This particular controversy is of especial significance since, as pointed out earlier, it allows us to establish *internally* that the *Perushim*-Pharisees and the *Soferim-*

Scribes are one and the same. For when the dictum "Holy Scriptures render the hands unclean" is affirmed in the very same tractate (Yad. 3:2) but without the Sadducees being involved, it is referred to as the *dibre Soferim,* "the words of the *Soferim.*" Moreover, the *dibre Soferim* are explicitly distinguished from the *dibre Torah,* the words of the Written Torah, as enjoying an independent and coordinate relationship: "We do not logically deduce the words of the Torah from the words of the *Soferim;* nor the words of the *Soferim* from the words of the Torah; nor the words of the *Soferim* from the words of the *Soferim*" (Yad. 3:2).

It is thus evident that the "words of the *Soferim*" are self-justifying and self-validating. They need have no logical connection to Scripture. They need not even be logically consistent with other dicta of the *Soferim.* They are *intrinsically* authoritative by virtue of their source: the *Soferim.*

This transcendent status of the *Soferim* is confirmed whenever their dicta are specifically referred to in the Mishnah. Thus their teachings are more rigorously binding that those of the Written Torah, for "if one says that there is no need to put on phylacteries so as to transgress thereby the words of the Torah, he is free of guilt. But he who says that five *totafot* are required [rather than four] thereby adding to the number prescribed by the words of the *Soferim* is guilty." (Sanh. 11:3).

Similarly, the degrees of consanguinity established by the *Soferim* are regarded as inviolate (Yeb. 2:4; 9:3), even as their categories of uncleanness are regarded as no less binding than those set down by Scripture (Par. 11:4-6; Teh. 4:7; cf. Zab. 5:12).

The Mishnah thus confirms that the Pharisees-*Soferim* are the teachers of the twofold Law whose dicta are venerated by the subsequent teachers of the twofold Law. The Pharisees-*Soferim* are linked together with the *Hakhamim,* the Sages, with the schools of Shammai and Hillel, and with the individual *tannaim* as the teachers of a non-Pentateuchal system of authoritative law and doctrine. The dicta of the Pharisees–Scribes are incorporated in the Mishnah along with the dicta of subsequent teachers of the twofold Law as binding dicta. And what has been preserved of their dicta are exclusively laws not written down in the laws of Moses.

The Mishnah likewise confirms that the *Perushim-Soferim* were antecendent in time to the individual *tannaim* who flourished after the destruction of the Temple in A.D. 70. The Pharisees-Scribes are referred to as a class of scholars rather than by the names of the individual scholars themselves. This comports with the assumption that the Pharisees-Scribes hark back to the first stage in the evolution of the scholar class, a stage in which only the heads of the scholar class, the so-called *Zugoth,* were differentiated by name. It is a striking fact that virtually no names other than those of the *Zugoth,* "the Pairs," are recorded in the Mishnah prior to the generation of Rabbi Yohanan ben Zakkai—not even the names of the first generation of the scholars belonging to the schools of Shammai and Hillel. This anonymity of the scholar class prior to A.D. 70 is confirmed by Josephus, Paul, and the Gospels, who speak of Pharisees and/or Scribes but not of individual scholars—with the exception of such individual scholars as Samaias and Pollion or Simon son of Gamaliel or Gamaliel, who were the leaders and spokesmen of the scholar class.

The compiler of the Mishnah was thus aware that prior to 70, the scholar class functioned as a class and not as individuals. He was also aware that the Pharisees-*Soferim* were the venerated progenitors, "the Fathers" of the twofold Law. He was also aware that prior to the establishment of an hereditary *nesiut,* "princeship," "principate," following the death of Hillel the *Zugoth* system had flourished for five generations. This system was a nonhereditary, co-leadership system, with the *Nasi* representing the majority point of view and the *Ab Bet Din* (Father of the *Bet Din*) representing the minority

point of view. These co-leaders were called *Zugoth,* or
"Pairs." There were five generations of *Zugoth as the
following textus classicus* reveals:*

Jose ben Joezer used to say, *"lo lismokh,"* Jose ben Johanan used
to say *"lismokh."*** Jose ben Penahyah used to say *"lo lismokh,"*
Nitai the Arbelite used to say *"lismokh."* Judah ben Tabbai used
to say *"lo lismokh,"* Shimeon b. Shetah used to say, *"lismokh."*
Shemaiah used to say *"lismokh,"* Abtalion used to say *"lo
lismokh."* Hillel and Manahem did not disagree. Menahem left
and Shammai entered. Shammai used to say *"lo lismokh,"* Hillel
used to say *"lismokh."* The first mentioned [of each Pair] were
Nesiim [Princes] and the others "Fathers" of the *Bet Din.* (Hag.
2:2)

If we allow approximately thirty years for a generation,
the *Zugoth* system flourished for about 150 years. This
would mean that the compiler of the Mishnah was aware
that the *Zugoth* system, and the *Bet Din* it presupposes,
began around 150 B.C., hence during the Hasmonean
Revolt. This dating coincides with Josephus' mention of
the Pharisees for the first time, even as it is compatible
with the decree of the *synagoge megale,* the *Kenesset
ha-Gedolah* investing Simon with the High Priesthood in
141 B.C. Indeed, the establishment of the *Bet Din* as a
permanent institution headed by the *Zugoth* may well
have gone hand-in-hand with Simon's investiture.

The Mishnah thus reveals itself to be a source no less
confirming of the Pharisaic Revolution than I Maccabees
and Josephus. As has been demonstrated, the Mishnah is

---

*The *Zugoth* are mentioned from time to time in the Mishnah and
associated with specific legislation. Cf. Eduyoth 4:1 (Yose ben Joezer);
Satah 9:9 (Yose ben Joezer and Yose ben Jochanan); Ta'an. 3:8, Sanh. 6:4
(Simon ben Shetah); Eduyoth 1:3, 5:6 (Shemaiah and Abtalion); Sheb.
10:3, Hag. 2:2, Git. 4:3, B. M. 5:9, Eduyoth 1:1-4, 'Arak. 9:4, Nid. 1:1
(Hillel); Ma'as Sh. 2:4, 9, 'Or. 2:5, Suk. 2:8, Eduyoth 1:1, 2, 3, 4, 7, 8, 10,
11, Kel. 22:4, Nid. 1:1 (Shammai).
**The Hebrew terms *lismokh* and *lo lismokh* are intentionally left
untranslated so as to avoid debate over the meaning, which, for the
purposes of this analysis, is largely irrelevant.

the repository of laws not written down in the Law of Moses; it is noncongruent with the Pentateuch formally, stylistically, linguistically, and substantively; its dicta are those of a scholar class exercising an authority nowhere bestowed upon them in Scripture; it regards the Pharisees-Scribes as the progenitors of the twofold Law and explicitly accords to the *dibre Soferim,* "the words of the *Soferim,*" an authority independent of Scripture and elevated above it; and finally, by recording five generations of *Zugoth* who presided over the non-Pentateuchal *Bet Din,* the Mishnah reveals that the scholar class of the twofold Law emerged during the Hasmonean Revolt.

The Mishnah, when set alongside the Pentateuch, the Prophets, and the Hagiographa, shows itself to be *absolutely* incongruent. This incongruence is so fundamental that only a revolution can account for a body of law and lore that purports to be the authoritative teachings of *the* Law. This supposition is doubly confirmed when we bear in mind that until the destruction of the Temple in 70 the Sadducees were still active champions of the literal Written Law, rejected the unwritten laws as spurious, and regarded the claims of a scholar class to sit on Moses' seat as fraudulent.

Without a revolution, there could have been no Mishnah. The Mishnah itself testifies to this proposition. The question we must face is thus not whether there was a revolution, but when and why the revolution occurred. It is here that the Mishnah as a work not written down before the beginning of the third century and as a repository of anonymous, nondatable legislation obstructs a clear-cut, neat answer to the question of when and why. But though obstructive, the Mishnah does not block us completely; for the Mishnah presupposes throughout that, as a *system,* the twofold Law was operative from the time of the first *Zug,* "Pair," and that this system was energized by a self-validating scholar class. The fact that we may not be able to determine when any *specific* oral laws set down in the Mishnah were promulgated does not mean that the *system* of oral laws was not operating from the period of the Hasmonean Revolt. Even if every single oral law in the Mishnah was formulated at a late date, this would in no way alter the fact that other oral laws had been operative, for the Mishnah itself reveals how frequently the *halakhah* underwent change.

Not only does the Mishnah presuppose throughout that the system of oral laws was operative long before the emergence of the schools of Hillel and Shammai, but it recalls a phase of the development of the *halakhah* which was structurally at variance with that which operated *after* the establishment of a hereditary *Nesuit,* or Principate. This phase had been marked, as pointed out above by the *Zugoth* system. This system provided for an elected, not hereditary, *Nasi* and *Ab Bet Din* to preside over the *Bet Din* and to serve as the spokesmen for the scholar class. The names of each *Zug* are preserved in the Mishnah. Hillel and Shammai were the last *Zug.*

With their death, a major structural alteration followed. Hillel's son Gamaliel became the hereditary *Nasi* with the title Rabban, and two schools, those of Shammai and Hillel, were allowed to offer alternative legal options. Hitherto, during the period of the *Zugoth,* the laws were determined by a majority vote of the *Bet Din* and were the only laws deemed authoritative.

The structural break is clearly recorded in the Mishnah. The *Zugoth* system is phased out even though the Pairs continued to be venerated as the esteemed teachers of the twofold Law. Hence, unless we are willing to posit that the compiler of the Mishnah invented the *Zugoth* phase and imagined a structure which had never existed, we are forced to conclude that the recollection of the *Zugoth* phase is a true recollection and that the *Zugoth* system reaches back to the period of the Hasmonean Revolt.

And supporting this assumption are I Maccabees and Josephus. I Maccabees testifies to a revolutionary break in the Zadokite High Priestly line when a *synagoge megale* without any Pentateuchal warrant elevated Simon to the High Priesthood. Josephus, in turn, testifies to the fact that the Pharisaic system of unwritten laws were operative when John Hyrcanus became High Priest and to the fact that the Pharisees were regarded by John Hyrcanus as his teachers.

Hence, both I Maccabees and Josephus would lead us to anticipate precisely what the Mishnah itself attests, namely, that the *Zugoth* go back to the time of the Hasmonean Revolt. Equivalently, if we were to begin with the testimony of the Mishnah, we would have calculated that sometime during the Hasmonean Revolt a dramatic revolutionary transformation had taken place when a non-Pentateuchal system of law was promulgated by a scholar class, who, without any Mosaic authorization, had placed themselves in Moses' seat. And since this novel system and this new class are presupposed by I Maccabees, Josephus, and the Mishnah; and since the Sadducee-Pharisee interlock presupposes that the Pharisees must have emerged in tandem with the Sadducees; and since the Sadducees could only have been born out a of a rejection of the Zadokite line; and since we can pinpoint this rejection as having occurred when first Jonathan and then Simon served as High Priests, we must posit that the Pharisees were those who declared the non-Zadokite Hasmoneans to be legitimate High Priests by authority of the Unwritten Law.

There is still a fourth body of sources, namely, the New Testament, which confirms, however indirectly, the Pharisaic Revolution. Paul's Epistles to the Philippians and the Galatians were written several decades before the destruction of the Temple. Hence, when Paul refers to his having been "as to the law a Pharisee" and to his precocious commitment to the *paradosis,* he is taking us even futher back in time to the very turn of the millennium. This would necessarily mean that Pharisaism had been fully consolidated as the definitive form of Judaism long before Paul was born. And since he differentiates this form from *other* forms of Judaism by virtue of its adherence to the *paradosis,* and since the *paradosis* consisted of laws not written down in the Law of Moses, its origins must be embedded within a revolutionary matrix. Similarly, the fact that Paul utilizes the very same proof-texting mode as that found in the Mishnah, without any qualification, and since this proof-texting mode is non-Pentateuchal and nonscriptural, it bespeaks the revolutionary activity of the Pharisees as having occurred long before his day.

The Synoptic Gospels likewise confirm the Pharisaic Revolution as one harking back so far in time that none of the Gospel writers raise any questions about the legitimacy of the Scribes-Pharisees. Jesus and his followers may have quarreled with them and may have deeply resented their rejection of Jesus as the Christ, but they do not challenge the Scribes-Pharisees on the grounds that they were a scholarly class which had only recently emerged with their teachings of the *paradosis* of the elders. Not at all. The Scribes-Pharisees are taken for granted as the authoritative teachers. Indeed, the author of Matthew 23, who is most rejective of the Pharisees, nonetheless insists that they sit in Moses' seat and that they sit there by divine right—"Therefore, do all which they tell you to do."

And finally, the Gospel writers, like Paul, quote Scripture in the Pharisaic mode. The proof texts are introduced again and again with the formula "as it is said," and they are freely drawn from all levels of Scripture, operating on the Pharisaic assumption that the Pentateuch, the Prophets, and the Hagiographa are a single, mutually reinforcing revelation.

It is thus evident from the New Testament that the Pharisees must have been sitting in Moses' seat long before Jesus' day, that they had long been differentiated from the Sadducees, that they had from time immemorial held to the belief in the resurrection and had clung to the *paradosis* of the elders.

The data pertaining to the Scribes-Pharisees in the New Testament are thus fully compatible with the data from I Maccabees, Josephus, and the Mishnah, the very data which had impelled us to posit the Pharisaic Revolution and to date its occurrence sometime during the Hasmonean Revolt.

Having established that (1) there had been a revolution sometime during the Hasmonean Revolt; (2) it was led by a scholar class; (3) this class was unauthorized by the Pentateuch; (4) it proclaimed the authority of laws not written down in the Pentateuch; and (5) through a non-Pentateuchal body, a *synagoge megale*, a new, non-Zadokite High Priestly line was legitimatized, we must seek to find an answer to the questions of the "why" and the "how" of the Pharisaic Revolution. But since none of our sources explicitly state that a revolution occurred, they can scarcely be depended upon to give us any data ask to why there was a revolution and as to how that revolution was successfully carried out. We must therefore work back from the structure of the phenomenon itself to the "why" and the "how."

The phenomenon reveals the following revolutionary components: (1) the Unwritten Law, the *paradosis;* (2) a scholar class sitting in Moses' seat; (3) exclusively non-Pentateuchal modes for teaching and for transmitting the Unwritten Law *(halakhah)* and lore *(aggadah);* (4) non-Pentatuechal language and formulas; (5) proof texting; (6) non-Pentateuchal institutions (*Kenesset ha-Gedolah, Bet Din,* synagogue); (7) non-Pentateuchal concepts (the world to come, resurrection). Structurally, the Pharisaic system is a differentiated system by virtue of its noncongruence with the Pentateuch, the Prophets, or the Hagiographa. This differentiation is evident when we put the Mishnah alongside Scriptures. Hence, in seeking the "why," we must search for an answer that will make intelligible the need for such a marked differentiation from scriptural models.

The phenomenon likewise reveals a tenacious clinging to scriptural elements. Thus, God's revelation of the Law to Moses is reconfirmed as unalterable; the prophets are held in the highest esteem because God spoke with them; and the Hagiographa is viewed as a rich repository of wisdom and inspiration because it was believed to express the Spirit of God. Indeed, so highly revered is Scripture as the very word of God that it is drawn upon for compelling proof texts, supportive of Pharisaic teachings. In answering the question as to "why" the Pharisaic Revolution, we must be able to account for this linkage.

Similarly, we have to make intelligible the preservation of the Temple cultus, the reconfirmation of the exclusive right of the Aaronides to offer sacrifices and to eat the heave-offering, and the continued underwriting of the system of ritual purity.

In short, we must account not only for the Pharisaic Revolution but also for the fact that it was a revolution committed as much to preservation as to innovation.

Let us then proceed, step by step, from the phenomenon to the explanation.

Firstly, since the innovative components are non-scriptural, we must look elsewhere for possible models. In doing so, we are struck by the fact that these components have Greco-Roman analogues:

1. The Pharisaic scholar class has its equivalent in the philosopher-sage, philosopher-statesman, philosopher–law-giver, and legislator of the Hellenistic-Roman world. This resemblance is explicitly pointed out by Josephus when he compares the Pharisees with the Stoics.

2. The teacher-disciple relationship, which is likewise non-Pentateuchal, is a mirror image of the relationship between Socrates and Plato and between the Stoic sages and their students.

3. Whereas the concept of unwritten laws was widespread among the Greek and Roman philosophers, it is nowhere articulated in Scripture.

4. Such law-making institutions as the *Kenesset ha-Gedolah* and the *Bet Din* are very reminiscent of the Greco-Roman legislatures, especially the Roman Senate. Indeed the Greek rendering of *Bet Din* was *boule,* the term Josephus continuously uses for Roman Senate.*

5. The formulation of laws as individual items, freed of any narratival connection, is the very formulation characteristic of the legal pronouncements of Greco-Roman legal bodies.

6. The belief that the *individual,* after death, enters into another world, whether Hades or the Elysium fields, along with the belief in the immortality of the soul echo and reecho throughout Greco-Roman literature.

7. Proof-texting was widespread in the Greco-Roman world, whether from ancient authorites to substantiate historical facts or whether from Homer, the tragedians, or the great philosophers.

It is thus apparent that whereas the components of the Pharisaic Revolution are incongruent with Scriptures, they are congruent with Greco-Roman models. It would therefore follow that the Pharisaic Revolution was seeking to incorporate within Judaism major structural components and major conceptual notions prevalent in the Greco-Roman world. These elements were essentially (1) a legislature *(Bet Din-Boule),* consisting of legal authorities, charged with responsibility for preserving, modifying, and developing the Law, whose authority did not derive from either priestly or inherited status, and (2) an elevated notion of the significance and importance of the individual and his yearnings and aspirations. The Pharisees must have been dissatisfied

---

*See E. Rivkin, *"Beth Din, Boule, Sanhedrin:* A Tragedy of Errors," *Hebrew Union College Annual,* XLVI (1975), 181-99.

with the Pentateuch because, by concentrating all authority in the hands of the priesthood, it made no provision for an ongoing legislative process. The Pentateuchal system was bogged down in a commitment to immutable laws administered by a priestly class whose power, authority, and privileges were tightly tied to preserving a system built on the joint interests of priests and peasants. It was a system that was not at all geared to fast-paced urbanization and its destructive impact on the individual, loosened from the soil, and dislodged from his rural moorings. The Pentateuch focuses almost exclusively on the agricultural blessings that will follow on obedience to God's Law and the agricultural disaster which the sinful people will reap should they prove disloyal to Yahweh. The ultimate punishment is to be driven from the land; the ultimate reward, to gather in overabundant harvests in peace and tranquility. And though the individual is promised a long and fruitful life, and though he is to benefit from the blessings which God will shower on an obedient Israel, there is no provision made for that individual who, though law-abiding himself, is swept into exile along with the majority who have sinned. Thus, salvation was ultimately dependent not on what the individual did but what the community of Israel as a whole did. This flaw in the Pentateuchal system distressed the psalmist who strained to reassure the individual that God's justice somehow extended to the individual as well. It so unsettled the author of the book of Job that he despaired of a resolution. And though this flaw may have been most grievously felt by the artisan, craftsman, and shopkeeper whose activities are nowhere taken into account in the Pentateuch, it was not excluded from the day-to-day experience of the peasant, especially when the coming and going of foreign armies disrupted the tranquil cycle of sowing and reaping.

The "why" of the Pharisaic Revolution, namely, the growing incongruence between the structure of experience and the structure of the Pentateuch, and the "when" of the Pharisaic Revolution, namely, sometime during the Hasmonean Revolt, have been dealt with. We are now left with the most difficult question of all: *How did a revolution of such magnitude take place?* How indeed was an upstart scholar class able to proclaim such revolutionary doctrines and to defy so brazenly the explicit provisions of the very Pentateuch which they themselves were reaffirming as God's immutable Written Law? How indeed were they able to gain so quickly, almost instantaneously, the enthusiastic support of the people, who for several hundred years had, without questioning, supported the Aaronide-Pentateuchal system as mandated by God for all generations? These questions, posed without any sources at our disposal to answer them, virtually defy resolution. Yet these questions must be dealt with, since the success of the Pharisees testifies to the fact that somehow or other they were able to seat themselves in Moses' seat with the acclamation, rather than the reproach, of the masses.

Perhaps the way out of our impasse is to focus on how the Pentateuch and the other books of the Bible may have served to make the claims of this scholar class seem less audacious and revolutionary than they really were. First let us consider the Pentateuch. Its claim to being the very word of God written down by Moses was not challenged by the Pharisees. They insisted, even as had their Aaronide predecessors, that God had chosen Aaron to be the father of an eternal priesthood and had made an everlasting covenant with Phinehas. But what the Pharisees noted was that within the very same Pentateuch, God had chosen not Aaron's son Eleazar but a nonpriest, Joshua, to succeed Moses as the leader of Israel. Ultimate authority was thus vested in a prophet-like figure, and not in an Aaronide priest. It is Joshua to whom God speaks when Moses dies; it is Joshua who conquers the land; it is Joshua who has the final word. Indeed, nowhere in the book of Joshua does God ever speak directly to either Eleazar or Phinehas. And if one proceeds from book to book of the Bible, God makes his will known to judges, like Gideon, and from prophet to prophet, one never finds God speaking directly to an Aaronide! The Pharisees could thus quote Scripture to prove that the transmission of ultimate authority had been from non-Aaronide Moses to non-Aaronide Joshua to non-Aaronide elders and to non-Aaronide prophets. The Aaronides, far from being the legitimate spokesmen of God, could be regarded as usurpers!

Second, the Pharisees could draw on the historical and prophetic books to demonstrate that those exercising ultimate authority had again and again carried out actions or issued commands that were at variance with the Written Law: Elijah offered up sacrifices on a high place even though he was not an Aaronide and even though the Temple was standing and functioning in Jerusalem. Similarly, Ezekiel, on the basis of prophetic authority, proclaimed a whole series of laws at variance with those in the Pentateuch. Indeed, the prophets never hesitated to do or say whatever Yahweh commanded them. And since the Aaronides regarded the prophets as loyal adherents to Yahweh—Ben Sira lists them all—the Pharisees could triumphantly claim that the words and deeds of the prophets bespeak unwritten laws!

Third, the Pharisees could point out the many contradictions within the Pentateuch itself which allowed for alternative options.

Fourth, the Pharisees could take advantage of the inherent ambiguity of language, insisting that the meaning could be "this" rather than "that." Similarly, there were endless possibilities in now stressing precise, now imprecise, usage.

Fifth, the Pharisees could confront the Aaronides with procedures and practices that were in vogue and taken for granted but which were not explicitly written down in the Pentateuch. What for the Aaronides was necessary inference, for the Pharisees was evidence of nonwritten laws. A most vivid example of such a potential confrontation involved the calendar. Although nowhere in the Pentateuch is the numbered-month calendar made explicit, it must have operated in a specific way. For the Aaronides, the fact that the Pentateuch does not explicate this calendar could be brushed aside as irrelevant. But for the Pharisees, the claim for this Aaronide calendar could be challenged on the grounds that it is not spelled out in the Pentateuch. Hence, a radically different calendar not only was allowable but was in consonance with the named months used by Haggai, Malachi, and Nehemiah.

Sixth, the Pharisees were able to find, snuggled within the historical and prophetic books of the Bible, hints, allusions—bordering at times on the explicit—to the belief in immortality. Thus, Enoch simply is taken by God (Gen. 5:24); the witch of Endor draws Samuel out of the earth (I Sam. 28:8-19); Elijah resurrects a child (I Kings 17:17-24), and he is himself swept into heaven on the wings of a chariot (II Kings 2:9-12); Ezekiel envisions the coming alive of the dry bones of those long dead (Ezek. 37:1-14); and Job hints of seeing his God when his flesh is gone (Job 19:25-27). Intimations of immortality and resurrection such as these could offset the failure of the Pentateuch to spell out these notions concretely and explicity. So long, however, as the non-Pentateuchal books of the Bible were deemed to be part and parcel of a single revelation, the Pentateuch could be read in the light of the prophets. And since we know from the Mishnah that the teachers of the twofold Law cite proof texts from the Prophets and the Hagiographa as no less authoritative than those drawn from the Pentateuch, we can assume that this proof-texting method was forged in the crucible of the revolution. It was a method that put the Sadducees on the defensive; for it pitted revelation against revelation, divine word against divine word, sacred authority against sacred authority. Brandishing proof texts, the scholar class could hardly be looked upon as revolutionaries. Indeed, they appeared to be zealous defenders of the faith, seeking to restore legitimate authority rather than undermining it. The Pharisees, so it seemed, were the traditionalists; the Aaronides, the innovators!

Seventh—and closely linked to the above—the Pharisees shattered the contextual matrix of Scripture when they adopted their mode of proof-texting. A biblical verse was considered to be a discrete entity, which could be lifted out of context and utilized as a meaning in itself. It could thus be used, either alone or in linkage with other biblical verses, as proof of a law or a doctrine. As such, it was immune to challenge from the verse which preceded and followed. Scriptures thus became a veritable arsenal, bristling with verses which could be used with lethal effect against the Sadducees.

When, therefore, we raise the question of the "how" of the Pharisaic Revolution, we can answer by pointing to the conjunction of pressing need (a system of Judaism structured to cope creatively with disruptive change) with historical opportunity (the collapse of traditional High Priestly leadership) with the determination and the ingenuity of a class thoroughly conversant in Holy Scriptures. When therefore the crisis of leadership threatened to extinguish the belief in the one and only God, the Pharisees were able to find within the Pentateuch, the Prophets, and the Hagiographa all the justification they needed to seat themselves in Moses' seat.

But, it may be asked, what of the organizational means by which the Pharisees marshalled the people behind their teachings so that they could assert their new-claimed authority effectively? Once again our sources are tight-lipped. I and II Maccabees tell us in considerable detail of an armed uprising led by the Hasmoneans, not the Pharisees, while Josephus largely paraphrases the account as given in I Maccabees. And as for the Mishnah, it has no interest whatsoever in interconnected history. There is the festival of Hannukah which is to be observed, but no chronicle narrating any of the events.

Yet we know that a revolution must have occurred during the period of the Hasmonean Revolt, and if it occurred, its leaders must have found the means for carrying it through.

The sources, however, do not leave us totally without recourse. I Maccabees tells us of a *synagoge megale* which elevated Simon to the High Priesthood. The Mishnah and the Tannaitic Literature likewise recollect the *Kenesset ha-Gedolah* as a body held in the highest esteem, which functioned *before* the time of the *Zugoth*. Among the acts of the *Kenesset ha-Gedolah* was the canonization of the books of the Prophets and the Hagiographa. It was thus a body exercising awesome authority.

Furthermore, in the Mishnah Yoma—cited in full above (chapter 3, "The Tannaitic Literature")—we read of the *hazan* of the *Kenesset* handing a copy of the Torah to the head of the *Kenesset* who, in turn, hands it over to the *segan*, who hands it to the High Priest who then reads from it as part of the prescribed ritual of the Day of Atonement—a ritual not prescribed by the Pentateuch.

And finally we find, after the Hasmonean Revolt, but not before, the *bet ha-kenesset*, the synagogue, active and flourishing.

Now what is striking is that the term *kenesset* is never used in Scriptures. The biblical words for an assembly are *edah, kahal,* and *kehillah,* not *kenesset.* Indeed, the term is known to us only through the tannaitic and cognate literatures. Hence the very usage *Kenesset ha-Gedolah* and *bet ha-kenesset* testifies to nonbiblical institutions.

If, then, we posit that the *synagoge megale,* the Great Synagogue, was a constituent assembly convoked to designate Simon as High Priest, though not of the Phinehas-Zadok line, then we may also posit that this non-Pentateuchal body also established the *Bet Din ha-Gadol,* the great *Boule,* or Senate, to exercise ultimate authority over the twofold Law. Such an act by the *Kenesset ha-Gedolah,* the Great Synagogue, would account for the fact that the Mishnah traces the *Zugoth,* the Pairs, back to this very time, and affirms that the first-mentioned was the *Nasi,* i.e., Prince, of the *Bet Din,* while the second mentioned was the *Ab Bet Din,* the Father of the *Bet Din.* Likewise, the fact that the *synagoge megale* was a constituent assembly and met for only a few days would explain why it was so venerated in the Tannaitic Literature even though there was no recollection of its having been a permanent body, such as the *Bet Din-Boule.*

If, further, we take note of the role of the *hazan* of the *Kenesset,* and of the *rosh* of the *Kenesset* vis-à-vis the High Priest on Yom Kippur, do we not have here some symbolic act which goes back to the moment when the scholar class first exercised their authority over the High Priest and the cultus by a public act in which the Torah is transmitted by the *hazan* of the *Kenesset* and the *rosh ha-Kenesset* to the High Priest who is to read from it as a necessary part of the ritual, even though such a reading is not prescribed in the Pentateuch?

Furthermore, if we posit the *Kenesset ha-Gedolah,* the Great Synagogue, to have been a constituent assembly, should we not consider the likelihood that the *bet ha-kenesseth,* the synagogue, was, in origin, the place where individual groupings of the Pharisees and their followers met to plan, to promote, and to pray for the success of their efforts? Like the conventicles of the Puritan Revolt, the committees of correspondence of the American Revolution, and the Jacobin clubs of the French Revolution, the *kenessioth,* the assemblies of the Pharisees and their followers, spun out a network of associations to attain their goals as they supported, with arms and prayers, the uprising of the Hasmoneans.

The "how" of the Pharisaic Revolution thus blends with the "when" and the "why." The ripening of need coincided with historical opportunity—the collapse of priestly leadership. This occurred when Jason bought the High Priesthood for himself from Antiochus and had Onias III, the rightful incumbent, exiled. This was a flagrant violation of Pentateuchal Law, not by alien outsiders but by the brother of the High Priest himself. This scandalous breach of the divine Law was further widened when Meneleus bought the High Priesthood for himself and ousted Jason. And since Meneleus was even willing to allow sacrifices of swine's flesh to Zeus to be offered up on the altar, the people were without legitimate High Priests to lead them. The situation was thus ripe for a new class of leaders to solve the leadership crisis by sitting themselves in Moses' seat and by proclaiming that God had given two Laws, not one—the *immutable* Written Law and the *flexible* Unwritten Law—that he had bestowed authority over this twofold Law, not to Aaron and his sons, but to the deserving leadership class of each age—Moses, Joshua, the Elders, the Prophets, and now the Pharisaic scholar class—and that he had promised eternal life for the soul and the resurrection of the body of each individual who had proved his loyalty to this *internalized* twofold Law.[1]

Chapter VII

On the Cathedra of Moses

The Pharisaic Revolution was a revolution indeed! A scholar class had gained ascendency over the Law and had reduced the Aaronide priesthood to cultic functionaries—a scholar class never referred to in the Pentateuch or in the historical books of the Bible or in the Prophets or the Hagiographa. It was a scholar class unmentioned in Ben Sira, unknown to Daniel, and unnoted by Josephus until the time of Jonathan the Hasmonean. Their unwritten laws are attested to in no pre-Hasmonean source, and their detractors and opponents, the Sadducees, are nowhere to be found in pre-Hasmonean literature. Yet in the early years of John Hyrcanus, the unwritten laws the Pharisees had transmitted from the Fathers, the *paradosis,* were the laws governing the people—laws deemed so authoritative that the masses arose in revolt against the Hasmonean family when John Hyrcanus abrogated them and Alexander Jannaeus persisted in nullifying them. The Scribes-Pharisees had seated themselves on the cathedra of Moses, and in doing so, they spun off a mutation so powerful that to this day this revolutionary form of Judaism, and not the unmediated Judaism of the Pentateuch, is regarded by all Jews as "traditional" Judaism.

This achievement, by any measure, was no mean feat, for the Pharisees never held sovereign power. They may have been responsible for legitimatizing the Hasmonean High Priesthood, but they were never themselves High Priests. They may have underwritten the governing powers of Simon the Hasmonean, but they were not themselves the governors. They may even have acquiesced in acknowledging Salome Alexandra as queen, but they were themselves no monarchs. They led no troops in battle, even though they may have inspired them. They did not send forth ambassadors, even though they may have approved of their missions. They may have been, at times, the power behind the High Priesthood or the throne, but only because they had stirred the masses of people with their "good news" of a twofold Law, and of its promise of eternal life and resurrection. The Pharisees were powerful because they had revealed the road to life eternal, a road whose milestones were marked by the fulfillment of the commandments of the twofold Law. Indeed, the word they coined for the Unwritten Law, the Law which was a prerequisite for life beyond the grave, was *halakhah,* "the walk," "the road," "the way."

The Pharisees were powerful, yet the very source of their power, the Unwritten Law, has effectively barred scholars from fully comprehending, or even acknowledging, it. The Pharisees wrote down neither their Oral Law or their Oral Lore, since their commitment to oral transmission was a principled one. It was necessary to maintain this principle inviolate lest they, the Pharisees, be charged with violating the Pentateuchal command forbidding any addition to or subtraction from the laws which Moses had written down. To such charges, the Pharisees could plead innocent, for they had added nothing to the written laws; nor had they deleted any written laws. Indeed, they affirmed, as vehemently as did the Sadducees, that not one jot or tittle of the Written Torah was to be altered. Their teachings were unwritten. They had been transmitted orally, and they would continue to be transmitted orally. There was thus no violation here of Pentateuchal writ, so long as the Pharisees did not insert their *halakhah* or *aggadah* in, or append them to, the five books of Moses as a sixth or seventh book. Since their hallmark was their oral teaching, the Pharisees could leave no written records of their Law and Lore. Hence, the very source of their power, the Unwritten Law and Lore, virtually makes it impossible for scholars to document, with contemporary sources, that power. The *halakhah* and *aggadah* are found in the Mishnah, the Tosefta, and subsequent literature, but these were written down long after the Sadducees had vanished as a force to be reckoned with.

To compound the dilemma, the Pharisees, in their efforts to sharply demarcate the Written from the Oral Law, meticulously refrained from adopting *any* biblical models for their unwritten teachings. As pointed out above, they devised their own formulas for expressing the *halakhah,* and they fashioned their own mode for rendering the *aggadah.* They rejected the historical narrative for the episode, the pericope, and the item. They deliberately turned away from poetry. They even disallowed orally transmitted chronicles since, even though unwritten, the chronicle, by following a biblical model, might open the Pharisees to the charge by the Sadducees that they, the Pharisees, were arrogating to themselves biblical modes and forms. As a consequence, there were no unwritten histories equivalent to the books of Joshua, Samuel, or Kings—only episodic snatches, structural markings and residuals, and occasional historical mementos.

And as if these barriers were not enough to block access to the history of the Pharisees and their teachings, the teachers of the Oral Law looked upon historical events as largely irrelevant, for the ultimate test of God's concern was to be in the world to come and not in this world. Here on earth the evil individual might reap a harvest of goodly things, but in the world to come, his pain, anguish, and wretchedness would stretch out unto all eternity. By contrast, the righteous individual might harvest wretchedness in this world, only to reap joys unending in the world to come. And on that day when the dead would rise up from their graves, the good soul would find itself in a new body free of pain and immune to aging, while the evil soul, having no such body to return to, staggered tormentedly through the aeons of time. Terrestrial history was thus, for the Pharisees, transient and without meaning. What counted was the life worthy of the world to come, the dogged trudging on the road to life eternal, the surmounting of every external and internal obstacle barring the way to the day of the resurrection. The Patriarchs had lived such paradigmatic lives and they were even now with their Father in heaven; Moses had lived such a life and was even now basking in celestial bliss; the prophets had lived such lives and were even now awaiting the day of resurrection; the teachers of the twofold Law lived such lives as they yearned for the life which death could never snatch away. The life and death of nations, the flurry of pointless happenings, the ebb and flow of directionless events, the struttings of mortal kings and finite emperors, the panting and puffing of ephemeral rulers, the rise and fall of tinsel civilizations—of what value were they when weighed alongside the righteousness of the *halakhah*-abiding, the goodness of the pious, the virtue of the sturdy believer? These lived lives above the jostlings of historical events, the constraints of time-bound structures, the happenstance of occurrences. What need, then, for the Pharisees to transmit their history if time, structure, and process are only peripheral and tangential to salvation? Facing such sturdy barriers to a reconstruction of the history of the Pharisees, the historian is caught in a cul-de-sac from which there is seemingly no escape.

Yet if we are willing to settle for only the briefest outline of the history of the Pharisees, we can discern, despite the sparseness of our sources, five phases and two structural stages:

1. The Pharisaic Revolution, which went hand-in-hand with the Hasmonean Revolt (*ca.* 167-142 B.C.). This phase is attested to by Josephus, the Tannaitic Literature, and I Maccabees.

2. The Pharisaic-Hasmonean coalition (142-*ca.*110 B.C.). During this period the Pharisees as the legitimizers of the Hasmonean priesthood and as the supporters of their right to govern are acknowledged by Simon (143-134 B.C.) and John Hyrcanus (134-104 B.C.) as the religious leaders of the people whose unwritten laws were the law of the land. This phase is attested to by Josephus explicitly in the case of John Hyrcanus, implicitly in Simon's case.

3. The split with the John Hyrcanus and the violent uprising against Alexander Jannaeus (103-76 B.C.). This phase is narrated by Josephus in some detail.

4. The Grand Compromise, following on the accession of Salome Alexandra as Queen, when the Pharisees were restored to power and their unwritten laws were reinstituted. Josephus is explicit in his account of the settlement.

5. The doctrine of the two realms. Following on the death of Salome Alexandra, the Pharisees acknowledge autonomy of the secular state in return for autonomy in the religious sphere. They thus had no compunction in switching their support from the Hasmoneans to the Herodians; nor did they challenge the sovereign rights of the Roman procurators or of King Agrippa. So long as the sovereign, whoever he might be, did not obstruct the Scribes-Pharisees from teaching the unwritten laws or block their teaching the "good news" of life eternal or interfere with their distinctive institutions, the *Bet Din* and the synagogue, the Scribes-Pharisees were willing to concede that the state authority was legitimate and deserved the loyalty of its Jewish subjects. This phase lasted till the outbreak of the revolt against Rome when some Pharisaic leaders sided, however reluctantly, with the insurgents. Josephus attests to this phase when he

informs us of the support which Pollion and Samaias gave to Herod against Antigonus the Hasmonean, and of the decision by the Pharisees that the people cooperate with the taking of the census ordered by Gaius.

Concomitant with these phases affecting the relationship of the Pharisees to state sovereignty, were two structural stages in the development of the scholar class itself:

1. The phase of the *Zugoth* ("Pairs"). This phase was ushered in with the Pharisaic Revolution when the *Bet Din ha-Gadol* was established as the *Boule*-Senate of the Scribes-Pharisees. The first named of each pair was the *Nasi*, or Prince of the *Bet Din ha-Gadol,* while the second named was called the *Ab Bet Din* (Father of the *Bet Din).* With only a few exceptions, the *halakhoth* promulgated by the *Bet Din ha-Gadol* were issued as the *halakhoth* of the entire *Bet Din ha-Gadol* and were not attributed to individual scholars, not even the *Nasi* or the *Ab Bet Din.* Furthermore, aside from the *Nasi* and the *Ab Bet Din,* the names of individual scholars are not known to us. Nor are titles, other than *Nasi* or *Ab Bet Din* used for the members of the *Bet Din ha-Gadol.* Neither they nor the *Nasi* and *Ab Bet Din* are ever called *Rabban* or *Rabbi.* It also appears that the *Nasi* representd the majority, while the *Ab Bet Din* represented the minority, and that until the second phase, the principle which divided the *Bet Din ha-Gadol* was that of whether it was necessary *le-smokh* or not *le-smokh* (see above p. 236). For on the one occasion when both members of the *Zug* were in agreement on this principle, that is, each member of the Pair affirmed *le-smokh,* one of them had to step aside to allow for another incumbent who held the contrary view. Phase one is attested to by the Tannaitic Literature, and with respect to one Pair, Pollion and Samaias, by Josephus.

2. The second phase was characterized by the dissolution of the *Zug* system. Following on the death of Hillel (*ca.* 4 B.C.), the office of *Nasi* became hereditary for

the descendents of Hillel. The *Nasi* from this time on was called by the honorific title *Rabban,* "our teacher." At the same time, two schools, those of Hillel and Shammai, were allowed to teach publicly their divergent views on what the *halakhah* should be. This contrasted with the past procedure which had limited discussion and debate to the sessions of the *Bet Din ha-Gadol.* Once the *halakhah* was determined by that body, it was exclusively the *halakhah.* Now, however, for the first time, two renditions of the *halakhah* were allowed, that of the House of Shammai and that of the House of Hillel. Until the destruction of the Temple in 70, however, individual scholars did not enunciate *halakhoth* in their own name, nor did they as yet have the title of *Rabbi.* This phase is attested to by tannaitic usage of *Rabban* for Gamaliel and Simeon the son of Gamaliel, and by the references to Beth Shammai and Beth Hillel without singling out, prior to 70, of individual Shammaites and Hillelites, and without reference to any individual with the title *Rabbi* before the establishment of the *Bet Din ha-Gadol* at Jamnia.

This sketchy outline is, regretfully, all that we can glean from the sources. To go beyond these bare bones is to clothe the history of the Pharisees with scholar-made garments. But though their history be largely irretrievable, the shards which have survived leave us in no doubt that from the time of the Hasmonean Revolt till the destruction of the Temple in the year 70, when the term *Pharisees* became, with the dying-out of the Sadducees, irrelevant, the Scribes-Pharisees sat in Moses' seat. This was true even during the generation of bitter civil war under Alexander Jannaeus, for it is evident from this bitter struggle that the people at large looked to Pharisees, and not to the Hasmoneans, as their leaders. The Scribes-Pharisees sat in Moses' seat *during* the Hasmonean Revolt, *after* the Hasmonean Revolt, *throughout* the years of the Hasmonean dynasty, and *under* Herod, the procurators, and King Agrippa. Matthew was only uttering a commonplace when he has Jesus say,

"The scribes and the Pharisees sit in Moses' seat, so practice and observe whatever they tell you" (Matt. 23:2-3). What were the teachings of these Scribes-Pharisees during all those years when their Law went forth from Zion? In seeking out an answer to this vital question, we once again find ourselves restricted by the fact that our sources—Josephus, the New Testament, and the Tannaitic Literature—are all from the first century and beyond. Nevertheless, we are not without recourse if we are careful to distinguish between the principles of Pharisaism, which were permanent, and the specific laws and specific lore which were continuously undergoing change. The unchanging were (1) the twofold Law; (2) the authority of the scholar class to reaffirm, modify, and alter the Law; and (3) the belief in the world to come and the resurrection. Although every oral law operative in the early years of John Hyrcanus may have been displaced by other oral laws, the principle of the twofold law was strengthened by each change, not weakened, and the principle of scholar-class supremacy was reinforced, not undercut. And decade in and decade out, laws in and laws out, the true believer could look to the world to come and the resurrection as the reward for adhering to the teachings of the scholar class.

If, then, we focus on these principles: (1) the twofold Law; (2) the authority of the scholar class to reaffirm, modify, and alter the Law; and (3) the belief in the world to come and resurrection, we can draw on those tannaitic texts that bespeak the earlier stages of Pharisaism and conjoin them with all those texts in Josephus and the New Testament which are exemplary of the three enduring principles.

Let us now analyze the appropriate tannaitic texts to elicit from them what the Pharisees taught.

It will be recalled that the Pharisees and the Sadducees disagreed with each other as to whether Holy Scriptures render the hands unclean (Yad. 4:6; see chapter 3, "The Tannaitic Literature," for the full text). What is striking is that nowhere in the Pentateuch is there even the remotest suggestion that the Torah could in any way be the source of uncleanness. The Pharisaic dictum "Holy Scriptures render the hands unclean" is thus a law not written down in the Law of Moses. For this reason it was rejected out of hand by the Sadducees who regarded as lawful only those laws written by Moses. This unwritten law was known to be the "words of the *Soferim*" and hence required no biblical underpinning: "We do not deduce the words of the Torah from the words of the *Soferim;* nor the words of the *Soferim* from the words of the Torah; nor the words of the *Soferim* from the words of the *Soferim*" (Yad. 3:2).

The operational significance of this Pharisaic dictum is revolutionary. Uncleanness of the hands has practical consequences only for the priesthood, for it renders *terumah,* "heave offering," but not *hullin* "common food," unclean. Consequently, if a priest touched the scroll of the Law, he was rendered unclean and was prohibited from eating *terumah* until he had taken a ritual bath and the sun had set. To all intents and purposes, therefore, the priesthood was effectively disqualified from handling the Torah, since it brought with it annoying penalties. Symbolically as well as operationally, the Pharisaic dictum of Holy Scriptures' rendering the hands unclean transferred authority over the Torah from the priesthood to the Scribes-Pharisees. The well-thought-out purpose of this legislation is evident from the fact that the Torah scroll, which was kept in the Temple court and from which the High Priest had to read during the Yom Kippur service, was exempted from this provision for, otherwise, the High Priest would be disqualified from continuing with his obligations. However, if this scroll was removed from the Temple court, it, too, rendered the hands unclean (Tosef. Kel. II:5:8).*

---

*Although the Tosefta reads "Ezra," the context makes it clear that the core issue centers on the removal of the scroll from the sanctuary.

Most decisively, the Pharisees demonstrated their overarching authority when they, and not the Sadducees, determined the procedures the High Priest was to carry out on the Day of Atonement. Here the Pharisees were literally trespassing on the Holy of Holies, for if ever a ceremony was devised to focus on the role of the High Priest as the Grand Expiator, it was his entry into the Holy of Holies one time a year, on the Day of Atonement. Hence, whoever determined the manner of the High Priest's performance of this ultimate act was clearly in Moses' seat. The Sadducees, appealing to what had always been the practice and to the literal meaning of the verse "For in the cloud I shall appear on the *kaporet*"(Lev. 16:3), insisted that the High Priest must light the incense *before* entering the Holy of Holies so that he would be enveloped in the cloud of incense when he appeared before the *kaporet*. By contrast, the Pharisees demanded that the High Priest light the incense only *after* he had entered the Holy of Holies. Operationally, this meant that every time a High Priest entered the Holy of Holies without having lit the incense in advance, he was publicly acknowledging to the entire congregation of Israel that the Pharisees sat on Moses' seat and even the High Priest was bound to do as they commanded.

Mishnah Yom. 1:1-36 preserves for us the careful and deliberate way in which the High Priest was briefed by the emissaries of the *Bet Din* and how he was made to swear that he would not deviate from any of the instructions that had been given him. And when, on occasion, a High Priest dared to defy the Pharisaic procedure, tradition records that the Sadducees themselves scolded the recalcitrant by admonishing him that "although we are Sadducees, we fear the Pharisees" (Yom. 19*b*; see chapter 3, "The Tannaitic Literature" for the full text.) This fear of the Pharisees is confirmed by Josephus when he assures us that the Temple worship was carried out in accordance with the expositions of the Pharisees and that whenever Sadducees served as magistrates they followed the regulations of the Pharisees "since the multitude would not otherwise put up with them" (*Ant.* XVIII:17; see above pp. 56-57 for the full text).

The Holy of Holies was not the only cultic area the Pharisees took over. Thus the Pharisees purified the lamp in the Temple following the festival as the Sadducees mocked them: "the *Perushim* are [as it were] immersing the orb of the sun [which is utterly pure]. (Tosef. Hag. 3:35:1; cf. Y. Hag. 79:1; see full text in chapter 3, "The Tannaitic Literature"). The mocking, of course, derived from the fact that since the lamp was within the area from which all nonpriests were excluded, and since the priests were meticulous in their observance of the laws of cultic purity, it was as though purity itself had to be purified! This seemingly absurd act was, however, highly symbolic. It put the priests on the same level as the masses. If the priests distrusted the masses with respect to ritual and cultic purity, the masses, in turn, distrusted the cultic purity of the priests. Hence the Pharisees insisted that the lamp be immersed following the festival, even though the priests alone came in contact with it.

Similarly, the Pharisees sought to exhibit publicly that their *halakhah* regulated the cultus. Thus, when the ceremony of the red heifer was to be carried out, it was carried out in accordance with Pharisaic procedures. These entailed (1) the rendering of the High Priest unclean; (2) his taking a ritual bath; (3) burning the red heifer when the sun was still high in the sky. The reason for this was that the Sadducees insisted that a ritual bath alone was not sufficient to dissolve uncleanness for all purposes, except for the eating of *terumah*. Since the High Priest had to be clean at the time when he burnt the red heifer, the Pharisees by requiring the High Priest to immerse while the sun was still high, publicly displayed that their teaching, and not that of the Sadducees, was authoritative. (Cf. Par. 3:7; Tosef. Par. 2:8; see also chapter 3, "The Tannaitic Literature" for full texts.)

No less impressive was the Pharisaic insistence that the costs of the *tamid,* the "daily sacrifice," should be defrayed by the Temple treasury. This was in contrast to the Sadducean view which held that a single individual might donate the costs of the *tamid,* a view supportable by a literal reading of Num. 28:4: "The one lamb which you [singular] shall offer in the morning, and the second lamb which you [singular] shall offer at twilight" (author's trans.). Since the biblical verse drawn upon by the Pharisees to refute the Sadducees, namely Num. 28:2, does not specifically deal with the *tamid,* the "daily sacrifice," we see that the Sadducees were, in contrast to the Pharisees, the literalists. (Cf. Men. 65*a*; see chapter 3 for full text.)

The Pharisees also were at odds with the Boethusians (Sadducees) as to the beating of the willows at the conclusion of the Feast of Tabernacles. The Pharisees insisted that the willows were to be beaten if the day happened to be the sabbath. This the Boethusians rejected. And the ground for the Pharisaic injunction? It is a *halakhah* that goes back to Moses on Sinai, i.e., it is an unwritten law which has no biblical support. (Cf. Tosef. Suk. 3:1; see chapter 3 for full text.)

Of especial importance was the Pharisaic take-over of the calendar, which put them firmly in Moses' seat. The Pharisees, and not the Sadducees, determined when the festivals and the holy days were to be celebrated. This is brought home to us in the controversy between the Pharisees and the Sadducees as to when the *omer,* signaling the barley harvest, was to be offered up. And since the day of the *omer* determined when the festival of Pentecost—forty-nine days following the waving of the *omer*—would fall, it was no little matter as to which view prevailed. To make certain that the Pharisaic reckoning and, by implication, the Pharisaic calendar, was the binding one, the Pharisees enjoined that a public ceremony should, year in and year out, proclaim that the day for the waving of the *omer* should be on the second day of Passover, and not, as championed by the Sadducees, on the morrow of the sabbath following the appearance of barley. The pains to which the Pharisees went to involve the people on a grand scale in the underwriting of Pharisaic hegemony is boldly evident in the following mishnah:

"How did they use to do it [i.e., prepare for the cutting of the *omer*]? The messengers of the *Bet Din [sheluhe Bet Din]* used to go out on the eve of the festival and make bunches while still attached to the soil, so that it would be easier to reap; and [all the inhabitants of] the towns nearby assembled there *in order that it might be reaped in great pomp.*

"When it grew dark, he [the reaper] would say, 'Is the sun set?' They [the people] would reply, 'Yes.' 'Is the sun set?' and they would [again] answer, 'Yes.' 'With this sickle?' They would anwer, 'Yes.' 'With this basket?' and they would answer 'Yes.' 'With this basket?' and they would answer 'Yes.'

"On the sabbath he would say to them, 'On this sabbath?' and they would answer 'Yes.' 'Shall I reap?' They would answer, 'Reap.' 'Shall I reap?' and they would answer, 'Reap.'

"He used to call out for each of these three [questions] and they would thrice answer, 'Yes! Yes! Yes!' "

Why such concern? Because of the Boethusians [Sadducees] who used to say: "The cutting of the *omer* is not to take place on the day following the festival" [but only on the morrow of the sabbath, i.e., on Sunday]. (M. Men. 10:3; cf. Men. 65*a-b*, B.B. 115*b*-16*a*; for full texts, see chapter 3.)

Setting the proper date for Pentecost is a vivid example attesting to the fact that the Pharisees had introduced a novel calendrical system without Pentateuchal warrant. There are, however, other texts that reveal that the Sadducees rejected the Pharisaic calendar. Thus we read in the Tosefta:

At first [the *Bet Din*] would accept testimony concerning the New Moon from anyone. It once occurred that the Boethusians hired two witnesses to mislead the *Hakhamim;* for the Boethusians [Sadducees] do not admit that *aseret* [i.e., Pentecost] can fall after the sabbath. (Tosef. R.H. 1:15)

Nor should this surprise us. As a revolutionary class proclaiming the twofold Law and denying that God had chosen Aaron and his sons to all perpetuity to sit on Moses' seat, no single act could have been more calculated to impress the people with the hegemony of the Pharisees than the introduction of a calendar nowhere to be found in the Written Law of Moses. Since this act was so daring and so rife with consequences, it is essential to spell out how truly revolutionary the Pharisaic calendar was.

Briefly put, the calendar of the Pharisees was a lunar-solar calendar. It was dependent for its operation on the witnessing of the new moon when it was "born" month in and month out. As a consequence, some months were twenty-nine, some thirty days. The fixing of the festivals thus followed on the determination of when the New Moon had appeared.

We know from the Mishnah, tractate Rosh ha-Shanah, that the process for proclaiming the New Moon was one that called for the active participation of the people at large. Everyone was to look for the new moon. Everyone was encouraged to go off to Jerusalem and there testify to the *Bet Din* of having seen the birth of the new moon. Once the *Bet Din* was convinced that the testimony was true, it would publicly proclaim the New Moon.

To impress on everyone how important it was to hie off to Jerusalem to testify, the Pharisees affirmed that even the sabbath laws might be violated so as to allow the individual to make his way to Jerusalem as quickly as possible. They also arranged for sumptuous banquets so that the witnesses would be encouraged to come again and again. Indeed, so as to make their stay as comfortable as possible, Rabban Gamaliel the Elder (R.H. 2:5) ordained that they be allowed to walk the same two thousand cubits which hitherto only residents had been allowed to do.

None of this is to be found in the Pentateuch. There are no provisions for observing the New Moon and bearing witness to its birth. There is no *Bet Din* to which witnesses are to come. There is no allowance to disregard the sabbath laws so as to be able to testify. And there is no lunar-solar calendar in the Pentateuch. The only calendrical system in the Pentateuch which is truly and strictly liturgical is the system utilized in the Aaronide texts exclusively. This calendar is a solar calendar of twelve months of thirty days each with four intercalated days each year. It is a calendar which was designed to make certain that the sabbath would always fall on the seventh day in a year divisible by seven. And since each year in this system falls one day short of a solar year, the extra day is added for forty-nine years. At the end of the forty-ninth year, a year of forty-nine days is intercalated and is called a jubilee year. In this calendar the festivals always came out on the same day each year. Pentecost—the only festival not assigned a fixed day because the onset of the barley harvest in this calendrical system would vary considerably over the forty-nine-year cycle—always fell on a Sunday, since the counting of the forty-nine days from the waving of the *omer* always began on the Sunday following the appearance of the barley.

There is thus no connection between the lunar-solar calendar of the Pharisees and the solar calendar of the Aaronide texts of the Pentateuch. Festivals fell on different days in different years, since the appearance of a New Moon would vary from year to year. Pentecost need not fall on Sunday since the Pharisees began counting from the second day of the festival and not from the first Sunday following on the appearance of barley. The holy days, according to the reckoning of the Sadducees, would become ordinary, profane days, while their ordinary, profane days could, by Pharisaic reckoning, become holy days. Most disruptive of all for the Sadducees was what the Pharisaic calender did to the Day of Atonement. The day most sacrosanct in the Pentateuch would in different years fall on different days. A Sadducean High Priest would thus be violating the very law of God whenever he entered the Holy of Holies on a day not prescribed by the Lord himself.

Indeed, the Pharisees extended their hegemony throughout all the domains of the law. Thus they rejected the Sadducean claim that false witnesses were to be put to death only after the defendant had been executed despite the fact that this claim seemed to be underwritten by a literal rendering of the dictum "life for life." Instead, the Pharisees argued that the false witnesses were to be put to death once the defendant was declared guilty by the court, even though the execution would not yet have been carried out. Rejecting the verse "life for life" as inapplicable, the Pharisees cited "Then you shall do to him as you thought to do to his brother" (Deut. 19:19; author's trans.)—the brother must still be living when the witnesses are executed. As for "life for life," this means that the witnesses are not to be put to death prior to the actual sentencing.

This particular controversy between the Pharisees and the Sadducees is brought alive in a recollection dating back to the *Zug*, "the Pair," Judah ben Tabbai and Simeon ben Shetah (*ca.* 85 B.C.). In reaction to Judah ben Tabbai's jubilant outburst that he had had a single false witness executed after the defendant had been acquitted so as to root out the Boethusian (Sadducean) notion that the witness was to be put to death only if the defendant had been executed, Simeon ben Shetah accused him of having shed innocent blood—not, mind you, because he sided with the Sadducees, but because he claimed that a single false witness was not to be put to death. Just as two witnesses were needed for conviction, so two witnesses had to give false testimony before they could be executed. Convinced by Simeon ben Shetah's reasoning, Judah ben Tabbai from that time on taught the *halakhah* in accordance with his colleague's opinion. (Cf. Tosef. Sanh. 6:6; see chapter 3, "The Tannaitic Literature" for the full text.)

The Pharisees likewise differed with the Sadducees on

such highly crucial issues as the liability of slaves for damage and inheritance. Thus the Sadducees held the slaveowner to be responsible for any damage to property caused by his slave on the grounds that the slave, like an ox or an ass, was property pure and simple and hence the slave had to be properly supervised by the master. By contrast, the Pharisees insisted that the slave was responsible for his actions, since as a volitional being, the slave might go forth on his own and maliciously cause damage so as to harm his master. (Cf. Yad. 4:7; see chapter 3 for complete text.) Similarly, whereas the Sadducees allowed the daughter to inherit the estate of the father should her brothers die following her father's death, the Pharisees bypassed the daughter and affirmed that the heir was to be the grandson or, in the event there was no grandson, the granddaughter.

And, finally, there are two precious tannaitic texts that crisply confirm that the Scribes-Pharisees sat in Moses' seat. The first of these, Sanh. 11:3, reads as follows:

There is greater rigor applied to the words of the *Soferim* than to the words of the Pentateuch. One who says, "There is no need to wear phylacteries," in order to transgress the Pentateuch, is free of guilt. [One, however, who says,] "Five *totafot* are required rather than four," in order to transgress by adding to the number prescribed by the words of the *Soferim,* is guilty.

The other dictum is set down in Yad. 3:2:

We do not deduce the words of the Torah from the words of the *Soferim;* nor the words of the *Soferim* from the words of the Torah; nor the words of the *Soferim* from the words of the *Soferim.*

The teachings of the Scribes have a status nonpareil. There is greater rigor applied to their words than even to the words of Moses himself. Furthermore, the dicta of the Scribes are sealed off from intrusion. The Scribes are sacrosanct in their own right. They need no support from the Written Law; nor need they conform to any logical consistency within themselves. Since the Scribes sit on Moses' seat, their teachings are equivalent in authority with any that Moses set down in writing.

An analysis of all of those tannaitic texts that in one way or another show themselves to be Pharisaic by virtue of a juxtaposition to the Sadducees reveal, despite their paucity, that the Scribes-Pharisees laid claim to full authority over the Law; they subordinated the High Priest and cultus to their prescriptions; they proclaimed their unwritten laws to be absolutely binding on the community of Israel.

The tannaitic evidence is thus clear enough: the Scribes-Pharisees did indeed sit on Moses' seat, and their twofold Law, with its promise of the world to come and the resurrection, was, for most Jews, the Torah, the Law. When, for example, Mishnah Sanh. 11:2 affirms that "the Torah went forth unto all Israel" from the *Bet Din ha-Gadol,* which met on the Temple Mount, the twofold Law was meant. When Mishnah Ab. 1:1 states that Moses received the Torah from Sinai and handed it down to Joshua, it is referring to the Written *and* Oral Torah. Indeed, in any tannaitic text where "Torah" is used, it means the twofold Law unless the context makes clear that the scroll of the Torah is meant.

Little wonder, then, that the author of Matthew 23 excoriates the Scribes-Pharisees as hypocrites and blind guides, and yet affirms that they sit on the cathedra of Moses as the authoritative teachers of the Law. But this Law could only have been the twofold Law, for it was precisely their teaching of the *paradosis,* the tradition, the Oral Law, which was their hallmark (cf. Matt. 15:1-9; Mark 7:1-13; Phil. 3:5-6; Gal. 1:13-14). Matthew thus attests to the accuracy of the picture as given in the tannaitic texts cited above.

But the Gospel of Matthew goes further, for it reveals to us some of the specific teachings and characteristics of the Scribes-Pharisees of the first century. The Scribes-Pharisees were active proselytizers, traversing sea and

269

land to make a single proselyte (23:15); they required the tithing of mint, dill, and cummin (23:23); prescribed the proper formula for an oath (23:16-22); insisted that the laws pertaining to cleanness and uncleanness be observed (23:25-26); placed a high store on law-abidingness, *dikaiosune* (23:27-28); sternly rejected those who challenged their authority by casting them out of the synagogues (23:29-36); took pride in the observance of the Law, making their phylacteries broad and their fringes long (23:5); yearned for recognition of their honorific status by the place of honor at feasts, the best seats in the synagogue, and respectful salutations (23:6-7); gave alms (6:2-4); fasted (6:16-18); prayed publicly (6:5-6). Although each of these actions draws the scorn of the author of Matthew, they are not actions from which the Scribes-Pharisees would wish to disassociate themselves. The Scribes-Pharisees would only reject the *interpretation* put on the motives underlying these actions, not the actions themselves. Matthew himself insists that "these you ought to have done, without neglecting the others" (23:23; cf. 6:2, 5, 16—"Truly . . . they have their reward") and that "unless your righteousness *[dikaiosune]* exceeds that of the scribes and Pharisees, you will never enter the kingdom of heaven" (5:20).

Matthew 23 is merely illustrative of what is to be found throughout the Synoptic Gospels. The Scribes-Pharisees are again and again associated with the synagogue (Mark 1:21; 3; Matt. 23:6, and *passim*). They proclaim the traditions of the elders (Mark 7:1-13; Matt. 15:1-9; cf. Gal. 1:13-14, Phil. 3:5-6); acknowledge the existence of demons (Mark 3:22; Matt. 12:24); insist that God alone can forgive sins (Mark 2:6-7; Matt. 9:2-3; Luke 5:20-21); look askance at eating with publicans and sinners (Mark 2:15-16; Matt. 9:10-11; Luke 5:29-32); attach great importance to fasting (Mark 2:18; Matt. 9:14; Luke 5:33); disallow the plucking of grain on the sabbath (Mark 2:23-24; Matt. 12:1-2; Luke 6:1-2); prohibit the healing of the chronically ill on the sabbath (Mark 3:1-6; Matt. 12:9-14; Luke 6:6-11); do not eat with unwashed hands (Mark 7:1-8; Matt. 15:1-2); determine which oaths are binding, which not (Mark 7:9-13); consider the dietary laws to be binding (Mark 7:14-23, with the Scribes-Pharisees being implied); assert that Elijah must come before the Son of man (Mark 9:9-13); allow divorce (Mark 10:2-4); disapprove of Jesus' overturning the seats of the money changers in the Temple and of his provocative proof text, "Is it not written, 'My house shall be called a house of prayer for all the nations'? But you have made it a den of robbers" (Mark 11:15-18); question Jesus' authority (Mark 11:27-33), along with the chief priests and the elders (Matt. 21:23-27; Luke 20:1-8); regard the tribute of Caesar to be a legitimate tax (Mark 12:13-17; Matt. 22:15-22; Luke 20;19-26); believe that the resurrection of the dead is set down in Scripture, in contradistinction to the Sadducees (Mark 12:18-27; Matt. 22:23-34; Luke 20:27-40; cf. Acts); deem that "Hear O Israel, the Lord our God, the Lord is one" and that "you shall love the Lord your God with all your heart" is the prime commandment, followed by "You shall love your neighbor as yourself" (Mark 12:28-33; Matt. 22:34-40); insist that the messiah would have to be from the seed of David (Mark 12:35-37; Matt. 22:41-46; Luke 20:41-44); prescribe, by implication, that the Scriptures be read every sabbath in the synagogues (Acts 15:21; 13:27); do not teach on the basis of personal authority (Mark 1:22; Matt. 7:28-29).

What is striking is that every one of these pictorializations is in accord with what we derive from the tannaitic data dealt with above. Indeed, entire tractates of the Mishnah are devoted to prayer (Berakoth), to tithing (Ma'aseroth, Maaser Sheni), the sabbath (Shabbat), fasting (Ta'anith), the uncleanness of hands (Yadayim), divorce (Gittin), the reading of Scripture (Megillah), vows (Nedarim). Other dicta are confirmed within the various tractates. The world to come and the resurrection are explicitly set forth as the ultimate reward (Peah 1:4;

Sanh. 10:1, 6:2; Ber. 9:5); the saying of the *Shema* was equivalent to assuming the yoke of the Kingdom of Heaven (Ber. 2:5); study of the twofold Law was deemed to be the most worthy of preoccupations (Peah 1:1), and to be a *hakham,* a sage, or a disciple of a sage *(talmid hakham),* even when a bastard, was to enjoy a status higher than that of an ignorant High Priest (Hor. 3:8).

Even more impressive than the congruence of image and idea is the way in which the unique literary forms of the Scribes-Pharisees suffuse the New Testament literature. As was pointed out above, the Scribes-Pharisees developed innovative modes for transmitting their unwritten Law and Lore, for they sought to sharply differentiate the Written from the Oral Law, so as not to be open to the charge of violating the Pentateuchal injunction prohibiting any additions to or deletions from the Law (Deut. 12:32). Not only were they meticulous in not writing down any *halakhah* or *aggadah,* but the Scribes-Pharisees scrupulously refrained from following any biblical models. Instead, they shaped and fashioned their own forms which were unique for Judaism. The Pentateuchal mode of intermingling laws with narrative is utterly abandoned. There is no narrative at all. The *halakhoth,* the oral laws, are transmitted as discrete items. The biblical formulas are never imitated; novel formulas are developed in their stead. So sharp are these formal differences that no one, even today, can put the Pentateuch alongside the Mishnah and discern any formal congruence. The Pentateuch begins with the creation of the world; the Mishna, with the reading of the *Shema.* The first laws commanded to Israel relate to the Passover, whereas the first tractate of the Mishnah deals with prayers not even mandated in the Pentateuch. Again and again in the Mishnah we meet up with legal formulas beginning with a question, "From what time do we read the *Shema* in the evening . . ." (Ber. 1:1), or with "There are four principal kinds of damages . . ." (B.B. 1:1), or "The general rule is . . . " (cf. Peah 5:8 and *passim*). When, from time to time, an *aggadic* item is inserted, it bears no likeness to any scriptural form, but is introduced by such a novel word as *maaseh*, "It is related of . . ." (Ber. 1:1 and *passim*).

Of especial interest, however, is the use of the scriptural proof text. Throughout the Mishnah, we encounter the formula *sheneemar*, "As it is written in Scripture" or "This is what Scripture meant to say." Such proof-texting is nowhere to be found in Scripture. On rare occasions, to be sure, allusions to other biblical writings are made, and perhaps here and there even a citation might be implied. But nowhere is proof-texting utilized as a method or a norm. Indeed, even as late as the writings of Ben Sira, we have no evidence of proof-texting. When Ben Sira proclaims God as the divine source of Wisdom, he does not quote chapter and verse to justify his claim. There is, in fact, not a single direct quotation from the Bible in Ben Sira even though his book bristles with biblical allusions and paraphrases biblical events and biblical laws. But we look in vain for *sheneemar*, "As it is said in Scripture," or *talmud lomar*, "Scripture therefore says thusly."

Proof-texting, along with the discrete item of law or lore, was thus a Pharisaic original. It is attested to only in the Mishnah, the Tosefta, and other tannaitic materials. It is not to be found in any apocryphal or pseudepigraphic work. Yet these Pharisaic forms are the very forms that underlie the Epistles of Paul, the Gospels, and Acts. Paul is forever citing Scripture in the Pharisaic manner. When he wishes to prove that God had made his covenant with Abraham before Abraham was circumcized, he drives his point home with a conclusive proof text from Scriptures (cf. Rom. 4:1-12, and *passim*). When Jesus confutes the Sadducees, he does so with a proof text so telling that the listening Scribe was mightily impressed (Mark 12:18-27). When he justifies driving the money changers out of the Temple, he does so with a proof text (Mark 11:17-18). When he seeks to refute the teaching of the Scribes that the Christ must be a scion of David, he cites Ps. 110:1. When he is dying on the cross, he likewise utters a verse from Psalms (22:1; Mark 15:34). Indeed, wherever one turns within the Gospels, one is offered proof text after proof text—a vivid testimony to how utterly normative this Pharisaic original had become. And underscoring this testimony is the unabashed adoption of the Pharisaic assumption that every verse in every book of Scripture, be it the Pentateuch, the Prophets, or the Hagiographa, was, in principle, co-equal and free of contextual constraints. This co-equality and this freedom from contextual constraint are likewise Pharisaic originals. (See above p. 242.)

But proof-texting does not exhaust the impact of Pharisaic forms on the New Testament. Scholars have long recognized that the Gospels are composite and reflect in their final version the unifying and architectural imprint of those who made use of traditions that had circulated orally in the early years of the Christian community. As evidence of this composite character, these scholars have pointed to the pericope, the discrete items, the individual dicta, which were knitted together by those who wished to communicate a total message about Jesus, his ministry, his crucifixion and resurrection. The Gospel-unifiers thus shaped a framework which could envelope the discrete traditions with a semblance of primordial unity. Once, however, this framework is set aside, it is rather evident that we have an array of free-floating pericopes, discrete items, unattached dicta hardly distinguishable in form from item-like *halakhah* and the pericope-like *aggadah*. Indeed, such episodes as Jesus' entering the synagogue on the sabbath and healing or his confrontation with the Sadducees or his going through the cornfields with his disciples on the sabbath—all virtually presuppose the *maaseh* form; for each is truly "a story about." And most importantly, the form is free-floating and not embedded within a larger narrative except through deliberate insertion. Each Gospel writer was free to draw on these unmoored items to fit within the narratival framework he had fashioned. The items in their original state were not within a tight narratival matrix as were the episodes in the Pentateuch but were taught as dicta and set forth as paradigms, in the Pharisaic mode.

The Gospels, Acts, and the Epistles of Paul—all attest to the hegemony of the Pharisees. The overarching framework of presuppositions, laws, and modes of communication was so Pharisaic that Jesus, Paul, and the earliest disciples could confront the Pharisees only with tools the Pharisees had devised and fashioned. Jesus was, like the Pharisees, a *didaskalos,* a teacher. He taught by word of mouth and example, even as did the Pharisees. So like them was he that on occasion he is addressed by them as Teacher *(didaskalos, rav).* He frequented their synagogues, read from the prophets on the sabbath, indulged in their mode of exegesis, regarded all three divisions of Scripture as co-equal, firmly believed in eternal life and resurrection. Paul, for his part, launched his mortal attack against the Law by wielding scriptural proof texts with all the abandon of a Pharisaic sage. Like the Pharisees, he, too, was pre-eminently a teacher and preacher who, with his disciples, went from synagogue to synagogue, public forum to public forum. His metier was the spoken word. His Epistles were imposed upon him by necessity. He would have preferred to have spoken directly to the Romans, the Thessalonians, and the Corinthians. Indeed, he recalls with pleasure his visits, chafes at the constraints on his being ever-present. His letters are conversations written down, preaching in ink, controversies on paper writ. They follow no biblical models. They are the oral dicta of a frenzied, zealous teacher whom distance has separated from his disciples, condemning him to write, lest his *oral* teachings be forgotten.

This power of Pharisaism to so bind Jesus, Paul, and the early disciples to the Pharisaic mode of thinking and teaching is explicable only if the Pharisees had been in Moses' seat for so long that no one could recall a time when they were not there. Matthew's plaintive plea that the Scribes-Pharisees were to be obeyed even when they hounded Jesus and his disciples because they, the Scribes-Pharisees, sat in Moses' seat is explicable only if they had been sitting there since time immemorial. Otherwise, Matthew would have exposed their claims as fraudulent. Pharisaism was clearly the Judaism of Jesus' day, adhered to by all but a handful of Sadducees, a smattering of Essenes, and by a minority, however growing and tempestuous they might have been, of malcontents who despaired of effective Pharisaic leadership against the crushing weight of Rome.

Pharisaic hegemony is no less attested to by Josephus. But with this difference: Whereas the Tannaitic Literature stumps us with its anonymity, with its unconcern for history, with its ellipticism, with its unhelpfulness as to the "when," the "where," and the "why" of this *halakhah* or that *aggadah,* Josephus extends his Pharisaic self-consciousness by his findings, as a historian, of patches from their past. He does not, to be sure, explicitly acknowledge that they had a genesis—as a follower of the Scribes-Pharisees, Josephus would perforce have believed that the twofold Law had been revealed at Sinai—but he does refrain from inserting them in his histories before the Hasmonean Revolt. Josephus' affirmation (1) that the Pharisees were around and active in the days of Jonathan; (2) that their *paradosis* was flourishing when John Hyrcanus became High Priest; (3) that the masses resisted the abrogation of the unwritten laws by John Hyrcanus so violently that there could be no social peace until Salome Alexandra reinstituted the laws of the Pharisees, makes thoroughly understandable the hegemony the Scribes-Pharisees are exercising in the time of Jesus even as it confirms the tannaitic assumption that the first *Zug,* "Pair," presided over the *Bet Din ha-Gadol* in the early Hasmonean period.

Josephus thus confirms explicitly what the New Testament and the Tannaitic Literature attest to implicitly.

With the help, then, of Josephus, we can more precisely delineate the teachings of the Scribes-Pharisees circulating during his lifetime and more fully appreciate why it was that they sat on the cathedra of Moses—and continued sitting there. Since Josephus testifies that he was a follower of the legal system of the Pharisees from the age of eighteen, and since this testimony is to be found in *The Life,* which he wrote as his days were drawing to their end and which is not modified by any statement to the effect that he had at any time abandoned his Pharisaic commitment, and since in the *War* (II:163; III: 374-75), *Antiquities* (I: 228-31; XVIII:14), and *Against Apion* (II:218-19), he affirms the belief in the world to come and the resurrection as normative, we must assume that whenever Josephus is speaking of the Law, he means the twofold Law, and whenever he is utilizing lore, as distinct from historical data, he is drawing on the Oral Lore of the Pharisees. Similarly, whenever he waxes eloquent on the perfection of the laws and their enduring excellence, he is referring to the system of laws taught by the Scribes-Pharisees. Likewise, whenever he stresses the utter loyalty of the Jews to the Law, a loyalty that transcended even the fear of torture and death, he means the twofold Law.

Josephus' writings are far too vast for an exhaustive paraphrase. For our purposes, it will be sufficient to demonstrate that some of the laws Josephus sets down as normative are not written down in the Pentateuch; that some of the lore he narrates as though it were biblical is not to be found in the Bible; that some of the concepts he assumes were held by the Patriarchs and by Moses were utterly alien to them; that some of his notions of the manner of leaders the Patriarchs and Moses were, are without scriptural warrant. Once these examples are set down, we shall be in a position to appreciate Josephus' hymn to the twofold Law.

Let us consider each of these categories in turn:

1. *Legislation.* Most striking in the realm of law is Josephus' attributing to Moses the establishment of the calendrical system known to us from tractate Rosh ha-Shanah:

This catastrophe [of the flood] happened in the six hundredth year of Noah's rulership, *in what was once the second month,* called by the Macedonians Dius and by the Hebrew Marsuan *[Marheshwan],* according to the arrangement of the calendar which they followed in Egypt. Moses, however, appointed Nisan, that is to say Xanthicus, as the first month for the festivals, because it was in this month that he brought the Hebrews out of Egypt; he also reckoned this month as the commencement of the year for everything relating to divine worship, but for selling and buying and other ordinary affairs he preserved the ancient order. *(Ant.* I:80-81; italics added)

Nisan is not mentioned in Exod. 12:1-20, nor for that matter, anywhere in the Pentateuch, though the month of Abib is (Exod. 13:4; 23:15; Deut. 16:1). Nor is the first month, as it is called in Exod. 12:18, designated as the commencement of the year for everything related to divine worship, in contradistinction to "selling, buying and other ordinary affairs."

By contrast, the Mishnah does single out the first of Nisan as the New Year for the festivals, and the first of Tishre as the New Year for the counting of the sabbatical years, for the Jubilees, and for the planting and for the tithing of vegetables. The calendrical system Josephus regarded as normative (cf. *Ant.* II:311, 318; III:248; IV:84, 327) and which he explicitly refers to as consisting of lunar months *(Ant.* II:318; III:240, 248; IV:78, 84) is thus not Pentateuchal but Mishnaic.

It is not surprising, therefore, that Josephus *(Ant.* III: 250-52) begins the counting of the *omer* from the second day of Passover, which was in accordance with the teachings of the Pharisees and not with those of the

Sadducees (Tosef. Men. 10:3; R.H. 1:15). It is also noteworthy that Josephus refers to the Mishnaic designation for Shebuoth, *Asartha,* as the normative usage.

If we turn from the calendar to other laws, we find that Josephus sets down legislation that is in accord with Pharisaic procedures. Thus he asserts that Moses ordained that the public *(ek tou demosios),* not an individual, defray the cost of the daily sacrifice *(Ant.* III:237)—a practice the Sadducees considered to be in violation of the meaning of the Law (cf. Men. 65*a*). Furthermore, he has Moses, in his farewell address, enjoin the people to acknowledge, "twice each day, at the dawn thereof and when the hour comes for repose," before God "the bounties which he has bestowed on them through their deliverance from the land of Egypt" *(Ant.* IV:212). This enjoinment may be found in the Mishnah (Ber. I:1, 2, 3) but not in Deuteronomy. Similarly, whereas the Mishnah makes mention of "seven good men of the city," Moses does not. Likewise, Josephus attributes to Moses the Mishnaic provision for thirty-nine lashes (Mak. 3:10), and not the forty of Deut. 35:3 *(Ant.* IV:238, 248), even as he has Moses allow for monetary compensation as an alternative to *lex talionis (Ant.* IV:280) in accordance with the Oral Law (B.K.83*b*).

2. *Lore.* Throughout *Antiquities,* Josephus freely elaborates on the biblical narrative by adding large amounts of lore not to be found in Scripture. This is astonishing, since Josephus is so generous in his praise of Moses as the spokesman of God *(Ant.* I:18-26), and it is hardly likely that he would have deviated in any substantive way from the Pentateuchal text unless his elaborations were regarded by him as enjoying co-equal status. Such a co-equal status was claimed by the Pharisees for their Oral Lore, the *aggadah.* Josephus was thus well within the boundaries of Pharisaism when he tells of Abraham's instructing the Egyptians in arithmetic and astronomy *(Ant.* I:167) and of baby Moses throwing

off Pharaoh's crown, flinging it to the ground, and crushing it underfoot (II:233).

3. *Concepts.* In the realm of doctrine, Josephus is most out of line with Scripture when, in describing the binding of Isaac, he has Abraham reassure Isaac that his soul will soon be with God, the Father:

"My child, myriad were the prayers in which I besought God for thy birth, and when thou camest into the world, no pains were there that I did not lavish upon thine upbringing, no thought had I of higher happiness than to see thee grown to man's estate and to leave thee at my death heir to my dominion. But, since it was by God's will that I became thy sire and now again as pleases Him I am resigning thee, bear thou this consecration valiantly; for it is to God I yield thee, to God who now claims from us this homage in return for the gracious favour he has shown me as my supporter and ally. Aye, since thou wast born (out of the course of nature, so) quit thou now this life not by the common road, but sped by thine own father on thy way to God, the Father of all, through the rites of sacrifice. He, I ween, accounts it not meet for thee to depart this life by sickness or war or by any of the calamaties that commonly befall mankind, but amid prayers and sacrificial ceremonies would receive thy soul and keep it near to Himself; and for me thou shalt be a protector and stay of my old age—to which end above all I nurtured thee—by giving me God in the stead of thyself."
The son of such a father could not but be brave-hearted, and Isaac received these words with joy. *(Ant.* I:228-32)

4. *Portraits of the Patriarchs and of Moses.* Josephus transmutes all the biblical heroes from seminomadic leaders into sophisticated philosophers, statesmen, orators, and military leaders. Here, for example, is his portrait of Abraham:

He was a man of ready intelligence on all matters, persuasive with his hearers, and not mistaken in his inferences. Hence he began to have more lofty conceptions of virtue than the rest of mankind, and determined to reform and change the ideas universally current concerning God. He was thus the first boldly to declare that God, the creator of the universe, is one, and that, if any other being contributed aught to man's welfare, each did so by His command and not in virtue of its own inherent power. This he inferred from the changes to which land and sea are subject, from the course of sun and moon, and from all the celestial phenomena; for, he argued, were these bodies endowed with power, they would have provided for their own regularity, but, since they lacked this last, it was manifest that even those services in which they cooperate for our greater benefit they render not in virtue of their own authority, but through the might of their commanding sovereign, to whom alone it is right to render our homage and thanksgiving. It was in fact owing to these opinions that the Chaldeans and the other peoples of Mesopotamia rose against him, and he, thinking fit to emigrate, at the will and with the aid of God, settled in the land of Canaan. (*Ant.* I:154-57)

It is amplified further on the occasion of Abraham's descent into Egypt:

For, seeing that the Egyptians were addicted to a variety of different customs and disparaged one another's practices and were consequently at enmity with one another, Abraham conferred with each party and, exposing the arguments which they adduced in favour of their particular views, demonstrated that they were idle and contained nothing true. Thus gaining their admiration at these meetings as a man of extreme sagacity, gifted not only with high intelligence but with power to convince his hearers on any subject which he undertook to teach, he introduced them to arithmetic and transmitted to them the laws of astronomy. For before the coming of Abraham the Egyptians were ignorant of these sciences, which thus travelled from the Chaldeans into Egypt, whence they passed to the Greeks. (*Ant.* I:166 68)

But even Abraham's multitalents pale before those of Moses who was "for grandeur of intellect and contempt of toils . . . the noblest Hebrew of them all" (*Ant.* II:229). Indeed, Moses has no peer whether as lawgiver, philosopher, statesman, orator, or general. This Josephus makes clear to his readers throughout his narrative. Thus in his prefatory remarks to his work he alerts the reader to Moses as being beyond compare:

But, since well-nigh everything herein related is dependent on the wisdom of our lawgiver Moses, I must first speak briefly of him, lest any of my readers should ask how it is that so much of my work, which professes to treat of laws and historical facts, is devoted to natural philosophy. Be it known, then, that that sage deemed it above all necessary, for one who would order his own life aright and also legislate for others, first to study the nature of God, and then, having contemplated his works with the eye of reason, to imitate so far as possible that best of all models and endeavour to follow it. For neither could the lawgiver himself, without this vision, ever attain to a right mind, nor would anything that he should write in regard to virtue avail with his readers unless before all else they were taught that God, as the universal Father and Lord who beholds all things, grants to such as follow Him a life of bliss, but involves in dire calamities those who step outside the path of virtue. Such, then, being the lesson which Moses desired to instill into his fellow-citizens, he did not, when framing his laws, begin with contracts and the mutual rights of man, as others have done; no, he led their thoughts up to God and the construction of the world: he convinced them that of all God's works upon earth we men are the fairest; and when once we had won their obedience to the dictates of piety, he had no further difficulty in persuading them of all the rest. Other legislators, in fact, following fables, have in their writings imputed to the gods the disgraceful errors of men and thus furnished the wicked with a powerful excuse; our legislator, on the contrary, having shown that God possesses the very perfection of virtue, thought that men should strive to participate in it, and inexorably punished those who did not hold with or believe in these doctrines. I therefore entreat my readers to examine my work from this point of view. For, studying it in this spirit, nothing will appear to them unreasonable, nothing incongruous with the majesty of God and His love for man; everything, indeed, is here set forth in keeping with the nature of the universe; some things the lawgiver shrewdly veils in enigmas, others he sets forth in solemn allegory; but wherever straightforward speech was expedient, there he makes his meaning absolutely plain. Should any further desire to consider the reasons for every article in our creed, he would find the inquiry profound and highly philosohical. (*Ant.* I:18-25)

Josephus is no less in awe when he reflects on Moses' passing:

He departed in the last month of the year, which the Macedonians call Dystros and we Adar, on the day of the new moon, having surpassed in understanding all men that ever lived and put to noblest use the fruit of his reflections. In speech and in addresses to a crowd he found favour in every way, but chiefly through his thorough command of his passions, which was such that he seemed to have no place for them at all in his soul, and only knew their names through seeing them in others rather than in himself. As general he had few to equal him, and as prophet none, insomuch that in all his utterances one seemed to hear the speech of God Himself. So the people mourned for him for thirty days, and never were Hebrews oppressed by grief so profound as that which filled them then on the death of Moses. Nor was he regretted only by those who had known him by experience, but the very readers of his laws have sadly felt his loss, deducing from these the superlative quality of his virtue. Such, then, be our description of the end of Moses. (*Ant.* IV:327-31)

Josephus' uninhibited inclusion of non-Pentateuchal laws, of non-Pentateuchal lore, of non-Pentateuchal doctrine, and of non-Pentateuchal portraits reveals his firm belief in a complementary system of revelation which he regarded as sharing co-equality with the Pentateuch. And since Josephus himself informs us that, from the age of eighteen, he had governed himself by the constitution of the Pharisees, we would anticipate that for him the Oral Law and Lore of the Pharisees were as authoritative as the Written Law itself. Hence we must assume that whenever Josephus uses the term "Law" unmodified, it is the twofold Law that he has in mind. His *Against Apion* is thus not a panegyric of the Written Law but of the twofold Law. As such, we can draw upon it freely to amplify our understanding of why the Scribes-Pharisees sat so securely on the seat of Moses.

The leitmotiv of Josephus' *Against Apion* is that Moses gave to the Jews, and through the Jews, to the world, a system of laws and beliefs of such divine splendor that they put to shame all the great lawgivers, such as Lycurgus and Solon, and such philosophers as Plato. Moses was unique, he had no peer:

Now, I maintain that our legislator is the most ancient of all legislators in the records of the whole world. Compared with him, your Lycurguses and Solons, and Zaleucus, who gave the Locrians their laws, and all who are held in such high esteem by the Greeks appear to have been born but yesterday. Why, the very word "law" was unknown in ancient Greece. . . .

Throughout all this [namely, leading the Israelites through the wilderness] he [Moses] proved the best of generals *[strategos]*, the sagest of counsellors *[sumboulos]*, and the most conscientious of guardians *[kedemon]*. He succeeded in making the whole people dependent upon himself, and, having secured their obedience in all things, he did not use his influence for any personal aggrandizement. . . . Having first persuaded himself that God's will governed all his actions and all his thoughts, he regarded it as his primary duty to impress that idea upon the community; *for to those who believe that their lives are under the eye of God* all sin is intolerable. Such was our legislator; no charlatan or imposter, as slanderers unjustly call him, but one such as the Greeks boast of having in Minos and later legislators. For among these some attributed their laws to Zeus, others traced them to Apollo and his oracle at Delphi, either believing this to be the fact, or hoping in this way to facilitate their acceptance. But the question, who was the most successful legislator, and who attained to the truest conception of God, may be answered by contrasting the laws themselves with those of others, and to these I must now turn. (*Against Apion* II:154-63; italics added)

Moses, in fact, succeeded where Plato and Lycurgus had failed. Plato's legislation, for example, proved to be utterly unworkable, and he despaired of teaching the masses elevated concepts of God. By contrast, the laws of Moses, though seemingly utopian, evoke the most devoted loyalty of the Jews:

Now suppose that our nation had not happened to be known to all the world and *our voluntary obedience to our laws* not a patent fact *[ten ethelousin hemon tois nomois akolouthian]*, and suppose that some one had delivered a lecture to the Greeks which he admitted to be the outcome of his own imagination, or asserted that somewhere outside the known world he had met with people who held such sublime ideas about God and had for ages continued steadily faithful to such laws as ours; his words would, I imagine, astonish all his hearers, in view of the constant vicissitudes in their own past history. In fact, those who have attempted to draft a constitution and code on any such lines are accused of inventing something miraculous, based, according to their critics, on impossible premises. I pass over other philosophers who have handled such topics in their writings. I need name only Plato, who, admired, as he is, by the Greeks for his outstanding dignity of character, and as one who in oratorical power and persuasive eloquence outmatched all other philosophers, is yet continually being, I may almost say, scoffed at and held up to ridicule by those who claim to be expert statesmen. And yet, on examination, his laws will be found to be frequently easier than ours, and more closely approximating to the practice of the masses. Plato himself admits that it is hazardous to divulge the truth about God to the ignorant mob. (*Against Apion* II:220-24; italics added)

Lycurgus, the most practical and hardheaded of Greek legislators, fared no better (II:225-35).

The Law (and it will be recalled that the Law throughout *Against Apion* is the twofold Law) is indeed unique, for it is rooted in the belief that God is one, perfect, omnipotent, and utterly blessed:

What, then, are the precepts and prohibitions of our Law? They are simple and familiar. At their head stands one of which God is the theme. The universe is in God's hands; perfect and blessed *[panteles kai makarios]*, self-sufficing and sufficing for all *[autos hauto kai pasin autarkes]*, He is the beginning, the middle, and the end of all things *[arche kai mesa kai telos houtos ton panton]*. By His works and bounties He is plainly seen, indeed more manifest than ought else; but His form and magnitude *[morphen de kai megethos]* surpass our powers of description. *No materials, however costly, are fit to make an image of Him; no art has skill to conceive and represent it.* The like of Him we have never seen, we do not imagine, and it is impious to conjecture. We behold His works: the light, the heaven, the earth, the sun, the waters, the reproductive creatures, the sprouting crops. These God created, not with hands, not with toil, not with assistants of whom He had no need; He willed it so, and forthwith they were made in all their beauty. Him must we worship by the practice of virtue *[areten]*; for that is the most saintly manner of worshipping God. (*Against Apion* II:190-92; italics added)

God's singularity and virtue are in glaring contrast to the anarchy and dissoluteness of Greek polytheism:

Who, in fact, is there among the admired sages of Greece who has not censured their most famous poets and their most trusted legislators for sowing in the minds of the masses the first seeds of such notions about the gods? They represent them to be as numerous as they choose, born of one another and engendered in all manner of ways. They assign them different localities and habits, like animal species, some living underground, others in the sea, the oldest of all being chained in Tartarus. Those to whom they have allotted heaven have set over them one who is nominally Father, but in reality a tyrant and despot; with the result that his wife and brother and the daughter, whom he begot from his own head, conspire against him, to arrest and imprison him, just as he himself had treated his own father.

Justly do these tales merit the severe censure which they receive from their intellectual leaders. Moreover, they ridicule the belief that some gods are beardless striplings, others old and bearded; that some are appointed to trades, this one being a smith, that goddess a weaver, a third a warrior who fights along with men, others lute-players or devoted to archery; and again that they are divided into factions and quarrel about men, in so much that they not only come to blows with each other, but actually lament over and suffer from wounds inflicted by mortals. But—and here outrageousness reaches its climax—is it not monstrous to attribute those licentious unions and amours to well-nigh all the deities of both sexes? Futhermore, the noblest and chief of them all, the Father himself, after seducing women and rendering them pregnant, leaves them to be imprisoned or drowned in the sea; and is so completely at the mercy of Destiny that he cannot either rescue his own offspring or restrain his tears at their death. Fine doings are these, and others that follow, such as adultery in heaven, with the gods as such shameless onlookers that some of them confessed that they envied the united pair. And well they might, when even the eldest of them, the king, could not restrain his passion for his consort long enough to permit of withdrawal to his chamber. Then there are the gods in bondage to men, hired now as builders, now as shepherds; and others chained, like criminals, in prison of brass. What man in his senses would not be stirred to reprimand the inventors of such fables and to condemn the consummate folly of those who believed them? They have even deified Terror and Fear, nay, Frenzy and Deceit (which of the worst passions have they not transfigured into the nature and form of a god?), and have induced cities to offer sacrifices to the more respectable members of this pantheon.

Thus they have been absolutely compelled to regard some of the gods as givers of blessings and to call others "(gods) to be averted." They then rid themselves of the latter, as they would of the worst scoundrels of humanity, by means of favours and presents, expecting to be visited by some serious mischief if they fail to pay them their price.

Now, what is the cause of such irregular and erroneous conceptions of the deity? For my part, I trace it to the ignorance of the true nature of God with which their legislators entered on their task, and to their failure to formulate even such correct knowledge of it as they were able to attain and to make the rest of the constitution conform to it. Instead, as if they were the most trifling of details, they allowed the poets to introduce what gods they chose, subject to all the passions, and the orators to pass decrees for entering the name of any suitable foreign god on the burgess-roll. Painters also and sculptors were given great license in this matter by the Greeks, each designing a figure of his own imagination, one moulding it of clay, another using paints. The artists who are the most admired of all use ivory and gold as the material for the novelties which they are constantly producing. And now the gods who once flourished with honours are grown old, that is the kinder way of putting it; and others, newly introduced, are the objects of worship. Some temples are left to desolation, others are but now being erected, according to individual caprice; whereas they ought, on the contrary, to have preserved immutably their belief in God and the honour which they rendered to Him. (*Against Apion* II:239-54)

So appealing are the laws of Moses that many in the Greek world are drawn to them:

From the Greeks we are severed more by our geographical position than by our institutions, with the result that we neither hate nor envy them. On the contrary, many of them have agreed to adopt our laws *[eis tous hemeterous nomous sunebesan eiselthein];* of whom some have remained faithful, while others, lacking the necessary endurance, have again seceded *[apestesan]*. (*Against Apion* II:123)

Indeed, serious proselytes are welcomed, since the ties that bind the community together are the laws, not birth:

The consideration given by our legislator to the equitable treatment of aliens also merits attention. It will be seen that he took the best of all possible measures at once to secure our own customs from corruption, and to throw them open ungrudgingly to any who elect to share them. To all who desire to come and live under the same laws with us, he gives a gracious welcome *[hosoi men gar ethelousin hupo tous autous hemin nomous zen hupelthontes dexetai philophonos],* holding that it is not family ties alone which constitute relationship, but agreement in the principles of conduct *[ou to genei monon, alla kai te proairesei tou biou nomizon einai ten oikeoiseta].* On the other hand, it was not his pleasure that casual visitors should be admitted to the intimacies of our daily life. (*Against Apion* II:209-10)

Throughout the world the laws of Moses stir admiration:

An infinity of time has passed since Moses, if one compares the age in which he lived with those of other legislators; yet it will be found that throughout the whole of that period not merely have our laws stood the test of our own use, but they have to an ever increasing extent excited the emulation of the world at large.

Our earliest imitators were the Greek philosophers, who, though ostensibly observing the laws of their own countries, yet in their conduct and philosophy were Moses' disciples, holding similar views about God, and advocating the simple life and friendly communion between man and man. But that is not all. The masses have long since shown a keen desire to adopt our religious observance *[kai plethesin ede polus zelous gegonen ek makrou tes hemeteras eusebeias];* and there is not one city, Greek or barbarian, nor a single nation, to which our custom of abstaining from work on the seventh day has not spread, and where the fasts and the lighting of lamps and many of our prohibitions in the matter of food are not observed. Moreover, they attempt to imitate our unanimity, our liberal charities, our devoted labour in the crafts, *our endurance under persecution in behalf of our laws.* The greatest miracle of all is that our Law holds out no seductive bait of sensual pleasure, but has exercised this influence through its own inherent merits *[kath'heauton isxusen* (force, power) *ho nomos];* and, as God permeates the universe, so the Law has found its way among all mankind *[kai hosper ho theos dia pantos tou kosmou pepthoiteken, houtos ho nomos dia panton anthropon bebadiken].* Let each man reflect for himself on his own country and his own household, and he will not disbelieve what I say. (*Against Apion* II:281-84; italics added)

Law and doctrine were to be *internalized* and reinforced
with relentless education:

Our legislator . . . took great care to combine both systems. He
did not leave practical training in morals inarticulate; nor did he
permit the letter of the law to remain inoperative. Starting from
the very beginning with the food of which we partake from
infancy and the private life of the home, he left nothing,
however insignificant, to the discretion and caprice of the
individual. What meats a man should abstain from, and what
he may enjoy; with what persons he should associate; what
period should be devoted respectively to strenuous labour and
to rest—*for all this our leader made the Law the standard and the rule,
that we might live under it as under a father and master,* and be guilty
of no sin through wilfulness or ignorance.

For ignorance he left no pretext. He appointed the Law to be
the most excellent and necessary form of instruction, ordain-
ing, not that it should be heard once for all or twice or on several
occasions, *but that every week men should desert their other
occupations and assemble to listen to the Law and to obtain a thorough
and accurate knowledge of it, a practice which all other legislators seem
to have neglected.*

Indeed, most men, so far from living in accordance with their
own laws, hardly know what they are. Only when they have
done wrong do they learn from others that they have
transgressed the law. Even those of them who hold the highest
and most offices admit their ignorance; for they employ
professional legal experts as assessors and leave them in charge
of the administration of affairs. *But, should anyone of our nation be
questioned about the laws, he would repeat them more readily than his
own name. The result, then, of our thorough grounding in the laws
from the first dawn of intelligence is that we have them, as it were,
engraven on our souls.* A transgressor is a rarity; evasion of
punishment by excuses an impossibility. (*Against Apion*
II:173-178; italics added)

This engraving of the laws on the soul shapes a unified
and harmonious people of God:

To this cause above all we owe our admirable harmony. Unity
and identity of religious belief, perfect uniformity in habits and
customs, produce a very beautiful concord in human character.
Among us alone will be heard no contradictory statements
about God, such as are common among other nations, not only

289

on the lips of ordinary individuals under the impulse of some passing mood, but even boldly propounded by philosophers; some putting forward crushing arguments against the very existence of God, others depriving Him of His providential care *[pronoian]* for mankind. Among us alone will be seen no difference in the conduct of our lives. With us all act alike, all profess the same doctrine about God, one which is in harmony with our Law and affirms that all things are under His eye. Even our womenfolk and dependents would tell you that piety must be the motive of all our occupations in life. (*Against Apion* II:179-81)

The Law demands a discipline so rigorous that only a people who have freely internalized the Law as God's will could possibly adhere to so demanding a regimen:

Practices which, under the name of mysteries and rites of initiation, other nations are unable to observe for but a few days, we maintain with delight and unflinching determination all our lives. (*Against Apion* II:189)

The self-discipline of the Jews even put the Spartans to shame:

We [in contrast to the Spartans] . . . notwithstanding the countless calamities in which changes of rulers in Asia have involved us, never even in the direst extremity proved traitors to our laws; and we respect them not from any motive of sloth or luxury. A little consideration will show that they impose on us ordeals and labours far more severe than the endurance commonly believed to have been required of the Lacedaemonians. Those men neither tilled the ground nor toiled at crafts, but, exempt from all business, passed their life in the city, sleek of person and cultivating beauty by physical training; for all the necessaries of life they had others to wait on them, by whom their food was prepared and served to them; and the sole aim for which they were prepared to do and suffer everything was the noble and humane object of defeating all against whom they took the field. Even in this, I may remark in passing, they were unsuccessful. The fact is that not isolated individuals only, but large numbers have frequently, in defiance of the injunctions of their law, surrendered in a body with their arms to the enemy.

Has anyone ever heard of a case of our people, not, I mean, in such large numbers, but merely two or three, proving traitors to their laws or afraid of death? I do not refer to that easiest of deaths, on the battlefield, but death accompanied by physical torture, which is thought to be the hardest of all. To such a death we are, in my belief, exposed by some of our conquerors, not from hatred of those at their mercy, but from a curiosity to witness the astonishing spectacle of men who believe that the only evil which can befall them is to be compelled to do any act or utter any word contrary to their laws. There should be nothing astonishing in our facing death on behalf of our laws with a courage which no other nation can equal. For even those practices of ours which seem the easiest others find difficult to tolerate: I mean personal service, simple diet, discipline which leaves no room for freak or individual caprice in matters of meat and drink, or in the sexual relations, or in extravagance, or again the absentention from work at rigidly fixed periods. No; the men who march out to meet the sword and charge and rout the enemy could not face regulations about everyday life. On the other hand, our willing obedience to the law in these matters results in the heroism which we display in the face of death. (*Against Apion* II:228-35)

And to what end this loyalty to the death? Eternal life and resurrection for each and every *individual* who had remained steadfast to the system of God-given laws which he had engraved on his conscience. This abiding faith in life everlasting stilled the clamor of this world of pain and suffering and stripped death of its frightening power:

For those . . . who live in accordance with our laws the prize is not silver or gold, no crown of wild olive or of parsley with any such public mark of distinction [*anakeruxis*]. No; each *individual, relying on the witness of his own conscience [all' autos hekastos hauto to suneidos exon marturoun pepisteuken] and the lawgiver's prophecy, confirmed by the sure testimony of God, is firmly persuaded that to those who observe the laws and, if they must needs die for them, willingly meet death, God has granted a renewed existence and in the revolution of the ages the gift of a better life [hoti tois tous nomous diaphulaxasi kan ei deoi thneskein huper auton prothumos apothanousi dedoken ho theos genesthai te palin kai bion ameino labein ek peritropes].* I should have hesitated to write thus, had not the facts made all men aware that many of our countrymen have on many occasions ere now preferred to brave all manner of suffering rather than to utter a single word against the Law. (*Against Apion* II:218-19)

With these words, Josephus openly reveals his Pharisaic loyalties, since the Sadducees utterly rejected any belief in rewards and punishments after death. This eloquent passage makes clear that the Law whose praises Josephus has been singing could only have been the twofold Law of the Pharisees.

This passage likewise firmly ties Josephus' faith as his life was drawing to an end, to the faith he clung to when he begged his companions to hold back from suicide lest they lose their immortality:

No; suicide is alike repugnant to that nature which all creatures share, and an act of impiety towards God who created us. Among the animals there is not one that deliberately seeks death or kills itself; so firmly rooted in all its nature's law—the will to live. That is why we account as enemies those who would openly take our lives and punish as assassins those who clandestinely attempt to do so. And God—think you not that He is indignant when man treats His gift with scorn? For it is from Him that we have received our being, and it is to Him that we should leave the decision to take it away. All of us, it is true, have mortal bodies, composed of perishable matter, but the soul lives for ever, immortal: it is a portion of the Deity housed in our bodies. If then, one who makes away with or misapplies a deposit entrusted to him by a fellow-man is reckoned a perjured villain, how can he who casts out from his own body the deposit which God has placed there, hope to elude Him whom he has thus wronged? It is considered right to punish a fugitive slave, even though the master he leaves be a scoundrel and shall we fly from the best of masters, from God Himself, and not be deemed impious? Know you not that they who depart this life in accordance with the law of nature and repay the loan which they received from God, when He who lent is pleased to reclaim it, win eternal renown; that their houses and families are secure; *that their souls, remaining spotless and obedient, are allotted the most holy place in heaven, whence, in the revolution of the ages, they return to find in chaste bodies a new habitation?* But as for those who have laid mad hands upon themselves, the darker regions of the nether world receive their souls, and God, their father, visits upon their posterity the outrageous acts of the parents. (*War* III:370-75; italics added)

Our analysis of *Against Apion* reveals that the fundamental teachings of the Scribes-Pharisees consisted of a Triad: (1) The singular Father God so loved the individual that he (2) revealed, through Moses, his twofold Law which, if internalized and steadfastly adhered to, (3) would gain for such an individual eternal life for his soul and the resurrection of his body. This Triad is one and the same as that Pharisaic Triad elicited from the Mishnah and the Gospels.

The learned sages who taught this Triad were held in the highest esteem. They were the exemplars of the people. Josephus leaves us in no doubt as to their preeminence in the closing lines of *Antiquities:*

And now I take heart from the consummation of my proposed work to assert that no one else, either Jew or Gentile, would have been equal to the task, however willing to undertake it, of issuing so accurate a treatise as this for the Greek world. For my compatriots admit that in our Jewish learning I far excel them. I have also laboured strenuously to partake of the realm of Greek prose and poetry, and after having gained a knowledge of Greek grammar, although the habitual use of my native tongue has prevented my attaining precision in the pronunciation. For our people do not favour those persons who have mastered the speech of many nations, or who adorn their style with smoothness of diction, because they consider that not only is such skill common to ordinary freemen but that even slaves who so choose may acquire it. *But they give credit for wisdom to those alone who have an exact knowledge of the Law and who are capable of interpreting the meaning of the Holy Scripture [monois de sophian marturousin tois ta nomima saphos epistamenois kai ten ton hieron grammaton dunamim hermeneusai dunamenois]. Consequently, though many have laboriously undertaken this training, scarcely two or three have succeeded, and have forthwith reaped the fruit of their labours.* (*Ant.* XX:262-65; italics added)

And that those who had this exact knowledge must have been the Pharisees is manifest throughout Josephus' works. (Cf. *War* II:162-63; *Life* 190-98.)

Stirred by faith in this Triad, the Jews transferred their loyalties from *a* reality without to *the* Reality within and were willing to lay down their lives for an *internal* constitution with greater readiness than were the Greeks and Romans to lay down their lives for an external constitution:

And from these laws of ours nothing has had the power to deflect us, neither fear of our masters, nor envy of the institutions esteemed by other nations. *We have trained our courage,* not with a view of waging war for self-aggrandizement, but in order to preserve our laws *[all'epi to tous nomous diaphulattein].* *To defeat in any other form we patiently submit, but when pressure is put upon us to alter our statutes [epeidan tines homas ta nomima kinein anakadzsi], then we deliberately fight, even against tremendous odds,* and hold out under reverses to the last extremity. (*Against Apion* II:271-72; italics added)

Robbed though we be of wealth, of cities, of all good things, our Law at least remains immortal *(ho goun nomos hemin athanatos diamenei);* and there is not a Jew so distant from his country, so much in awe of a cruel despot, but has more fear of the Law than of him. If, then, our attachment to our laws is due to their excellence, let it be granted that they are excellent. If, on the contrary, it be thought that the laws to which we are so loyal are bad, what punishment could be too great for persons who transgress those which are better? (II:277-78)

Here, then, in Josephus' *Against Apion,* we have eloquent testimony to the enduring achievement of the Pharisaic Revolution: a system of *internalized* laws mapping the road to salvation. It was a system of laws and belief which was nonpareil. Here is Josephus' final summation:

I have shown that our race *[to genos]* goes back to a remote antiquity. . . . [As for our lawgiver, Moses] his sterling merits have found a witness of old in God, and, after God, in Time.

Upon the laws it was unnecessary to expatiate. A glance at them showed that they teach not impiety, but the most genuine piety: that they invite men not to hate their fellows, but to share their possessions; that they are the foes of injustice and scrupulous for justice, banish sloth and extravagance, *and teach men to be self-dependent and work with a will;* that they deter them from war for the sake of conquest, *but render them valiant defenders of the laws themselves;* inexorable in punishment, not to be duped by studied words *[asophistoi logon paraskeuais],* always supported by actions. For actions are our invariable testimonials. I would therefore boldly maintain that we have introduced to the rest of the world a very large number of beautiful ideas. What greater beauty than inviolable piety? What higher justice than obedience to the laws? What more beneficial than to be in harmony with one another, to be a prey neither to disunion in adversity, nor to arrogance and faction in prosperity; in war to despise death, in peace to devote oneself to crafts or agriculture; *and to be convinced that everything in the whole universe is under the eye and direction of God [panta de kai pantaxou pepeisthai ton theon epopteuonta diepein]? (Against Apion* II:288-95; italics added)

Chapter VIII

"God So Loved the Individual . . ."

Josephus' testimony is eloquent. The Jews alone of all the peoples of antiquity had *internalized* a system of laws for which they were willing to lay down their lives. Unlike the laws of the Greek city states or the laws of Rome, the twofold Law was binding on the individual wherever he might be, whether in Jerusalem, or Antioch, or Corinth, or Ephesus, or in Rome itself. Adherence to it was independent of the comings and goings of state sovereignty. It was the twofold Law of God himself and therefore obligatory wherever God was. And since this God was the one and only God, his sovereignty over the individual was not altered by the rise and fall of cities, the ebb and flow of empires, the ups and downs of civilization. His eye peered into the innermost recesses of the individual's soul and discerned every flutter of good and of evil. From this all-seeing God no individual could hide his innermost thoughts and feelings. And this God—omnipotent, sovereign, and caring Father—could be depended upon to grant to each and every Law-abiding individual a share for *his* very own soul in the world to come, and resurrection for *his* very own body at some distant time known to God alone.

The vast majority of the Jews, then, who followed the teachings of the Pharisees, carried wherever they went an internalized constitution, a *politeuma*. Whereas for the

Greeks and Romans this constitution encircled the individual, binding him from without, the *politeuma* of the Scribes-Pharisees was encircled by the individual and bound him from within. And whereas a Greek or Roman citizen might or might not feel the pangs of guilt when he violated a law of the city or empire, and certainly felt no guilt when, having left Athens or Corinth, he no longer obeyed the laws of his native city, his Jewish counterpart had no way of escaping his feelings of guilt whenever he violated the laws of the divine *politeuma* which, from the very dawn of conscience, had been engraved on his soul.

The Scribes-Pharisees were thus the most ardent advocates of the kingdom of God within. They were the grand internalizers. They achieved what neither the Pentateuch nor the prophets nor the Greek philosophers had achieved. They had so stirred the masses of people with their vision of the glory road leading to a life beyond death, a road whose directional markers were the Written and the Oral Law, that the overwhelming majority of the Jews were willing to forgo even priestly mediation. They were ready to face God the Father directly with only their inner *politeuma* to reassure them that he would reward their steadfastness to the kingdom within by bestowing upon them a world of felicity without end.

The cultus, the priesthood, the Temple, ceased to be the focus and the essential concern. The laws regulating the sacrifices were no longer the simple written laws; they were the *halakhoth.* Discriminating between the clean and the unclean, the holy and the profane, was no longer an exclusive priestly prerogative, for it was the scholar class who prescribed the criteria. The sons of Aaron might still exercise the priestly monopoly, but the procedures they were to carry out were firmly set down by the Scribes-Pharisees. The total cultic system was subordinated to the teachings of the Oral Law. To offer sacrifices was no more or less elevated a commandment of God than reciting the *Shema* twice daily. The High

priest's entry into the Holy of Holies on Yom Kippur was
neither more nor less salvationary than the carrying out
of any number of acts rendered sacred by the twofold
Law. God's ultimate judgment would follow from a
judicious weighing of all the *halakhoth* one had carried
out, alongside of all the *averoth,* "transgressions," one
had committed. A High Priest who failed to follow the
prescribed procedures on Yom Kippur was as culpable as
an individual who prepared a fire on the sabbath. A Jew
living in Rome who could not participate in the Temple
worship, but who carried out whichever of the *halakhoth*
were doable in the Diaspora, was as certain of the world
to come and the resurrection as his Judean counterpart
who carried out the *halakhoth* that were applicable to
those who resided in the Holy Land. God the Father's
ultimate decision was dependent on the totality of his
relationship to each and every individual. Loyalty to the
politeuma within, not intermediation from without, was
what tipped the scales.

The Scribes-Pharisees thus went a step beyond the
prophets, the Aaronide priests, and the psalmists. The
prophets had stressed the primacy of the heart; the
Aaronide priests made no pretense that the altar atoned
unless the sinner brought his sacrifice with contrition; the
psalmist opened the gates of the sanctuary only to those
who are of "clean hands and of pure heart." Internalization was thus the goal of prophet, priest, and psalmist.
But this goal was elusive, since the Aaronide system as
spelled out in the Pentateuch is a system of cultic and
priestly intermediation. Though one should have clean
hands and a pure heart, having such qualities were not in
and of themselves sufficient for atonement. They were
prerequisities, but they were not enough. The sacrifices
had to be brought to the proper place, offered at the
proper time, for the proper purpose, by the proper
priesthood. To deviate was to defy God's divine
ordinances mandated for all generations. Similarly,
however much the prophets and psalmists and priests

pleaded for the inner commitment, they were up against the barriers set by their restrained concept of reward and punishment. So long as the individual measured his salvation by terrestial longevity, earthly abundance or scarcity, this-worldly security or exile, the fertile or barren womb of the here and now, he could gamble that evildoing was as likely to reap rich rewards as doing good, if not richer. The cry of the psalmist and the sufferings of Job only too eloquently testify to this assumption.

But with the Scribes-Pharisees all of this was transmuted. By proclaiming that God the Father looks into the heart and soul of each individual, measures the outer action by the inner motive, evaluates the degree of quality of each individual's loyalty to the internalized *politeuma,* and then, following on such piercing scrutiny, determines whether that individual's soul is to suffer eternal punishment or eternal felicity, the Scribes-Pharisees struck a mortal blow at gambling with one's salvation. If one truly believed that God the Father rewarded and punished in the world to come, then one had no alternative but to peer deeply into the inner recesses of one's mind and heart, lest one be blind to what God the Father sees all too clearly. In such a system, internalization cannot be bypassed. Intermediation is not an option. Neither the altar nor the priesthood nor the scholar class can effect atonement. They can point out the way, but the individual must himself walk upon it. They can make known the obstacles, but only the individual can remove them. They can make known the *politeuma* leading to salvation, but only the individual can determine whether he will be a loyal and steadfast citizen. And since there are no absolute guarantees, no unqualified certainties, no foolproof assurances, the individual is compelled to establish a direct relationship to God the Father and wrestle, sometimes in pain, sometimes in ecstacy, and sometimes, as with Paul, in sheer desperation, with where one stands with the loving-judging Father.

The Scribes-Pharisees thus went far beyond the priests, prophets, and psalmists. They stripped the empiric world of its ultimate relevancy. It was, to be sure, the world in which one earned or lost eternal life; but it was not the world in which ultimate judgment was rendered. The righteous might suffer torment of body and soul, even die a martyr's death, but his soul would soar up to God the Father. The wicked might revel in every pleasure, bask in prosperity, wallow in sensuality, and die aged and unbowed—only to enter into a life of endless torment, unrelieved agony, and eternal pain. Indeed, suffering in this world was a sign of righteousness, for how else was God to test one's unflagging commitment to the internalized *politeuma*. To obey God when the rewards are immediately to hand is, after all, only a form of expediency; to obey him when there is no evidence that he cares is to meet the true test of inner faith.

The Scribes-Pharisees also went far beyond the philosophers of the Greco-Roman world. Socrates, Plato, Aristotle, and, above all, the Stoics spoke eloquently and persuasively of an internalized standard—a standard that would elevate the individual above the raging tumult and disorder of the world of sense perception and allow him to enjoy the felicity that comes from a world of eternal ideas, from a changeless order of reality, from a realm of immutable Truth. With such an inner standard as trustworthy beacon, one could pilot one's way through the surging seas and treacherous shoals of life, for even if one foundered, he need not give way to despair. But, as Josephus points out, such an internalized standard was a real option only for a handful of philosophers and the statesmen who were their disciples. It was no option for the masses, since they had been nurtured on polytheism. For them there could be no single internalized standard, for they did not have a single God. Each god was sovereign in his or her own realm. Each god had his or her special virtues and special vices. Each had his or her temples, priests, and devotees. To internalize the pantheon of the Greeks and Romans was to internalize chaos, conflict, and discord. It was to internalize congeries of mutually exclusive demands, prohibitions, and ego ideals. It simply made a one-to-One relationship impossible, for there was no One.

Indeed, to the degree that internalization was an option for the people at large, it followed from loyalty to the *politeuma* of the city or state. If one was an Athenian, then, irrespective of the variety of gods one worshiped, one was loyal to the Athenian *politeuma* and not to that of Sparta. But a city or a state is not itself a god. Disloyalty could be punished within the boundaries of the *politeuma* but not without. There was no single God who could visit punishment on a disloyal citizen wherever that individual might be and however far from Athens he might flee. One might internalize the notion of loyalty to whatever *politeuma* was in force but not the *politeuma* itself.

There was a further difference as well. The gods of the Greek and Roman worlds were poor models for human emulation. Even by Greek standards, the gods behaved in ways that were not tolerated in well-run societies. By contrast, there were any numbers of individuals who had led exemplary and noble lives. These were individuals who had internalized certain ideals to which they were staunchly loyal. A Socrates was thus far more of an ego ideal for the virtuous person than was Zeus. For the individual, then, there was not available in the Greek pantheon any single god who could serve as the perfect exemplar of all those attributes which a person might wish to emulate. For the Greeks and Romans, humans were more divine than the gods.

Not so with the Scribes-Pharisees. As heirs to the Pentateuch, the Prophets, and the Hagiographa, they reaffirmed their absolute commitment to the one and only God. This God, unlike the Greek gods, was a perfect

God—a God who was good and gracious and loving and merciful and just. If he gave way to anger, it was only to rectify an injustice. If he showed any negative human passion, it was only to underscore his absolute commitment to his essential attributes. He was a God who was a *living* model for emulation. And since this God was one, his commands could be internalized by each and every individual; and because he was omnipotent and omnipresent, he could watch over each individual and judge him at all times and in all places. From his eye one could not hide. One might flee from Zeus to Apollo, but how could one flee from God to God?

Because God was one, and because God was exemplary, and because God had revealed the road to eternal life and resurrection, the masses of Jews were won over to internalization of the twofold Law as the way out of a cul-de-sac, a cul-de-sac into which the Pentateuch had driven them by limiting salvation to this world. For them, the teaching of the Scribes-Pharisees was the good news they had longed for, a gospel of hope, redemption, and salvation. Each and every person who had faith in the internalized twofold Law was on the glory road to life eternal. As Josephus expressed it with unmatched eloquence: "Each individual relying on the witness of his own conscience and the lawmaker's prophecy, confirmed by the sure testimony of God, is firmly persuaded that to those who observe the laws and, if they must need die for them, willingly meet death, God has granted a renewed existence and in the revolution of the ages the gift of a better life" (*Against Apion* II:218-19).

This, then, was the core of the Pharisaic Revolution: a firm and unwavering belief in an alluring Triad: (1) God the just and caring Father so loved each and every individual that (2) he revealed to Israel his twofold Law—Written and Oral—which, when *internalized* and faithfully obeyed, (3) promises to the Law-abiding individual eternal life for his soul and resurrection for his body. Internalization of the divine will as the ultimate, the most certain, and the only enduring reality—this was the grand achievement of the Scribes-Pharisees.

And it was this achievement that served as the bedrock of emergent Christianity. Jesus was nurtured on the twofold Law. At the very dawn of his intelligence, the grand faith of the Pharisees in the Triad was inscribed within his conscience. God was indeed the loving and caring Father. God had revealed his will to Israel in the twofold Law. God had promised that everyone who served with love and loyalty would enjoy eternal life and resurrection. For Jesus, as for the Pharisees, the ultimate reality was within, not without. It was this reality that shone forth from the cross, when wracked by pain and suffering, the one God was affirmed, not denied.

And Jesus' disciples, blurred by sorrow, reached out to the Triad—in faith and in hope—and saw Jesus risen from the dead. The promise of the Scribes-Pharisees was a true promise indeed! God does raise from the dead. The Son of man lives on. The Messiah reveals his authenticity by illuminating God's power to quicken the dead, even as the Scribes-Pharisees had again and again demonstrated from Scriptures. The Resurrected Christ was the living truth of a core Pharisaic teaching. The Triad was reinforced, but with one modification—God had revealed in addition to the twofold Law, Jesus as the Christ. Christ must be *internalized* if the promise of eternal life and resurrection and the coming of the Kingdom of God was to be fulfilled.

Christ was to be *internalized!* Faith in him was not to be measured by the bludgeonings of fate or the pummelings of chance. Christ within shielded one from the batterings without. This was what faith in Christ was all about. That Christ did not come back at once, that he did not ward off the blows rained on his loyal disciples, that he seemed so helpless—these empirical signs of his nonexistence did not blur, for believing Christians, his felt presence and his utter reality. Like the Scribes-Pharisees, the Christians were immune to the "reality" without because they had *the* reality within. And the reality for both was the Triad: (1) The Father God, (2) the revelation of his will (twofold Law for the Pharisees, Christ for the Christians), (3) eternal life and resurrection.

The middle term is the crux. It was here that the Christians parted company with their teachers. The Scribes-Pharisees could not acknowledge Jesus as having risen from the dead. Resurrection was not the issue, for it was the very core of Pharisaic teaching. Jesus' resurrection, however, was very much the issue. For Scribes-Pharisees, Jesus could not have been resurrected because during his lifetime he had challenged the Scribes-Pharisees with claims that they had firmly rejected. Jesus had not knuckled under to their authority. He persisted in teaching as though he were indeed the Son of man. He thus defied the very class that held the keys to eternal life and resurrection. No one challenging their authority could possibly have been selected by God to be raised from the dead. If a messiah were ever to come, not only would Elijah precede him, but he would prove to be the Messiah, not by rising from the dead but by fulfilling his messianic role while still alive. The Christian claims that Jesus had been resurrected and that it was this resurrection that proved beyond doubt he must be the Messiah, were, from the Pharisaic angle of vision, utterly fraudulent.

There was one follower of the Pharisees, however, who was shocked into belief that Jesus had indeed been resurrected. This ardent devotee of the Pharisees who had prided himself in his blameless adherence to the twofold Law was Paul. He exemplifies, as no one else, the inner core of Pharisaism and the inner core of Christianity. His agonizing experience reveals the bridge he built from *internalization* to *internalization,* from *Triad* to *Triad.* His Christ is the living witness of Pharisaism's creative power.

Paul, by his own testimony, was "as to the law a Pharisee, as to zeal a persecutor of the church, as to righteousness under the law blameless" (Phil. 3:5b-6). He attests to his precociousness when he recalls in Gal. 1:14 that he was "advanced in Judaism beyond many of my own age among my people, so extremely zealous was I for the traditions of my fathers *[pardoseis mou pateron]."* This zealousness Paul associated with his violent efforts to overthrow the church (Phil. 3:6, Gal. 1:13). Paul's "as to righteousness under the law blameless" and his zealous persecution of the Church testify to his having *internalized* the Pharisaic Triad deep within his conscience. This meant that he was always striving to prove to God and to himself that he was worthy of eternal life and resurrection. If only he could be blameless under the Law! If only he could eradicate those who proclaimed that Jesus, a challenger of the Scribes-Pharisees, had been raised from the dead! Such blamelessness and such zeal would earn for his soul a goodly portion in the world to come and for his body, in God's own time, resurrection.

We know that for Paul this internalization failed. The more blameless he thought himself to be, the more insecure he became. The more zealous he was in persecuting the Church, the more was his inner self thrown into tumult. The Pharisees had taught unequivocally that there was to be a resurrection of the righteous dead, those who had been blameless—or sufficiently blameless—in their adherence to the twofold Law. Yet here were Christians proclaiming that Jesus had been seen risen from the dead. They affirmed this as a fact. Since the belief that resurrection was not only possible but inevitable was not in question, the only point at issue was whether the Christian claim was factual. Had Jesus risen from the dead or had he not?

At first Paul vehemently rejected the claim as fraudulent. He sought to root it out, so that it would not endanger the salvation of his fellow Jews. But the more zealous his persecution, the more haunting became the question: Did Jesus rise from the dead, or did he not?

Paul's certainty was undermined. His *internalized* defenses began to crumble. The barrier of the twofold Law which was designed to protect the individual from the poundings of the outer and the inner worlds, to dissolve doubt and renew faith, to block the onslaughts of sin—this barrier suddenly tumbled, and Paul collapsed into the arms of Christ. He was transfigured. Jesus had indeed risen. The nonfact was a fact. The Pharisees, not the Christians, had taught fraudulently. The twofold Law was not the way to eternal life and resurrection. It cannot hold back the power of sin. Sin lurks behind the Law; it is provoked by the Law; it can, at any time, overwhelm the Law. The power of the Law is illusory. Sinful man, impulse-torn and sin-sodden, cannot be redeemed by the Law, the agent provocateur of sin, but only by the freely given love of Jesus Christ who, in dying, deprived sin of life. Christ's love and grace could do what the Law could not—dissolve the power of sin itself.

Christ, and not the Law, was to be internalized. So long as one had Christ within, one had joy unbounding. One was without fear, however much terror abounded. One was ready to face the beasts at Ephesus or submit, now to this kind of martyrdom, now to that, with serenity and anticipation. Christ's grace and Christ's love raised one above the claws and pangs of death. Eternal life beckoned with alluring certainty. Paul might well have paraphrased Josephus (*Against Apion* II:271-72): And from Christ, nothing has the power to deflect us, neither fear of our masters, nor envy of the institutions esteemed by other nations. We have trained our courage, not with the view of waging war, but in order to hold onto Christ. To defeat in any other form we patiently submit, but when pressure is put on us to abandon Christ, then we deliberately fight even against tremendous odds, and hold out under reverses to the last extremity.

Paul thus built a bridge from internalization to internalization; from Triad to Triad. Paul, more effectively than the writers of the Gospels and Acts, won over Christians to his concept of Christ, for Paul's portrait of Christ, unlike the others, is not blurred by terrestrial events and happenings. Christ for him is exclusively the resurrected Christ, the Christ who lived in order to die, who died in order to rise from the dead, who rose from the dead so that his grace would allow humans to overcome sin. For Paul, Christ was not the Jesus who lived an exemplary life, however exemplary it must have been, who stirred his disciples with parables, who wrangled with Pharisees, who drove the money changers from the Temple. No, for Paul, Jesus was the gift from God the Father to dissolve the illusion that the twofold Law can save and that human beings, unaided, can resist the allure and the provocation of sin. Little wonder, then, that for Paul, Christ's second coming was secondary to his never having gone away. Christ had to be absorbed within before he could appear without. And if Christ was within, there was no pressing need that he ever show himself without. The *internalized* Christ was the *eternalized* Christ.

The Pharisaic revolution thus seeded the Christian revolution. It seeded it with its Triad and with its focus on internalization. The power of Christianity is thus, in a vital way, an extension of the power of Pharisaism. Christianity, to be sure, mapped its own roads to salvation. Out of its commitment to Christ it bred vigorous offshoots, creative shapes and forms, exciting variations and mutations. The power of Christ has proved to be an enduring power, even as the love of Christ has never failed to embrace believing Christians. Yet the primordial source of the Christian Triad is the Pharisaic Triad. Paul's certainty that Christ was resurrected was rooted in the certainty that there could be a resurrection. Paul's Father is the Father of the Scribes-Pharisees; Paul's internalized Christ is the counterpart of the internalized twofold Law of the Pharisees; Paul's hope for eternal life and resurrection is the Pharisaic

307

hope. Paul's unwavering faith in Scripture is one and the same as the faith of the Scribes-Pharisees. Paul's Triad and the Pharisaic Triad may not be congruent, but they are strikingly similar in form, in structure, and in symbolic power.

The Pharisaic and Christian revolutions seeded still a third spiritual revolution when Muhammad revealed his own version of the Triad. For him, as for the Pharisees and for the Christians, God was the Father who had revealed the way to eternal life. The Triad, as form, is thus identical. What Muhammad altered was the middle term: God's will was made known to Muhammad in its purest form; and it is this will that the true Muslim must internalize. The teachings of the Koran displaced the twofold Law; the words of Muhammad, Christ. Islam emerged as living witness to the power of Pharisaism and to the power of Christ.

Pharisaism thus generated two blooming offshoots: Christianity and Islam. Each of these religions has demonstrated remarkable creative powers. Each has succeeded in winning over millions of followers. Each has generated a wide array of differentiated forms. Each has been able to preserve itself in the face of novel problems and unanticipated developments. Each has stirred its followers with its reassurance that reality is within and not without, that felicity without end awaits the faithful at life's journey's end, that *eternal* person-hood is the ultimate reward for *internal* steadfastness. So powerful indeed have been both Christianity and Islam that neither has made significant headway against the other except through coercion.

But no less remarkable has been the fate and destiny of Pharisaism. The Scribes-Pharisees seeded Christianity, but they were not supplanted by the Christians. They seeded Islam, but were not overcome by it. Their own original creation, the Triad, held firm. Only a handful of their followers were drawn to the gospel of the risen Christ as preached by Jesus' disciples; even fewer were drawn to Paul's gospel of the Law as the agent provocateur of sin, and of Christ who died so that sin not live. The overwhelming majority of the Jews remained loyal and steadfast to the good news of the Scribes-Pharisees and clung to the hope embodied in the Triad they taught. Indeed, with the destruction of the Temple, and with the disappearance of the Sadducees, the heirs of the Pharisees, now called Sages, Rabbis, Tannaim, went from strength to strength. Now that the Temple was gone, there was no real alternative to the internalization of the twofold Law. And as the Jewries of the Diaspora expanded and flourished, only internalization could preserve Judaism. And as Jews found themselves a permanent minority within Christian, Sassanian, and Moslem societies, internalization was their only shield and buttress. Little wonder, then, when the Oral Law was finally written down in the Mishnah by Judah the Prince around A.D. 210, it served as the internal *politeuma* for Jews wherever they might be, and it became the sacred text for the scholars of the post-Mishnah generations. The Mishnah served as the foundation both for the Palestinian Talmud and the Babylonian Talmud; these, in turn, served as the foundations for the *geonic* responsa, the commentaries, the rabbinic responsa, the compendia, and the codes. And the process is by no means at an end as countless disciples of the Sages, *talmide hakhamim,* continue to pour over the folios of the Talmud and ponder the meaning and application of the twofold Law—the twofold Law, it should be stressed, not the Written Law alone. The Pentateuch was never again read by the followers and the heirs of the Pharisees except through the prisms of the Oral Law; the prophets were never understood outside the boundaries of the Oral Law; Proverbs, Ecclesiastes, the Song of Songs, Job, Daniel, and the Psalms were never interpreted as incongruent with the Pharisaic Triad. The Pharisaic Revolution was utterly triumphant, for it was not the

Pentateuch or the prophets but the Triad of the Pharisees that became normative Judaism.

And when we ask ourselves the source of this generative power, we find it in the relationship the Pharisees established between the one God and the singular individual. The Father God cared about *you;* he was concerned about *you;* he watched over *you;* he loved *you;* and loved *you* so much that he wished *your* unique self to live forever. One's earthly father was here today and gone tomorrow; but the one Father-God was here forever. One's earthly father was frail; one's heavenly Father, omnipotent. One's earthly father was now just, now unjust, now kind, now harsh, now dependable, now whimsical; one's Father in Heaven was always just, kind, merciful, and dependable. And the heavenly Father was ever present. One could talk to him, plead with him, cry out to him, pray to him—person to Person, individual to Individual, heart to Heart, soul to Soul. It was the establishment of this personal relationship, an inner experience, that accounts for the manifest power of Pharisaism to live on. It accounts for the power of Christ to live on. It accounts for the teachings of Muhammed to live on. For it would seem that there is no viable human alternative to the reality *within,* a reality that reassures each one of us that he or she is a precious person, a unique individual worthy of eternal life if each of us remains steadfast to a *politeuma* pressed deep within our souls where no external force can ravage it. *Internalization* is the only road to salvation.

In that still-living testimony of the Pharisaic transmutation, the Mishnah, we read in that crisp, nonbiblical style which the Scribes-Pharisees developed for the transmission of *halakhah* and *aggadah,* the following text:

How did they used to warn the witnesses in capital cases? They brought them in and warned them, "Perhaps you will state what is mere supposition, or hearsay, or evidence from other witnesses, or [you will say] 'We heard it from the mouth of a trustworthy person,' or perhaps you were unaware that we would test you with enquiry and cross-examination. "You must know that capital cases are not like cases involving property. In cases involving property, a man may pay money and make atonement, but in capital cases his blood [i.e., the blood of the one who is executed] and the blood of his seed hang on to him [the witness] until the end of the world. For thus we have found in the case of Cain who saw his brother, as it is said, *'thy brother's bloods crieth'* [Gen. 4:10]—it does not say *'thy brother's blood,'* but *'thy brother's bloods';* [which means] his blood and that of his progeny. For this reason man was created a singular individual: to teach you that anyone who destroys a single soul of humankind, Scripture reckons him as having destroyed the entire world. [Contrariwise] whoever preserves alive a single soul of humankind, Scripture reckons him as having preserved alive the entire world.

"[These verses are also meant] to tell us of the greatness of the Holy One praised be He. For when a human mints many coins with a single seal, all of them are identical with each other. But when the King of kings, the Holy One, blessed be He, stamps every individual with the seal of the first man, no one individual is identical with another. Therefore, every individual is required to say, 'Because of me the world was created.'" (Sanh. 5:1)

The Pharisaic Revolution is encapsulated in this Mishnah: the innovative, nonbiblical form; the articulation of a nonbiblical dictum; the drawing on biblical proof texts; the novel nonbiblical terminology; the unabashed assumption that the prescription as given here is binding law, though not spelled out in the Pentateuch. But transcending these formal attestations to the Pharisaic Revolution is the teaching itself: God so loves the individual that he created one person, not many. He so cherishes the individual that to kill an innocent person is equivalent to destroying the world and to save a person's life is equivalent to preserving the world. And God so commits himself to the uniqueness of the individual that he stamps out every person in his image, yet no individual is identical with another. With a God so caring of every individual, is it any wonder that the Scribes-Pharisees spun off an internal revolution of enduring power?

Notes

Introduction

1. Cf. Emil Schürer, *A History of the Jewish People in the Time of Jesus Christ* (New York, 1902), Second Division, vol. II, 10-28. The core of Schürer's definition reads as follows:

"In the New Testament also and in Josephus, the Pharisees evidently appear as a decided fraction of the people. In the same sense also must their name be explained. It is in Hebrew *perushim,* in Aramaic *perishin,* stat. emphat. *perishaya,* whence the Greek *pharisaioi.* That these literally mean 'the separated' is undoubted. The only question can be, to what to refer the term? Are they those who separate themselves from all uncleanness and all illegality, or those who separate themselves from certain persons? The first is spoken for by the circumstance that in Rabbinic Hebrew also the substantives *perishah* and *perishut* occur with the meaning 'separation,' scil. from all uncleanness. But if only a separation from uncleanness, without any reference to persons, were intended, other positive epithets would have been more obvious (the 'clean,' the 'just,' the 'Pious,' or the like). Besides, a separation from uncleanness is at the same time a separation from unclean persons. If, then, the latter is in any case to be included, it seems obvious to derive the name from that 'separation,' which took place in the time of Zerubbabel and then again in the time of Ezra, when Israel separated from the heathen dwelling in the land and from their uncleanness (Ezra vi.21, ix.1, x.11; Neh. ix.2, x.29). . . .

"For the Pharisees must have their name from a

separation, which *the bulk* of the nation did *not* undergo with them; in other words, *from a separation made by them, in consequence of their stricter view of the notion of uncleanness, not only from the uncleanness of the heathen, but also from that with which, according to their view, a great portion of the people were affected."* (*Ibid.*, p. 210)

Schürer then equates the Pharisees with the *"Chaberim"* (sic.). This definition is echoed by R. Travers Herford:

"The word *[perushim]* means 'separated' and the separation is *obviously* that between the members of the association, *haberim* [Herford has *haberim* in the original Hebrew] on the one hand, and the *Am-ha-aretz,* the people of the land, on the other. The higher grades of *haberim* were all within the association, marked off from each other, but all alike separated from the *Am-ha-aretz.*

"The *Perushim* as a class marked the actual line of separation, and that is clearly what their name implies. As the lowest order of the *haberim,* they would be the most numerous, because the severer tests of the higher grades would be satisfied only by a smaller and smaller number of men" (*The Pharisees* [New York, 1924], p. 32).

And this definition is re-affirmed by Louis Finkelstein:

"It was the characteristic of the plebeian scholars, the so-called scribes, that they did not at once proceed to create a political party for the advancement of their views. Instead they organized themselves and their followers into a Society for the stricter and more thorough observance of that part of the Law which was being most widely ignored and flouted among the provincials—the rules of Levitical purity.

"Universal obedience to these regulations seemed to the plebeians a necessary prerequisite to the recognition of Israel as a 'kingdom of priests and a holy nation.' They correctly understood that it was this the Lawgiver had in mind when he associated the laws of purity with approach to the Temple. It was clear perversion of his intent, and nothing more than a quibble, to maintain, as the provincials did, that only those who visited the Temple were required to be pure. . . .

"The members of the Society called one another *haber,* comrade. The expression 'members of the synagogue' *(bene ha-kenesset)* was sometimes used to distinguish the masses of the Order from their leaders, the scholars or Scribes *(Soferim).* But the wall between them and other Jews gained for them most commonly the name of 'Separatists'

(Hebrew *perushim,* Aramaic *perishaia;* Grecized into *Pharisaioi,* whence the English, Pharisees.) This was not intended in any derogatory sense; it implied merely separation from impurity and defilement. . . .
"As late as the Mishnah, compiled three and one-half centuries after the organization of the Society, the term Pharisee was still used as an antonym of *'Am ha-Aretz.'* 'The clothes of the *am ha-aretz,'* we are told, 'are impure for the Pharisee; the clothes of the Pharisee are impure for those who eat the heave-offering" (*The Pharisees* [Philadelphia, 1962], I:74-76).
　　Cf. Salo W. Baron, *A Social and Religious History of the Jews* (Philadelphia, 1952), II:35-54; George F. Moore, *Judaism* (Cambridge, 1927) I:56-71; A. Finkel, *The Pharisees and the Teacher of Nazareth* (Leiden, 1964), pp. 42-57.
　　Most recently Jacob Neusner has, in an array of studies, most notably *The Rabbinic Traditions of the Pharisees before 70,* 3 vols. (Leiden, 1971), *From Politics to Piety: The Emergence of Pharisaic Judaism* (Englewood Cliffs, 1973), and *Early Rabbinic Tradition: Historical Studies in Religion, Literature, and Art* (Leiden, 1975), pictured the Pharisees as a sect which (1) "laid great stress on eating with the right people, specifically those who obeyed the purity laws . . . (2) "held a 'tradition of the Elders' about this matter, which required that one wash hands before eating and performing other ritual ablutions . . . (3) "laid stress on eating the right kinds of food . . . tithed with great care . . ." (*Politics to Piety,* p. 80). For Neusner, "the Pharisees were the Jews who believed one must keep the purity laws outside of the Temple . . . in one's own home, the laws of ritual purity were to be followed in the only circumstance in which they might apply, namely the table. Therefore, one must eat secular food (ordinary everyday meals) in a state of ritual purity *as if one were a Temple priest.* The Pharisees arrogated to themselves—and to all Jews equally—the status of the Temple priests, and performed actions restricted to priests on account of that status. The table of every Jew in his home was seen as being like the table of the Lord in the Jerusalem Temple. The commandment 'you shall be a kingdom of priests and a holy people,' was taken literally: Everyone is a priest, everyone stands in the same relationship to God, and everyone must keep the priestly laws. At this time [prior to 70], only the Pharisees held such a viewpoint, and eating unconsecrated food as if one were a Temple priest at the Lord's table thus was

one of the few significations that a Jew was a Pharisee and a sectarian" (*Ibid.*, p. 83).

It should also be noted that Neusner shrinks away from analyzing the texts in the Tannaitic Literature in which the *Perushim* are juxtaposed to *Zedukim:* "the difficult question of meaning of *perushim* in M. Hag. 2:7, b. Sotah. 22b, b. B.B. 60b, Tos. Ber. 3:25, M. Yad. 4:6-7, Tos. Yad. 2:20, 4:8, b. Yom. 1:5, Tos. Hag. 3:35, b. Nid. 33b, Tos. Yoma 1:8, or Mak. 1:6, Sifré Deut. 190 and in the other texts examined by Ellis Rivkin in 'Defining the Pharisees' (*Hebrew Union College Annual,* 40-41, 1969-70, pp. 205-249) is not raised" (*The Rabbinic Traditions,* p. 2). In a massive treatise of 1207 pages, devoted to culling and analyzing the rabbinic traditions about the Pharisees, Neusner excludes the only tannaitic texts in which the term *perushim* as meaning Pharisees is confirmed by the juxtaposition of *Perushim* to *Zedukim,* "Sadducees"!

Neusner's three-volume study, *The Rabbinic Traditions About the Pharisees Before 70,* concludes with a definition of the Pharisees as preeminently a table-fellowship: "Then [i.e., during the last half century or so before the destruction of the Temple] the Pharisees were (whatever else they were) *primarily a society for table-fellowship,* the high point of their life as a group . . ." (p. 318). How this definition differs from that of Schürer, Herford, and Finkelstein is difficult to discern.

Although from time to time scholars have advanced other definitions (e.g., Jacob L. Lauterbach, "The Pharisees and their teachings," *Rabbinic Essays* [Cincinnati, 1951] pp. 109-10, who argues that the name Pharisees, "Separatists," was fastened on the nonpriestly teachers of the Sanhedrin when they were expelled from that body by John Hyrcanus), they have failed to gain significant scholarly recognition. Of these alternative definitions, only that formulated by Solomon Zeitlin has any affinity to the definition delineated in this book. Although I take issue with Zeitlin's postulation that the Pharisees were the people at large, and that the Pharisees emerged in the early postexilic period, I am indebted to him for the methodological breakthrough reflected in his insistence that only the texts in which the term *Perushim* is juxtaposed to *Zedukim* (Sadducees) can be drawn upon for establishing an objective definition of the Pharisees. As will be evident in chapter 3, I have adopted Zeitlin's methodological insight but refined it by making it explicit.

Although Zeitlin's method represented a major breakthrough, scholars failed to appreciate its significance and continued to identify the *perushim* in Hag. 2:7, as the

Pharisees, even though these *perushim* are juxtaposed to the *am ha-aretz* and not to the *Zedukim,* "Sadducees."

Of Zeitlin's many contributions to Pharisaic studies, the most impressive is his *Ha-Zedukim we-ha-perushim, Horeb 2* (1936), pp. 56-89, now available in English translation: *Studies in the Early History of Judaism,* II (New York, 1974), pp. 259-91. For my own appreciation of Zeitlin's seminal thinking, see E. Rivkin, "Solomon Zeitlin's Contribution to the Historiography of the Intertestamental Period," *Judaism,* 14 (1965) 354-67.

Chapter I

1. It is important to note that Josephus uses the Greek term *haeresis* whenever he refers to the Pharisees, Sadducees, Essenes, and the fourth *haeresis* launched by Judas of Galilee. But what precisely is a *haeresis*? The translators of Josephus sometimes translate the word *haeresis* as "school of thought," sometimes, "sect." H. St. J. Thackeray, for example, in this translation for the Loeb edition of the *War* (II:118) renders *haeresis* as "sect" in the passage which tells of the revolutionary Judas, but "school of thought" (II:162) in the passage quoted above. In his translation of the *Life* (10, 191), Thackeray uses "sects" in preference to "schools of thought" as the English equivalent of *haereseis.* Ralph Marcus, however, who translated some of the *Antiquities* for the Loeb series, uses "school of thought" (XIII:171, 285). Louis H. Feldman, for his part of *Antiquities* dealing with the three *haereseis,* did not have any choice but to translate Josephus' *philosophian (Ant.* XVIII:9), *philosophias* (XVIII:10), *philosophia* XVIII:11), *philosophion* (XVIII:23), and *philosophetai* (XVIII:25) as "philosophy" and "philosophies." Nonetheless, in his footnote to XVIII:12, Feldman refers to the three "sects,"while Marcus in his footnote to *Ant.* XIII:171 likewise uses "sects." Indeed, the notion of sects is fastened indelibly in the reader's mind by virtue of its usage by Thackeray (*War* II:119 ff.) as a major margin heading: "The three Jewish sects."

For a modern reader, "sect" is certain to evoke emotional associations which "school of thought" does not arouse. One thinks of a dissenting religious body, especially one that is heretical, or of "a group within an organized religion whose adherents recognize a special set of teachings or practices" or of "a comparatively small recently organized exclusive religious body, especially one that has parted company with a long established communion" or of a religious denomination, other than the established one." The word "sect" is thus an imprecise word which may run the gamut of meaning from a school of thought to a small heretical group (cf. *Oxford English Dictionary,* s.v. "sect").

No such impression, however, is conveyed when we use the term "school of thought" exclusively. It is totally benign, free of any involvement with the history of any religious system. Its meaning is imprecise, but not because it has several possible precise meanings. It carries with it no connotations of number, of tight organization, or of deviation. A school of thought may have many followers or few, may have an organizational embodiment or not, may be very popular or attract only a handful. Hence, if *haeresis* is translated "sect," it means something quite different to an English reader than if it were translated as "school of thought."

When Josephus chose the word *haeresis* to designate what Pharisees, Sadducees, and Essenes, and the followers of Judas of Galilee were, he must have been reasonably certain that the word would evoke an appropriate image. His readers could know only what the word *haeresis* meant in their day; they could not possibly know any future meaning it might develop. And Josephus was not attempting to invest the word with a new meaning. He had no inkling that his use of *haeresis* to describe the Pharisees, Sadducees, and Essenes would at some future time be translated as "sect." Nor could he have had any premonition that this word *haeresis* would give birth, under Christian auspices, to the meaning "heresy," a doctrine deviating from the authoritative teaching of the established Church.

It is evident from Josephus' assertion that there had been three *haereseis* among the Jews and that Judas of Galilee was the father of a fourth. Jews followed the teachings of one of these four. No other crystallized schools of thought existed. *And since Josephus refers to the Pharisees as the leading* haeresis, *they could not have been a sect!* The Pharisees could not have deviated from the established or dominant form of Judaism of their day if they were the established and dominant school of Judaism!

Perhaps the meaning of the word *haeresis* can best be clarified if we analyze what sort of characteristics Josephus attributes to an *haeresis.* Such an analysis reveals that a *haeresis* stood for certain doctrines and teachings. Judas of Galilee founds a fourth *haeresis* when he champions a doctrine that is novel: no lord but God, hence no tribute to Rome. The

Pharisees are an *haeresis* that has as distinguishing characteristics an accurate interpretation of the laws, a belief simultaneously in Providence and free will, a faith in rewards and punishments after death. The Sadducees and Essenes likewise advocate doctrines that differentiate them from the *haeresis* of the Pharisees and the *haeresis* of Judas of Galilee. Josephus uses only one synonym for *haeresis,* namely, "philosophy." Both in his introduction to the description of the three *haereseis* in *War* (II:119) and in the sentence that brings that section to an end (II:166), he refers to the *haereseis* as the three forms of philosophy among the Jews. So, too, in his reference to the Pharisees in the *Life* (12), Josephus asserts that some of their teachings are similar to those of the Stoics. He also identified an *haeresis* with philosophy in the *Antiquities* (XVIII:9, 11, 23, 25) when he first states that Judas of Galilee introduced a fourth philosophy, and then goes on to describe the teachings of the other three.

Josephus thus makes clear his intent. He wishes his readers to view the Pharisees, Sadducees, and Essenes as "schools of thought" and as "philosophical systems." He chose the word *haeresis* because it conveyed the idea of those who commit themselves to a body of doctrine, or those who are drawn to a set of teachings. He was in effect saying that Jews rally around three diverse forms of Judaism. His usage of *haeresis* along with the synonym "philosophy" excludes any notion of sect as "a party dissenting from an established church" or "as a group within an organized religon whose adherents recognize set of teachings or practices."

The correct meaning of *haeresis* is of great significance for constructing an objective definition of the Pharisees. If, in our minds, *haeresis* is linked to number or to deviation or to denomination, then the Pharisees we conjure up will conform to our notion of a sect. If, on the other hand, *haeresis* is neutral with respect to number, deviation, and denomination, then we can examine the evidence to determine whether the Pharisees were a *haeresis,* a school of thought, that was in reality a sect, or whether it was a *haeresis* that enjoyed the support of the vast majority of the Jewish population. When, therefore, Josephus refers to the Pharisees as the leading *haeresis* which cultivates harmonious relations with the community, he is implying strong support by the majority of Jews.

2. The rendering set down in the text is a free rendering, foreswearing literality for intelligibility. I have, however, made every effort to ferret out Josephus' meaning, despite

the opaqueness of some of his language and syntax. So elusive indeed is Josephus' Greek that even the most competent scholars have come up with significantly different translations.

To give the reader some notion of the difficulties, and, at the same time, to alert one to alternatives to the free rendering I have adopted for the text, I am setting down Louis Feldman's translation for the Loeb Edition, to be followed by two independent translations, the first by Professor Seymour Topping of the Classics Department of the University of Cincinnati and the second by Professors Martin Yaffe and Anthony Damico of the Department of Foreign Languages, North Texas State University. I am most appreciative of the graciousness of Professors Topping, Yaffe, and Damico in expending so much time and effort to help me try to understand what Josephus was trying to say.

a. *Translation by Louis Feldman.*

"The Pharisees simplify their standard of living, making no concession to luxury. They follow the guidance of that which their doctrine has selected and transmitted as good, attaching the chief importance to the observance of those commandments which it has been fit to dictate to them. They show respect and deference to their elders, nor do they rashly presume to contradict their proposals. Though they postulate that everything is brought about by fate, still they do not deprive the human will of the pursuit of what is in man's power, since it was God's good pleasure that there should be a fusion and that the will of man with his virtue and vice should be admitted to the council-chamber of fate. They believe that souls have power to survive death and that there are rewards and punishments under the earth for those who have led lives of virtue or vice: eternal imprisonment is the lot of evil souls, while the good souls receive an easy passage to a new life. Because of these views they are, as a matter of fact, extremely influential among the townsfolk; and all prayers and sacred rites of divine worship are performed according to their exposition. This is the great tribute that the inhabitants of the cities, by practising the highest ideals both in their way of living and in their discourse, have paid to the excellence of the Pharisees.

"The Sadducees hold that the soul perishes along with the body. They own no observance of any sort apart from the laws; in fact, they reckon it a virtue to dispute with the teachers of the path of wisdom that they pursue. There are but a few men to whom this doctrine has been made known, but these are men of the highest standing. They accomplish practically nothing, however. For whenever they assume some office, though they submit unwillingly and perforce, yet submit they do to the formulas of the Pharisees, since otherwise the masses would not tolerate them." (*Ant.* XIII:12-17)

b. *Translation by Martin Yaffe and Anthony Damico.*

"For the Pharisees economize on their regimen, in no way giving in to luxury, and follow the guidance of what their doctrine has after due consideration transmitted [orally] as good, since they have been led to believe that the guarding of what it has wished to propagate is much to be prized. In matters of honor, they defer to those preceding them in age, not being rashly inclined to the contradicting of what has already been introduced. Though they estimate that everything is accomplished by fate, they do not in every case deprive the human will of initiative but find it seemly that for God there is a fusion between the council-chamber of fate and those human beings who wish to accede to it with virtue [*aretē*] or vice. It is their belief that there is an immortal strength to souls, and beneath the ground are rewards and punishments for those whose pursuit in life has been one of virtue or vice—for some souls eternal imprisonment has been set forth, for others an opportunity for resurrection. And because of these views they happen to be most persuasive to the vulgar, and whatever is considered divine in the way of prayers and rituals happens to be accomplished in line with their interpretation. So much of their influence [*aretē*] have cities borne witness to in the pursuit of every position of authority, both in the regimen of life and in matters of doctrine.

"As for the Sadduccees, their doctrine dissipates souls together with bodies, and is on guard that there never be any alteration in this or in the laws; for they count it a virtue to debate with the teachers of wisdom, which they covet. This doctrine has come to but few men, who are, however, foremost in positions of esteem—yet they accomplish none of their views, so to speak; for whenever they arrive in positions of rule, they thereupon accede to what the

Pharisees say, albeit unwillingly and of necessity, because of their not being tolerated otherwise by the masses." (*Ant.* XIII:12-17)

c. *Translation by Seymour Topping.*

"The Pharisees reduce their standard of living, not giving in to any softness. What their doctrine transmits [orally] as good, they heed its authority; and they consider it worth fighting to guard the things their teaching dictates. With respect, they yield to those of advanced age, and they are not roused to contradict with arrogance what they [the elders] proposed.

"They believe everything is done by fate, but they do not deprive the human will of some impulse in them; for God has consented to a fusion of the council-chamber of fate with the will of men wanting to go over to virtue or vice.

"They believe that the souls are immortal, and that men receive punishments or honors in the underworld according to the virtue or vice they practised in life, the latter being intended to eternal imprisonment, the former having the opportunity of resurrection.

"Hence, they are plausible to the people, so that whatever pertains to prayers to God or to the sacrifices is done according to their interpretation. The cities have borne witness to their great virtue by their [the cities'] pursuit of the best both in their manner of life and in their teachings.

"The Sadducees believe that the souls perish together with the bodies, and are on guard that no alteration whatsoever in the laws be countenanced. They reckon it a virtue to dispute with the teachers of wisdom [i.e., the Pharisees] whom they hound [or harass].

"Only a few men hold their belief, but they are the first in rank. They do nothing, so to speak. For when they reach office, unwillingly and by necessity, they go over to what the Pharisees advocate, because otherwise they would be unacceptable to the people." (*Ant.* XIII:12-17)

3. There is indeed a text—*Ant.* XVII:41-45—which uses the term *pharisaoi* in connection with a clique of religious fanatics who were very much involved with the palace intrigues going on behind Herod's back. Most scholars have simply taken for granted that these *pharisaoi* are the Pharisees even though they are incongruent with the picture of the Pharisee

as drawn by Josephus in all other passages where the word *pharisaoi* is used. It is for this reason that I have not included this passage in the body of the text.

Nonetheless since scholars have written in using this passage as though the term *pharisaoi* were a sufficient guarantee that the Pharisees are meant, it is vital that this text be set down in full and critically analyzed.

The text in question occurs in connection with the alleged anti-Herodian activites of Pheroras and his wife. The passage reads as follows:

> "For there was also a clique *[morion]* of Jews priding itself on its adherence to ancestral custom and claiming to observe the laws which the Deity approves, and by these men, called Pharisees, the women [of the court] were ruled. These men were able to help the king greatly because of their foresight, and yet they were obviously intent upon combatting and injuring him. At least when the whole Jewish people affirmed by oath that it would be loyal to Caesar and to the king's government, these men, over six thousand in number, refused to take this oath, and when the king punished them with a fine, Pheroras' wife paid the fine for them. In return for her friendliness they foretold—for they were believed to have foreknowledge of things through God's appearance to them—that by God's decree Herod's throne would be taken from him, both from himself and his descendents, and that the royal power would fall to her and Pheroras and to any children they might have.
>
> "These things, which did not remain unknown to Salome, were reported to the king, as was the news that the Pharisees had corrupted some people at court. And the king put to death those of the Pharisees who were most to blame, and the eunuch Bagoas, and a certain Caras, who was outstanding among his contemporaries for his surpassing beauty. He killed also those of his own household who approved of what the Pharisees said. Now Bagoas had been carried away by their assurance that he would be called the father and benefactor of him who would some day be set over the people with the title of king, for all the power would belong to him and he would give Bagoas the ability to marry and to beget children of his own." (*Ant.* XVII:41-45)

This passage bristles with difficulties. *Pharisaoi* are explicitly mentioned. They are linked to the exact observance of the Law and to religious concerns. They refuse to take the oath of loyalty to Herod. Hence they seem at first glance to have some points in common with the Pharisees described elsewhere in Josephus' writings. Yet on closer scrutiny, one discovers that there is no congruence whatsoever.

In the first place, these *pharisaoi* are not called a *haeresis,* a school of thought, but rather a *morion*—a faction, a sect—of Jews. The term *morion* definitely connotes a comparatively small number, and this notion is confirmed when the *pharisaoi* who refused to take the oath are said to have numbered six thousand. If these *pharisaoi* are identical with the Pharisees, then why did Josephus use the term *morion* rather than *haeresis?*

Second, these *pharisaoi* are described as laying claim to being exact observers of the country's laws, and not expounders or interpreters of the laws. This is in contrast with Josephus' reiterations that the Pharisees were the most accurate expounders of the laws.

Third, among the distinguishing characteristics of these *pharisaoi* are their influence with women and their foreknowledge of things to come. The Pharisees elsewhere in Josephus do not share these characteristics.

Fourth, the *pharisaoi* are pictured as meddlers in palace intrigue and as persistent opponents of Herod's rule. This contrasts sharply with Pollion and Samaias' positive relationship with Herod.

Fifth, the *pharisaoi* who refused to take the oath of allegiance to Caesar and Herod were punished with a fine, whereas Pollion, Samaias, and their disciples were not punished at all.

Sixth, these *pharisaoi* are not juxtaposed to the Sadducees or Essenes.

At the heart of the dilemma is thus a stark contradiction. If Josephus is rendering an accurate account of the relationship between Pollion and Samaias and Herod, then the Pharisees were honored and respected by Herod and they, in turn, did not oppose his rule. What, then, are we to do with the *pharisaoi,* if they are the Pharisees, in view of the fact that they were active in attempting to overthrow Herod? The contradiction is heightened when the oath of loyalty is taken into account. Here was a demand that took place at a specific time. Pollion, Samaias, and their disciples refused to take the oath. The *pharisaoi* refused to take the oath. Pollion and Samaias and their disciples are exempted and are not punished; the *pharisaoi* are fined. If the *pharisaoi* are the Pharisees, then how does Herod at one and the same time treat the *pharisaoi* punitively and the Pharisees benignly? It therefore appears the *pharisaoi* in this text cannot be the Pharisees whom Josephus has been portraying consistently throughout his writings.

How, then, are we to account for the fact that the Greek word *pharisaoi* is one and the same? The answer is to be found in the fact that the Greek word is a modified transliteration of the Hebrew *perushim,* with a Greek plural ending attached, *pharisai-oi.* If, then, it can be demonstrated that the Hebrew *perushim* can mean either Pharisees, i.e., with a capital "P," or separatists of one sort or another, the *pharisaoi* in this passage need not be the Pharisees. Such a demonstration is set forth in detail on pp. 162-66. The criteria for determining when the term *pharisaoi* meant Pharisees and when it meant separatists, dissenters, fanatics, etc., would be dependent on the *context,* and not in the spelling of the word itself. Since the *pharisaoi* of the Pheroras-Herod episode are so unlike the *pharisaoi* of the rest of Josephus, the one precludes the other. Herod's dual treatment of the *pharisaoi,* "Pharisees," and the *pharisaoi,* "fanatics," is conclusive: The Pharisees Pollion and Samaias *and* their disciples were so respected by him that he exempted them from a loyalty oath, since their loyalty could be taken for granted; the *pharisaoi,* on the other hand, were engaged in Rasputin-like palace intrigue to unseat him and were fined when they refused to take the oath of loyalty.

It would seem that Josephus simply would not tamper with his source, which had transliterated the Hebrew *perushim* meaning separatists, and not the Hebrew *Perushim* meaning Pharisees.

Chapter II

1. A recent impressive dissertation on the terminological use of "scribes" and "Pharisees" in the Gospels is that by Michael J. Cook, "The Problem of the Scribes and Pharisees in the Gospel According to Mark" (Hebrew Union College, 1974); see his conclusions in "Judaism, Early Rabbinic," *Interpreter's Dictionary of the Bible, Supplement.* Among the variety of views in specifically New Testament scholarship disputing the synonymity of "scribes" with "Pharisees," see especially F. C. Grant, *The Earliest Gospel* (New York, 1943), p. 50; V. Taylor, *The Gospel According to St. Mark,* 2nd ed. (New York, 1966), p. 209; J. Jeremias, *Jerusalem in the Time of Jesus,* ET

(Philadelphia, 1969), pp. 246, 258-59; also D. Chwolson, *Das letzte Passamahl Christi,* 2nd ed. (Leipzig, 1908), pp. 112 ff.; A. Büchler, *Die Priester und der Cultus* (Vienna, 1895), pp. 84 ff.; A. T. Olmstead, *Jesus in the Light of History* (New York, 1942), 178 ff.; P. Winter, *On the Trial of Jesus* (Berlin, 1961), pp. 126-27, 209 n.25. For additional views and analysis, see Cook.

2. In the story of Jesus' eating with tax collectors and sinners, Mark associates the Scribes and Pharisees with the denunciation of such conduct. Now to be sure, the text is uncertain, for the reading generally preferred is "the scribes *of* the Pharisees" even though some manuscripts read "the scribes *and* the Pharisees." If the first reading is accepted, then there is an implication that the term *Pharisees* is not synonymous with the term *Scribes.* It could imply either that only some Pharisees were Scribes, but all Scribes were Pharisees, or that groupings other than the Pharisees likewise had Scribes (thus it might be contended that the Sadducees had Scribes as well). But we have already established that the second possibility is not viable, for Mark presents the Scribes as anti-Sadducean without any qualification such as "the scribes of the Pharisees." As for the first implication, it cannot be denied that if "the scribes *of* the Pharisees" is indeed the correct reading, then the Scribes would be a distinct group within the wider group of Pharisees. The scholar must therefore weigh the probabilities. He can call upon the alternate reading, "the scribes *and* the Pharisees," as preferable, since there can be no absolute proof that "the scribes *of* the Pharisees" is the correct reading. Or he can adopt the following procedure: analyze all the other texts to determine whether *contextually* the Scribes and Pharisees are or are not necessarily the same class. Should this eventuate, we would posit the Scribes and Pharisees had been mistaken for separate entities, when in reality the "Scribes" are the Pharisees, and the Pharisees are the "Scribes." Such an assumption would make intelligible why there should be some passages where we have Scribes without Pharisees, and Pharisees without Scribes.

3. *Pharisaoi* as a Greek word is noncommunicative; for it is a transliteration of the Hebrew *Perushim.* It would need translation or clarification for those who did not know who the Pharisees were. *Scribes* might have been helpful, but it was ambiguous, since the Greek *grammateis* does not mean a lawyer or a teacher of the Law, though the Hebrew term *Soferim* in Jesus' day in Judea did have this meaning. *Nomiko* or *nomodidaskalos,* however, clearly conveyed lawyer a

teacher of the Law. When, therefore, a Greek or Roman questioned a Christian as to who these Pharisees were, the answer was, "Why they are *nomikoi* ("lawyers"); they are *nomodidaskaloi;* they are teachers of the Law." And the same must have been the case with the *grammateis,* the Scribes. It is not hard, therefore, to see that by the time Luke was written, the translation and explanation had become separate entities bereft of differentiating criteria.

And that which holds true for Luke holds equally true for Matthew and Mark: a clarification or a translation was taken for a separate and distinct class. The process which accounts for this confusion is by no means anomalous in the development of the Gospel tradition. The immediate disciples of Jesus were Jews who could not but express themselves in the language of their fellow Jews. Since the names for institutions and for classes were known to them, they needed no translation or explanation. The scholar class that determined the Law was an entity sharply differentiated from other classes, such as the priests, and the people as a whole. Only one such scholar class existed, and this scholar class was referred to by names which betray a Hebrew source, namely, "Scribes" (i.e., *Soferim*) or "Pharisees" (i.e., *Perushim*). Although it cannot be determined with precision which of the two terms was preferred, the fact that Mark uses *Scribes* without *Pharisees* more frequently than either Matthew or Luke, and the fact that in each of the Synoptics the Scribes appear unjoined to the Pharisees in the account of Jesus' arrest, trial, and crucifixion—i.e., that part of the narrative which is most likely to have had the earliest formulation in the tradition—these facts may point to the term *Soferim,* "Scribes," as the term preferred, if not exclusively used, by Jesus and his immediate disciples. Had "Scribes" been the only name by which the scholar class was known, then the multiplying of scholar classes by the subsequent tradition might have proved difficult. But so long as the term *Pharisees* was also in vogue to designate this class—and as a transliteration of the Hebrew *Perushim, pharisaoi* must have arisen in Judea and circulated there—a false differentiation was almost inevitable. And this differentiation was abetted by the nature of the two terms. As a transliteration, *pharisaoi* does not communicate any information other than its Hebrew origin. It does not evoke any image in its own right. It could be evocative only for an individual who already knew what the term designated. For one who lacked this information, *pharisaoi* was a meaningless transliteration referring to some group or other. It could be a class, a sect, a fraternal order, or for that matter, any group at all. It might, but need not be, a scholar class.

Not so with the *grammateis*, "the Scribes." Here the Greek translation of *Soferim* delimited the scope of the term. Although *grammateis* does not necessarily carry with it the notion of lawyers or teachers of the Law, it does convey the idea of a class that has intellectual concerns. Confronted with the two terms *pharisaoi* and *grammateis* an individual who had no knowledge of what they referred to not only might not recognize them as synonyms—especially if his sources used the terms now separately and now together—but would conclude that the *grammateis* must have been the scholars of the Pharisees. The *pharisaoi* would be the rank and file while the *grammateis* would be the leaders. He would come to this conclusion not because he had evidence for this differentiation but because *grammateis* conveys some usable information whereas *pharisaoi* only reveals itself as a transliterated proper noun. We have already had occasion to see in our analysis of Luke-Acts that the author of Luke or his sources went a step further and sought to clarify the meaning of *grammateis*. The Scribes are not secretaries or writers or intellectuals in general, but a class of legal authorites, lawyers, *nomikoi*, and teachers of the Law, *nomodidaskaloi*. In making this effort, the author of Luke opened up the possibility that *nomikoi* and *nomodidaskaloi* might be mistaken for separate classes, for the simple reason that *"grammateis"* as a word is *not* synonymous with lawyers or teachers of the Law, though it does not exclude the possibility of lawyers or teachers of the Law being covered by its range of meaning.

Chapter VI
1. As for the question as to why the authors of I and II Maccabees made no explicit mention of the Pharisaic Revolution, the answer lies in the fact that the author of I Maccabees wrote his version of the Hasmonean Revolt *after* John Hyrcanus split with the Pharisees, while the author of II Maccabees was writing for Jews living in the Hellenistic Diaspora. Since the author of I Maccabees is lavish in his praise of John Hyrcanus (I Macc. 16:23-24), he must have been a follower of the Sadducees. His aim would necessarily be to picture the Hasmonean Revolt as exclusively the achievement of the Hasmonean family and not at all owing to the support of the Pharisees. Nonetheless, as we have see

the author quotes in full from the proclamation of the *synagoges megales,* which invested Simon with the High Priesthood and thus leaves the telltale evidence of the Pharisaic Revolution.

The author of II Maccabees likewise had good reasons for not mentioning the Pharisaic Revolution, since he was himself not a Pharisee. Writing as he did long after the emergence of Pharisaism and dependent on the voluminous account of Jason of Cyrene, which seemingly was packed with military actions and political events, the author could hardly have viewed the Hasmonean Revolt as the occasion for the triumph of Pharisaism. His religious interest in these events stemmed from a conception of Judaism that was neither Pharisaic nor Sadducaic but Hellenistic.

Large numbers of Jews lived in Hellenistic cities prior to the Hasmonean Revolt and prior to the emergence of the Pharisees. Many of these Jews were fully attuned to the Hellenistic culture which surrounded them at the same time that they were loyal to Judaism. As loyal followers of Judaism, they looked upon Jerusalem as their mother city and the Temple cultus as their shrine. They could therefore not remain unaffected by the Hasmonean Revolt and its consequences, even though they did not participate in these events. At no time were they confronted with those problems that were peculiar to the Palestinian situation and which had generated, along with the Hasmonean Revolt, the Pharisaic Revolution. They were only concerned with interpreting the events in such a way that it not only conformed with their conception of Judaism but confirmed it. They were not interested in innovations, for these could only disrupt a form of Judaism that had proved viable.

The form of Judaism that had evolved in the Greek cities prior to and simultaneously with the Hasmonean Revolt was Hellenistic, i.e., it was a form of Judaism that had translated Pentateuchal-theocratic Judaism into Hellenistic concepts. In Alexandria, this form of Judaism is evident in the Letter of Aristeas and subsequently, in a more elaborate philosophical form, in Philo. A similar form had likewise sprung up in Antioch. All attempts at linking this type of Judaism with Pharisaism have failed, for there is no linkage. This form of Judaism antedated Pharisaism; and since it had already proved its adequacy for Hellenistic Jews, the triumph of Pharisaism in Palestine could not successfully challenge it. It was a form of Judaism that had developed its distinctive variation while the theocracy was still unchallenged, and in the very process of affirming loyalty to Pentateuchal-theocratic Judaism. The expansion of the Pharisaic Diaspora was achieved by the emigration of Jews who were already Pharisees out of Palestine and who immigrated into the Hellenistic cities during the Hasmonean Revolt and especially during the Civil War in the reign of Alexander Jannaeus. The older Hellenistic Jewish communities continued to exist alongside the Pharisaic communities, even though the latter in many cities represented more and more the majority of the Jewish population. The older Hellenistic communities remained loyal to their Hellenistic Judaism.

The Second Book of Maccabees was written for followers of this Hellenistic form. The author offered an interpretation of the Hasmonean Revolt that accorded with the ideas that prevailed among these Jews. He therefore has no interest whatsoever in Pharisees or Pharisaism. Rather is he concerned with emphasizing that God grants eternal life to those who remain steadfast to his laws, particularly the dietary laws and the laws of polytheism. For this reason he includes the story of the martyrdom of Eleazar who refused to eat swine's flesh and of Hannah and her seven sons who affirmed God and his laws with the full realization of the agonizing deaths that awaited them. Likewise, the author is careful to point out that any ruler who is disrepectful of God's holy sanctuary is punished by God.

Hellenistic Jewry was thus encouraged to remain loyal to their form of Judaism, even in the face of persecution and death. As a reward for their steadfastness, they could be assured of resurrection.

This concept of eternal life after death and resurrection was by no means a monopoly of the Pharisees. It was good Hellenistic Jewish doctrine. This is especially evident in the Fourth Book of Maccabees which takes one incident in the Hasmonean Revolt and draws confirmation of the belief in immortality. What is crucial is not a shared belief in immortality or resurrection but in how it is attained. For the Pharisees, the *halakhah,* the Oral Law, was the road to salvation, whereas for the authors of II and IV Maccabees, salvation is gained through the willingness to suffer martyrdom rather than violate the Written Law by eating forbidden foods or worshiping other gods.

Bibliographical Note

Readers interested in exploring alternative definitions of the Pharisees and their history will find extensive bibliographies compiled by A. Michel and J. ·Le Moyne following their comprehensive article "Pharisiens" in the *Supplement au Dictionnaire de la Bible* (Paris, 1964); and Louis Finkelstein, *The Pharisees* (Philadelphia, 1962) II:903-45. Jacob Neusner's "Bibliographical Reflections" in his *The Rabbinic Traditions of the Pharisees Before 70* (Leiden, 1971) III:320-68, will give the reader a good notion of Neusner's assessment of the literature from a point of view fundamentally at odds with that espoused in *A Hidden Revolution*. Also, Ralph Marcus' "The Pharisees in the Light of Modern Scholarship," *Journal of Religion*, XXIII (1952), 153-164, is still worth reading.

Index

Aaron and Aaronides, 251
  Ben Sira and, 191-207
Abraham, 279, 280
Abtalion, 26, 177
Acts. *See* New Testament
Afterlife, 57, 259, 291, 329. *See also*
  Resurrection doctrine; Soul
Aggadah, 128, 274, 279
  Pharisees and, 254
Antigonus the Hasmonean, 71,
  72, 257
Antiochus III, 206
Antiochus IV, 207, 223
Aristeas, Letter of, 328
Aristotle, 300
Atonement, Day of, 260-61, 266-
  67

Baeck, Leo, 172n
Ben Sira
  as Pentateuchal literalist, 191-
  204
  pre-Pharisaic society described
  by, 188-207
Beraitoth, 128-29
Boethusians. *See* Sadducees, in
  Tannaitic Literature

Caesar, tribute to, 94
Calendrical system
  Josephus on, 278-79
  Pharisaic, 263-66
Christianity, Pharisaic Revolution
  and, 303-11
Church Fathers, 31

Damico, Anthony, 319, 320
Demetrius (King), 35, 216
Diogenes, 47, 48, 49, 67, 68, 70

Ecclesiasticus, the Wisdom of Ben
  Sira. *See* Ben Sira
Eleazar, 191, 193, 198, 217
Essenes, 185, 323
  in Josephus, 34, 66
Ezra, 185, 197

False witnesses doctrine, 267
Feldman, Louis, 319
Fourth philosophy, 318
  in Josephus, 53, 54, 58, 59-60
Free will, 54, 67-68

Gamaliel (Rabban), 26, 173, 175,
  177, 235, 258, 265
God, individual and
  concept following Pharisaic
  Revolution, 310-11
Goldschmidt, Lazarus, 170n

Haberim texts, 173-75
Haeresis defined, 316-18
Hakhamim, 234
  as synonym for Pharisees, 138-
  42
    juxtaposed to Sadducees-
      Boethusians, 142-58
    connection with *Perushim-So-
      ferim,* 158-60
Hakme Yisrael, 142-45
Halakhah, 128, 274, 329
  Pharisees and, 253-55, 3~

331

Halakhah (continued)
two renditions of, 258
See also Hakhamim; Law
Hasmonean Revolt, 186, 187, 188,
189, 215, 249, 327, 328, 329
Hasmoneans
Pharisees and, 256
vs. Zadokites, 217-21
Hellenism, Jews and, 328-29
Herod (King), 50-53, 71, 72, 94,
95, 257, 321, 322, 323
High Priesthood, 239
Ben Sira and, 190-207
Day of Atonement and, 260-61
transfer of power in, 211-21
Zadokite vs. Hasmonean, 217-
21
Hillel, 26, 177, 235, 257, 258
Hypocrites, relationship to Phari-
sees, 121-23
Hyrcanus, John, 26, 68, 70, 73,
221-23, 256, 276, 327
rift with Pharisees and abroga-
tion of Pharisaic law, 33,
35-42, 256

Individual, God and
concept following Pharisaic
Revolution, 310-11
Inheritance laws, 268

Jannaeus, Alexander, 26, 33, 37,
43, 69, 258
Scribes and, 105-21
Jason, 207, 217, 250, 251
Jesus
Pharisees and, 26, 79-80, 83, 84,
91-98, 100, 101, 103, 273-76,
303-11
proof-texting, 273-74
Joarib, 217
Johanan ben Zakkai, 145-47, 154,
177
Jonathan the Hasmonean, 34, 35,
185, 186, 276
Josephus, 26, 27, 184, 187, 203,
235, 236, 238, 256-57, 261
on Abraham, 279-81
on calendrical system, 278-79
on discipline of Law, 290
internalization of Law, 289,

294-95
on Mosaic Law, 283-95
on Moses, 279-80, 281-84
and Pharisaic Revolution, 221-
23
in relationship to Pharisees, 32,
292
on resurrection and afterlife,
291-92
on suicide, 292
on twofold Law, 176-95
See also Pharisees, in Josephus
Josephus, works of
Against Apion, 104n, 277, 302
The Antiquities, 25, 32, 33, 34,
35, 38, 43, 44, 45, 50, 51, 52,
57, 58, 59, 67, 78, 185, 187,
222, 262, 277, 278, 279, 280,
281, 282, 283, 293, 320, 321
The Jewish War, 32, 33, 38, 43,
47, 48, 53, 54, 55, 56, 60, 63,
222, 277, 292
The Life, 33, 63, 66, 277
non-Pentateuchal material in,
276-83
Joshua (High Priest), 185, 251
Judah Aristobulus, 43, 47
Judah ben Tabbai, 139-42, 267
Judah ha-Nasi, 127
Judaism
in Hellenistic culture, 328-29
preserved through internalization, 309-11
Judas of Galilee, 53, 54, 59

Korah, 193-95, 196
Koran, twofold Law displaced by,
308

Law
as core of Pharisaism, 72-73
Ben Sira's concept of, 191-206
discipline of, 23-24, 290
internalization of, 289, 294-311
in the Mishnah, 223-24, 234,
235, 237
twofold (Written and Oral),
23-24, 28, 46, 67, 129, 159,
161-62, 179, 233, 253, 254,
259, 269, 283
in Josephus, 276-95

Koran and, 308
Mishnah and, 234, 235, 237
  origin of concept of, 183-90
Unwritten (Pharisaic), 38, 41-
  43, 68-70, 72-73, 77-78, 89-94,
  145-60, 253
  usage in tannaitic texts, 269
Written (Pentateuch; Sadducean), 41-43, 91, 145-56 *passim*
See also Mishnah; Moses; Tannaitic Midrash; Tosefta
Lawyers, 115-19, 325-26, 327
Lycurgus, 283, 284

Megillat Ta'anit
  scholion, 31
Meneleus, 207, 217, 251
Mishnah (Oral Law), 27, 126, 217,
  178-79
  categories in, 229
  contents of, 127
  encapsulation of Pharisaic Rev-
    olution in, 310-11
  New Moon proclamation in,
    265
  Pentateuch and, 223-37
  Pharisaic Revolution and, 223-
    39
  proof-texting in, 225-26
  reciting of *Shema* in, 224
  repository of teachings of schol-
    ar class, 232-38
  resurrection of dead in, 229-31
  scholar class and, 223-24, 235
Moore, George Foot, 172n
Morion, 323
Moses, 81, 83, 87, 89, 95, 113, 124,
  152, 183, 191, 192, 195, 196,
  197, 199, 205, 217, 219, 220,
  221, 231-32, 248, 251, 253,
  255, 265, 269
  Josephus on, 79-280, 281-92
  Pharisees on the seat of, 252-95
  See also Pentateuch
Muhammad, 308, 310

Nasi, 257-58
Nehemiah, 212
New Testament, 26, 31, 32
  Fourth Gospel (John), 79, 98-
    104, 124

Galatians, 78-239, 305
  influence of Pharisaic literary
    forms on, 272-75
  Pharisaic Revolution confirmed
    in, 239-41
Philippians, 77, 239, 305
Scribes terminology, 325-27
Synoptic Gospels and Acts,
  79-98 *passim*, 102-3, 104-23,
  178, 240, 269-76, 326-27
See also Jesus; Paul

Onias III, 219, 250

Paul, 97, 98, 104, 123, 178, 235, 299
  Pharisees and, 77-79, 239-40,
    273, 275-76, 304-9
  proof-texting, 273
Pentateuch, 187, 217
  Ben Sira's understanding of,
    191-204
  calendrical systems in, 218-19,
    266
  Mishnah and, 223-37
  Pharisees and, 243-48
  Soferim and, 185-86
Perushim, 125
  identification with *Soferim*, 158,
    233-34, 235
  juxtaposed to term *Sadducees*,
    132-42
  meaning "heretics" or "separa-
    tists" (not "Pharisees"), 165-
    73, 324
  Perushim-Hakhamim connec-
    tion, 139-42
  Perushim-Hakhamim-Soferim
    connection, 158-60, 235
  usage with Sadducees-Boethu-
    sians absent from text, 158-61
  usage of word in unambiguous
    texts, 133-38
  translations
    not translated by scholars as
      "Pharisees," 162-66
    translated by scholars as
      "Pharisees," 129-30
Pharisaic Revolution
  calendrical system of, 218-19
  conditions underlying, 211-15
  241-45

Pharisaic Revolution *(cont.)*
core of, 302-3
encapsulated in Mishnah, 310-11
enduring achievement of, 294-95, 308-11
Greco-Roman influence on, 242-43
a hidden revolution, 214-15
High Priestly line in, 217-21
how accomplished, 245-51
New Testament and, 239-41
relationship of authors of I and II Maccabees to, 327-29
sources for knowledge of, 215
Josephus, 221-23
I Maccabees, 215-21
Mishnah, 223-39
time of, 213-15, 241, 245, 256
Pharisaoi terminology, 321-27
Pharisees
authority of, 253, 268-69
calendrical system of, 218-19, 263-66, 303-11
concurrence between Tannaitic and New Testament accounts of, 271-72
cultic practices of, 259-69
and Day of Atonement, 260-61, 266-67
as defined by
composite of sources surveyed, 176-79, 183
Fourth Gospel, 104
Josephus, 67-75, 178
modern scholars, 27-28, 312-16
New Testament, 78-79, 85, 97-98, 104, 123-24, 178
Paul, 78-79
Synoptics and Acts, 97-98, 178
Tannaitic Literature, 176-79
and development of Judaism, 26-27, 309-11
doctrines of, 259-71, 293
on false witnesses, 267
God-individual relationship interpreted by, 310-11
and *halakhah*, 253-55, 329
heirs of, 309

High Priesthood and, 211-21, 239
history of, 183-90, 255-57
Holy of Holies and, 261-62
inheritance laws of, 268
internalization of and salvation through Law, according to, 289, 294-311
Jannaeus and, 43-48, 258
and liability of slaves, 267-68
literary forms used by, 272-75
on Moses' seat (as lawgivers), 252-95
Pentateuch and, 243-48
Pharisaic-Hasmonean coalition, 256
pre-eminence of, 293-94
proof-texting, 273-74
as proselytizers, 269-70
resurrection concept of, 23, 28, 96-97, 110-11, 113, 303-11
as revolutionaries, 15, 28
role of, 28
Salome Alexandra and, 43-49, 256
scholar class, 231-52
Scribes-Pharisees terminology, 325
secular and religious autonomy doctrine of, 256-57
split with John Hyrcanus by, 33, 35-42, 256
and *tamid* (daily sacrifice), 263
and unclean hands doctrine, 156-58, 259-60
and the Unwritten Law, 38, 41-43, 68-70, 72-73, 77-78, 89-94, 145-60, 253
on the Written Law, 253
See also Law: twofold; Pharisaic Revolution; Pharisees, in Josephus; Pharisees, in New Testament; Pharisees, in Tannaitic Literature
Pharisees, in Josephus, 31-75, 276-95
as activists, 61-65
attitude toward Roman state, 58-65, 70-73
break with John Hyrcanus, 33, 35-42

and belief in afterlife, 57
definition of, 67-75, 178
doctrines, beliefs, values of, 54,
56-57, 73-75, 318-21
fate vs. free will, 54, 67-68
Law and, 38, 41-43, 67, 68-70,
72-73
Pharisaism as a way of life,
66-67
pharisaoi terminology, 321-24
piety *(eusebes)* of, 48-49
political power of, 49-53
rebellion against Alexander
Jannaeus, 43-48
relationship with Salome Alexandra, 43-49
as scholars, 55-56, 70
social class, 65
use of force, 67
Pharisees, in New Testament, 31,
32, 76-124, 269-76
in Acts, 90-98 *passim*
authority of, 81-88, 98-104, 113-18
beliefs, 96-97, 269-76
confusion of terms for, 120
defined, 78-79, 97-98, 88, 104,
123-24, 178
in Fourth Gospel, 98-104
hostility toward, 81-88, 93
hypocrisy of, 89-90
Law and, 89-94
in Luke, 90-98, *passim*
in Mark, 88-98, *passim*
in Matthew, 81-88, 269-71
in Paul, 77-79, 88
purity of, 86
relationship to hypocrites, 121-23
relationship to Jesus, 26, 79-80,
83, 84, 91-98, 100, 101, 103
relationship to Scribes, 104-21
resurrection doctrine of, 96-97,
110-11, 113
righteousness of, 78-87
scholar class, 83-84, 92
Pharisees, in Tannaitic Literature,
125-79
defined, 176-79
doctrines of, 259-69

evidence for Pharisaic-Sadducean opposition, 131-56, 259-69
Hakhamim as term for, 138-56
(see also Hakhamim)
Perushim as term for, 129-30 *(see also Perushim)*
ritual purity of, 160-61
as spokesmen for Unwritten
Law, 145-60
in unambiguous texts, 133-38
Philo, 328
Phinehas, 191, 193, 196, 198, 217
Plato, 242, 283, 284
Pollion, 50-53, 70, 71, 72, 235, 257,
323, 324
Proof-texting, 225-26, 243, 247-48,
273-74
Ptolemies, 206, 212

Rabban title, 258
Resurrection doctrine, 259
Hellenistic Jewish, 329
influence of Pharisaic doctrine
on Christianity, 303-11
in Mishnah, 229-31
Pharisaic, 23, 28, 96-97, 110-11,
113
as reward for life under Law,
291-92
See also Afterlife; Soul
Revolution, Pharisaic. *See* Pharisaic Revolution
Ritual purity, 160-61

Sadducees, 185, 253, 292, 323
author of I Maccabees and, 327
disappearance of, 258
Sadducees/Zadokites, 219-22
Written Law and, 237
See also Sadducees, in Josephus;
Sadducees, in New Testament; Sadducees, in Tannaitic Literature
Sadducees, in Josephus, 34, 66,
222-23
doctrines of, 54, 56-57, 319-21
hostility to Pharisees, 37
Law of, 41-43, 187
Sadducees, in New Testament,
95-96, 98, 104n, 117, 240
doctrines of, 96-97, 109-10

Sadducees, in Tannaitic Literature, 125, 131-32, 133-34, 233-35
  "Beothusians" as synonym for, 134-42, 229
  juxtaposed to *Hakhamim*, 142-58
  vs. Pharisees, 131-56, 259-69
Salome Alexandra, 26, 33, 53, 68, 69, 70, 71, 253, 276
  relationship with Pharisees of, 43-49, 256
Salvation
  Christian, 23
  halakhah and, 329
  internalization of Law and, 294-311
Samaias, 50-53, 70, 71, 72, 235, 257, 323, 324
Scholar class, 55-56, 70, 83-84, 92, 129, 223-24, 231-52
  authority of, 259
  development of, 257-58
  teachings of, in Mishnah, 232-38
Scribes, 80-82, 88-90, 102, 185, 186
  authority of, 113-18
  doctrines of, 109-13, 259-69
  pre-Hasmonean, description of, 197-206
  relationship to Pharisees, 104-21
  Scribes-Pharisees terminology, 325-27
  See also Pharisees
Seleucids, 206, 212
Shammai, 26, 177, 235
Shema, 272, 297
Shemaiah, 27, 177
Simon ben Shetah, 27, 139-45, 177, 267
Simon son of Gamaliel, 61-65, 69, 70, 235, 258
Simon the High Priest, 188, 193, 196, 215-16, 217, 219, 221, 223, 249, 256, 327-28
Socrates, 242, 300, 301
Sofer. See Soferim
Soferim, 185-86
  as a designation, 203-4
  in Mishnah, 233-35

Pharisees-*Soferim,* 158-60, 202-3, 220
  pre-Hasmonean *Soferim*-Scribes (Ben Sira), 197-206, 220
Soul
  after death, 54
  Pharisaic vs. Sadducean doctrine, 318-21
  See also Afterlife; Resurrection
Stoics, 66, 67, 75, 242, 300
Synoptic Gospels. *See* New Testament

Talmud
  Babylonian, 31, 126, 128
  Palestinian, 31, 126, 128
  Soncino, 167-70
Tannaitic Literature, 25, 26, 27, 31, 203, 229
  dating of, 125
  scholar class and, 129
  scope of, 125-26
  Scribes-Pharisees' teachings in, 259-69
  use of "Torah" in, 269
  See also Mishnah
Tannaitic Midrash, 126-29
Topping, Seymour, 319
Torah
  as Twofold Law, 269
  See also Moses
Tosefta, 126-27, 273
Twofold Law. *See* Law

Wisdom
  of Ben Sira, 191-27
  Soferim and, 200-201

Yaffe, Martin, 319
Yohanan ben Zakkai, 235

Zadok, 191, 196, 198
Zadokites vs. Hasmoneans, 217-21
Zealots, 61, 63, 65
Zedukim, 125, 131-32, 133-34, 156-67
Zerubbabel, 185
Zugoth system, 235-39, 257, 276
  dissolution of, 257-58